A HISTORY
of
Rock Creek
PARK

WILDERNESS & WASHINGTON, D.C.

D0874954

SCOTT EINBERGER

Charleston · London

THE
History
PRESS

Published by The History Press
Charleston, SC 29403
www.historypress.net

Copyright © 2014 by Scott Einberger
All rights reserved

Front cover, top: Klingle Road Ford in Rock Creek Park. *John DeFerrari Collection*; *bottom*:
Boulder Bridge over Rock Creek. *John DeFerrari Collection*.
Back cover, bottom left: Rock Creek Park superintendent Jim Redmond (right) and maintenance
worker Michael Deas during park awards ceremony, circa 1980. *National Park Service*.

First published 2014

Manufactured in the United States

ISBN 978.1.62619.574.5

Library of Congress CIP data applied for.

This book is dedicated to the memory of Stewart Udall, whose writings as U.S. secretary of the interior in the 1960s and afterward helped bring the author to the pathway of environmental history and sustainability.

Stewart Udall (second from left) with Department of the Interior staff members and their families on a special visit to the Rock Creek Park Nature Center in 1962. *National Park Service.*

CONTENTS

CONTENTS

CONTENTS

ACKNOWLEDGEMENTS

Researching and writing this book has been one of the most enjoyable and personally gratifying experiences in my life, but it could not have been completed without help from others. First and foremost, a huge thank-you goes out to my wife, Andria Hayes-Birchler, whose support, listening skills and input every step of the way proved invaluable. A massive mountain of thank-yous also goes out to Simone Monteleone, cultural resource program manager for Rock Creek Park, for providing stellar feedback, edits and guidance. Bill Yeaman, natural resource specialist for Rock Creek Park, also deserves a major thank-you for providing important insight into his early experiences in the park and for edits to the manuscript. Thank-yous also go out to work associates and friends Michael Zwelling and Barbara D'Emilio for editing and providing important feedback. Additionally, thank you to Tazwell Franklin, archives specialist at the National Park Service's National Capital Region Museum Resource Center, and Laura Barry, research services librarian for the Historical Society of Washington, D.C., for assisting the author in securing select photos and documents. Finally, thank you to the friendly and professional staff of The History Press, most notably Banks Smither and Julia Turner, for making this book a reality.

INTRODUCTION

Rock Creek has an abundance of all the elements that make up not only pleasing but wild and rugged scenery. There is perhaps, not another city in the Union that has on its very threshold so much natural beauty and grandeur, such as men seek for in remote forests and mountains.
—John Burroughs, American naturalist (1868)

Serving as the national capital's creek, forest and backyard, Rock Creek Park is one of the finest and largest urban nature parks in the world. At over double the size of New York City's famed Central Park, its 1,754 acres is home primarily to eastern deciduous forest, rolling hills sloping down toward Rock Creek and trickling streams. For decades, visitors have enjoyed its natural features. Hikers, joggers and cyclists by the thousands explore the park each nice-weather weekend, while unique features such as a planetarium, outdoor amphitheater, horse center and professional tennis stadium bring in nontraditional national park visitors with other ideas of fun.

These rich natural features and myriad recreational opportunities are well known to D.C. residents. Less known, however, is the park's past. In every nature park, there is history, and perhaps nowhere more so than in Rock Creek Park. From Civil War to civil rights, water pollution to water-wise solutions and eccentric poets to exercising presidents, Rock Creek Park history includes them all. These unknown, mostly unpublished histories of the park—the "stories behind the scenery"—form the backbone of the book you are beginning.

This said, it's important to note that just as in ecology where "everything is connected," so it is, too, with history. Rather than operating in a vacuum, history is majorly influenced by its surroundings. And so Rock Creek Park's past has been largely influenced by its rich natural heritage and natural resources. Also though, the park has been heavily influenced by the city in which it has evolved. This is not just any city—it's *the* city, the nation's capital. These two factors are the reason for the subtitle of this book: "Wilderness and Washington, D.C." Nature (wilderness) combining with urbanity (Washington, D.C.) is a major part of the Rock Creek Park story. Yet Rock Creek Park has been influenced by other factors as well, perhaps most notably the fact that it includes ninety-nine other distinct sites and parks.

Indeed, since the mid-1970s, the time of a major organizational restructuring of the National Park Service's National Capital Region parks, Rock Creek Park has been both the name of the 1,754-acre park that was established in 1890 as well as the name of the larger administrative unit. While most visitors understand that Rock Creek Park the park is the large swath of forest bounded generally between Broad Branch Road and Oregon Avenue on the west and Sixteenth Street on the east, many would be surprised to know that Rock Creek Park the administrative unit includes ninety-nine other park sites outside the main Oregon Avenue–Sixteenth Street stem. Most notably, these additional units include the Rock Creek and Potomac Parkway as well as several narrow stream–valley parks that feed directly into Rock Creek. Less noticeable due to the fact that these sites are slightly away from the creek, Rock Creek Park the administrative unit also includes Old Stone House in Georgetown, Meridian Hill Park at the southern edge of the Columbia Heights neighborhood and several former and still standing Civil War fortifications, among other lands and parcels. In promoting Rock Creek Park's diversity, this book will shed light on many of the administrative units in addition to the main 1890 stem of Rock Creek Park.

The History of Rock Creek Park: Wilderness and Washington, D.C. has been arranged chronologically, beginning with the park's American Indian past and continuing all the way to the present. Each chapter is made up of several short essays. These articles are listed in the table of contents, thus allowing you the option of flipping to specific sections you find interesting or reading the book cover to cover to get the full experience. You may also choose to visit specific history locations and read the book's corresponding essay right then and there, at the actual spot.

Whichever way you read this book, the bottom line is that Rock Creek Park is more than just pretty scenery. The park story is a gluing together of nature, humankind and a great city. In some instances, it's humankind and the city working against nature. This story—some of which will be sobering, some of which will be gratifying, all of which will hopefully be thought provoking—begins here.

Part I

Before the Park

1

THE PRE-PARK LANDSCAPE

About 85 percent of Rock Creek Park today is composed of dense forest cover, and with the upper half of the Rock Creek and Potomac Parkway also being lined with woodland, it might seem like a "pristine ecosystem" has always ruled supreme in the Rock Creek Valley. This is not entirely the case. While bits and pieces of the Rock Creek Valley have been forested for centuries, historic maps show dozens of homesteads, farms, water-powered mills and even plantations near and along the creek. Many pre-park peoples undoubtedly relished in the beauty of the Rock Creek Valley just like we do today, but they primarily took advantage of the stream valley's abundant natural resources. How American Indians and early European Americans used and worked the land that eventually became Rock Creek Park and its administrative units is the subject of this first chapter.

ANCIENT AMERICAN INDIANS AND THEIR QUARRIES

Jaws in Rock Creek Park

For at least thirteen thousand years, people have utilized the rich natural resources of the Rock Creek Valley to their benefit. Although we will never know the names or thoughts of specific ancient American Indians of the pre-park era due to the fact that they did not have writing systems, we can nevertheless turn to the valuable field of archaeology for important clues.

Evidence suggests that ancient American Indians did not live in present-day Rock Creek Park but rather camped in the area, taking advantage of the abundant natural resources and then moving on. For millennia, different groups were gatherer-hunters. They gathered oak nuts and, more recently, American beechnuts and chestnuts; collected wild berries and fruit from the pawpaw tree; and made certain plants their pharmacy. With more difficulty, they fished the creek and hunted big game, which around eleven thousand years ago included "caribou, elk, moose, black bear, peccary, wolf, lynx, beaver, mastodon, mammoth, and musk ox."[1] Undoubtedly, these people of the pre-park era also utilized the waters of Rock Creek for drinking and at least fording but probably also cooling off and cleaning.

Aside from collecting foodstuff, ancient American Indians quarried rock outcroppings to make tools for various uses in cooking, eating, hunting, art and warfare, according to archaeologists. Perhaps the two most notable ancient quarries of Rock Creek Park are located along the Piney Branch tributary and in Soapstone Valley.

Studied meticulously by William Henry Holmes of the American Bureau of Ethnology and his team of archaeologists between 1889 and 1894, the Piney Branch quarry consists of thousands of oval-shaped quartzite cobbles, or preforms. Prior to Holmes's research, due to the fact that the preforms resembled tools used by Paleolithic peoples of Europe that inhabited the continent between 500,000 to 100,000 years ago, it was commonly believed that people inhabited North America during this ancient time. Holmes disproved this theory by replicating the process by which Piney Branch quarry users quarried and then built their tools. By showing that the quartzite cobbles were simply discards—litter—Holmes was able to prove that the quartzite hillsides were quarried not 100,000 years ago but "only" about 4,500 years ago. In a letter to the manager of Rock Creek Park in 1925, Holmes wrote:

> *When, forty years ago, I began the study of the ancient remains of the eastern states, the archeologists of Washington, New York, Boston and other cities were gathering rudely chipped stones such as are found on the slopes of Piney Branch. They filled museum cases with them and labelled [sic] them "American Paleolithic Implements," and the archeologists of the world accepted without hesitation the view that these chipped stones were the implements of a race preceding the Indian, a race of glacial age, that,*

Diorama of American Indians at Piney Branch Quarry. Archaeologist William Henry Holmes helped design this diorama that was then shown at Chicago's World Fair of 1893. *National Archives and Records Administration.*

in the scale of culture had never risen above the use of rude stone tools. I examined carefully these specimens and visited the Piney Branch sites and soon reached the conclusion that this was all wrong, and that these chipped stones were not implements at all, but rejectage [sic] of the difficult chipping process, the failures of the Indian blade maker, left on the quarry site as simple refuse. The successful blades, not one in twenty attempts, were carried to the villages and finished to serve as weapons of war and the chase, and in various primitive arts. For a score of years controversy over this interpretation raged, but there is today, so far as I know, not in any museum of the world, a single American shaped stone of any kind labelled [sic] as belonging to the glacial period or to a stone age culture corresponding with that of the Old World.[2]

Quartzite is a strong, hard rock, but a different kind of rock was quarried for a different purpose in a narrow valley just west of Rock Creek and Broad

Branch. Soapstone Valley, today overrun by invasive English ivy ground cover as well as a sewer pipe, was another important ancient American Indian site. Soapstone, a softer rock than quartzite, was quarried in the namesake valley and then carved into bowls used for eating and grinding. Quarrying in the Soapstone Valley, especially around the present-day Connecticut Avenue area, was alive and well around four thousand years ago.[3]

Aside from quarrying and living off the land, at least one significant burial took place around 1,300 years ago in the Rock Creek Valley. Recently, archaeologists working at the intersection where the Whitehurst Freeway crosses the Rock Creek and Potomac Parkway uncovered perhaps "the most important ancient American Indian find yet made in the District of Columbia." In a shallow, two-foot pit, they uncovered a burial site with the remains of a thirty- to forty-year-old woman. Along with the bones of this woman, whom the author refers to as "Whitehurst Woman," were artifacts including "a comb carved from a deer antler, two stone pendants, a carved sandstone phallus, a triangular knife, 14 great white shark teeth, a bone from a large bird, six antler disks, a wooden bead, and cloth woven from the pawpaw tree and native grasses."[4]

Due to the fact that similar burials have been excavated in upstate New York, archaeologists now have proof that these early New Yorkers were travelers. Furthermore, mid-Atlantic-region American Indians at the time of European contact spoke Algonquian languages, more common among native speakers of the Great Lakes region. Hence, the Whitehurst Freeway find completes a missing link: New York Algonquian speakers brought their language and culture southward.[5]

One question regarding Whitehurst Woman remains a mystery, and this involves why she was buried with so many artifacts. Most likely, objects such as the great white shark teeth and wooden beads were placed in her grave for religious purposes, but it also could symbolize her high stature in society. We'll never know for sure, as we were not living there at the time and no written record was passed down.

Quarrying, foraging, fishing, hunting and burying—this was the way things were in the Rock Creek Valley for millennia. But when British captain John Smith sailed up the Chesapeake Bay and past the mouth of Rock Creek in the early 1600s, a sea of change was about to occur that would involve disease, death and eventually forced migration to the surviving native inhabitants of the area in and around Rock Creek. Armed with not only guns and germs but also pen and paper, European Americans moved into the area. The rest, quite literally, became history.[6]

NINIAN BEALL AND THE ROCK OF DUMBARTON

Redheaded Hercules at the Mouth of Rock Creek

One of the first European Americans to own land along Rock Creek and probably the very first to actually settle it was a man named Ninian Beall. Beall (pronounced "Bell") was not raised in Maryland but across the Atlantic. The story of how he got to the banks of Rock Creek is most definitely unique.

Born in 1625 in rural Scotland, Beall fought against the British army at the Battle of Dunbar. He was unfortunately captured during the battle and became a prisoner of war, sentenced to five years of indentured service in Barbados. During the voyage across the ocean to the Caribbean island, two-thirds of his fellow prisoners died from disease and malnourishment, but Beall was one of the lucky ones to survive.

In 1652, Richard Hall of Calvert County purchased the rights to Beall and brought him to Maryland, where he served out his sentence and eventually won his freedom. The six-foot, seven-inch-tall Scotsman who sported long red hair and had a muscular build eventually married, fathered twelve children and, for the rest of his life, called the area of Maryland in and around present-day D.C. home. Starting out as a farmer and land speculator on a fifty-acre plot, Beall gained more property through the years and ultimately came to acquire an astounding twenty-five thousand acres.[7]

While much of this land was located along the Patuxent River, one particular plot was located along Rock Creek. He called this land, which eventually became Georgetown, the Rock of Dumbarton, named after a rocky bulge in his native Scotland where the River Leven meets the River Clyde. The name "Dumbarton" stuck and is the reason why today there is a Dumbarton Oaks and Dumbarton Oaks Park.[8]

Beall's Rock of Dumbarton was an eight-hundred-acre rectangular tract located on the west side of Rock Creek bordering the Potomac River. Although it is unknown to what extent Beall cultivated the land, his last will and testament suggests that he primarily used it for livestock grazing. "I do give and bequeath unto my son George my plantation and tract of land called the Rock of Dumbarton lying and being at the Rock of Dumbarton and being at Rock Creek…with all the stock thereon both cattle and hogs," Beall's will reads. Early maps show that the redheaded Scotsman also built a home at Rock of Dumbarton, where he stayed occasionally in addition to his other residences.[9]

While Beall purchased the Rock of Dumbarton rather late in his life in 1703, for decades prior, he roamed the land on both sides of the creek as well as through the greater D.C. area. With his imposing figure, Beall served as both an early Maryland politician as well as an American Indian negotiator, eventually being titled "Commander-in-Chief of Provincial Forces." In charge of a group of rangers who patrolled the land attempting to keep peace, Beall was rewarded upon his retirement with a gift of "three Negro slaves for proper use and benefit." In what might seem astounding today, the gift of human bondage was paid for in fact out of public funds—taxpayer's dollars.[10] While it is unknown how many additional slaves Beall had, it is probable that some of them worked and lived on his land along Rock Creek.

At any rate, when he passed away at age ninety-two in 1717, Beall's son George inherited a large portion of the Rock of Dumbarton. George eventually sold it to George Gordon, who in 1751 founded the town of George, or George Town, on the exact plot of land.[11]

Old Stone House

Washington, D.C.'s Oldest Building Was Preserved Thanks in Part Due to a Myth

Many Georgetown tourists are surprised when, walking along bustling M Street, they observe a quaint old house with a colorful garden sandwiched between designer retail stores and gourmet cupcake shops. This is Old Stone House, a small National Park Service site administered by Rock Creek Park. Built first in 1765 and completed by the 1780s, Old Stone House serves as an exceptional example of an upper-middle-class Georgetown home of the late colonial and early American period. Furthermore, the humble house is D.C.'s oldest building still on its original foundation and the only original nine-tenths of an acre property left from the founding of Georgetown in 1751. How has it survived for 250 years? One reason is that it's famous by association; the other is that it was owned by the same family for over 100 years.

A member of Georgetown's upper-middle class, Cassandra Chew purchased the house and property in 1767 after the original owners had built a humble home that included today's bookstore room as well as probably the two bedrooms on the second floor. A widow, Chew added on and up to the house. By 1780, the current configuration was completed.

While it is unclear who lived in the house (Cassandra's daughter and her husband might have resided there with her), an interesting twist to the Chew family can be found in looking at their connection with Robert Peter, Georgetown's first mayor. Peter purchased another Georgetown home for Cassandra and also provided for Mary generously in his will. Due to these facts and the fact that Peter was a married man, some historians believe that he had an affair at some point in time with Cassandra and was Mary's father.[12]

Whether or not this was the case, according to at least one National Park Service record of the house, when Cassandra died in 1808, Mary did in fact inherit Old Stone House. Upon Mary Chew Brumley's own death in 1826, her daughters were then willed the house. Two of these daughters were Sarah Maria Suter and Ann Suter, the last name "Suter" being an important name in the house's story, as we'll see below. Sarah would continue to own part of Old Stone House until the mid-1870s.[13]

Throughout most of the time that Chew and her heirs owned the house, Georgetown was an industrial and commercial hub for the region. Indeed, while Georgetown was incorporated into the District of Columbia when the national capital was established in 1790, it outpaced the federal city (currently downtown Washington) in economic growth and prosperity for decades. Many of the original homes of Georgetown were eventually razed over the years, especially along M Street, to make way for more modern and larger (and sometimes more efficient) structures, but Old Stone House miraculously remained unscathed.

At essentially the exact time that Old Stone House left the hands of the Chew family in the 1870s, rumors began circulating that it had served as George Washington's headquarters in 1791 when he spent some time in the nation's capital planning for it with controversial Frenchman Pierre Charles L'Enfant. National Park Service historian Cornelius Heine notes that, as early as 1874, a plaque outside the house read, "George Washington's Engineering Headquarters." In 1899, a new marker stated, "George Washington's Headquarters while surveying Washington in 1791."[14]

Over the years, some came to believe that George Washington worked out of Old Stone House not in 1791 but during the Revolutionary War. U.S. Speaker of the House Sam Rayburn, in pushing Congress to purchase the house for posterity in 1950, told the chamber that "I am very interested in the passage of this bill, not because it means a thing in the world to me but because I do think the few landmarks we have in the United States ought

"General George Washington" at Old Stone House. As late as 1951, the year this photo was taken, celebrations were held at Old Stone House promoting our first president's legacy and mythical connection to the house. *National Park Service.*

to be preserved as an inspiration to the generations that are coming…This old building was the headquarters of the Father of our country during the Revolution."[15] Regardless of the dates of Washington's supposed visits to the house, books were written on these "facts," and commemorative living history events were held outside.

These myths probably stemmed in part from the fact that one John Suter of Georgetown had a popular tavern—known as Suter's Tavern, or Suter's Inn—where Washington, Thomas Jefferson and L'Enfant met for a few days in 1791 to discuss and write up plans for the District of Columbia. Located a couple blocks away from Old Stone House, the tavern passed to John Suter's son, John Suter Jr., after his father passed away. Coincidentally, Suter Jr. also rented out the front room of Old Stone House from Mary Smith Brumley and used it as his clock shop. In addition, due to the previously mentioned last names of Mary's daughters, Sarah Maria Suter and Ann Suter, some evidence suggests that Suter Jr. married Brumley, had children with her and lived in Old Stone House.[16]

Old Stone House, circa 1960. The National Park Service acquired the house and property in 1950, renovated, restored and then opened it to the public in 1960. *Library of Congress.*

It is unknown whether the family who purchased Old Stone House in the 1870s started the "Washington's headquarters" rumor in order to bring in more customers to a business located inside or whether Georgetown citizens created the myth in order to boost local folklore and commerce. What is known, however, is that the myth that Old Stone House was used by America's first president is just that—a myth. Heine points out that, in 1929, when a bill in Congress was introduced to make "Washington's Engineering Headquarters" a national monument with an engineering theme, local historians came out in droves against the idea on the grounds that Old Stone House's proclaimed history was all a hoax. "The face of the Old Stone House has been a haven of historical markers. These have been false in their message," noted Columbia Historical Society president Allen C. Clark at the time.[17]

Heine himself put the myth to rest by conducting significant research in the 1950s and finding no evidence of America's first president ever using Old Stone House. "History is dependent upon facts based upon written records. Without such records, even in view of a lingering tradition, history cannot be written. In this aspect of the Old Stone House story, it would be impossible in view of the complete lack of written evidence to refer to the structure as the 'Engineering Headquarters of George Washington,'" he notes. Heine was also able to prove that Suter's Tavern was not located at Old Stone House but down by the Georgetown waterfront.[18]

The George Washington Headquarters at Old Stone House theory is now long abandoned. More importantly, though, Washington, D.C.'s oldest building remains intact and well preserved as a historical site 250 years after it was constructed.

James Lingan's Funeral

The War of 1812 in Montrose Park

On the northern end of Georgetown, a park site known as Montrose Park represents the quintessential city park. It's got grassy fields, a playground and tennis courts. Montrose Park is an administrative unit of Rock Creek Park. Historically known as Parrott's Woods, the grounds that became the park hosted the funeral of perhaps the first person in U.S. history to die in defense of freedom of the press. The person's name was James Lingan, and he was also one of the first casualties in the War of 1812.

As a brief background, just like the Iraq War that took center stage during the first decade of the twenty-first century, the War of 1812 was controversial from the get-go. A three-year war in spite of what its name suggests, it began when President James Madison reluctantly declared war on Great Britain with the ultimate goal of getting the small yet powerful island nation to back off its policy of impressing. Great Britain was at war with France and, in order to recruit additional help in its war effort, had begun impressing, or forcefully taking, U.S. merchant vessels, their cargos and their crews in open water. In this fashion, hundreds of U.S. citizens were forced into the Royal Navy against their wills. While many U.S. citizens approved of what they considered the "Second War for Independence," others did not see the need for what they called "Mr. Madison's War." This came to the forefront in Baltimore and, sadly, during a war-related funeral in Parrott's Woods, today known as Montrose Park.[19]

Parrott's Woods was the property of Richard Parrott, who built a mansion and ropewalk on the grounds as well as a water-powered mill just down the hill along Rock Creek. The ropewalk, essentially a unique outdoor factory where rope was made, actually supplied the U.S. Navy during the war. Because of this, Parrott was probably very nervous when the British marched on Washington and burned several important government buildings in August 1814. One account actually claims that Parrott's ropewalk was burned by the British, but this is very likely inaccurate, as it was written over one hundred years after the matter and no other documents claim that British troops even reached Georgetown.

While his ropewalk wasn't burned, Parrott's property was nevertheless involved in the war in that it served as the site for the funeral of James Lingan on September 12, 1812. Lingan very well might have the distinction of being the first person in U.S. history to die in defense of freedom of the press. Furthermore, he was one of the first three fatalities of the War of 1812—ironically, he was killed by Americans rather than the British navy. Lingan was a Revolutionary War hero, prisoner of war and Georgetown tobacco merchant; the story of his murder and resulting funeral in Parrott's Woods ultimately began a couple months beforehand just north, in Baltimore.[20]

Lingan's friend Alexander Hanson, editor of Baltimore's *Federal Republican*, began writing against the war in his newspaper. "The last hope of civilization, law, and order was old Mother England," wrote Hanson, as he lobbied fellow citizens to throw down their weapons instead of fight a needless war. This enraged some members of the opposition who considered Hanson a traitor. With emotions running high, a pro-war mob burned and looted his print shop. Hanson, escorted by Henry "Light-Horse Harry" Lee—who, like Lingan, was also a Revolutionary War veteran, not to mention father of Robert E. Lee—fled to the home of a friend in Georgetown. Their friend was James Lingan. But the trio traveled back up to Baltimore too soon.[21]

Thinking the excitement would be over, Lee and Lingan helped Hanson set up shop in a new office. The mob reappeared, however, and soon there was a stakeout. Things reached a fever pitch, and the small group of men, trapped in their shop and fearing for their lives, shot and killed a couple of the mobsters. Eventually, Baltimore police escorted the three men to jail, where they were told that they would get protection and a fair trial. That night, however, the watchmen turned their backs. The mob stormed the jail cell.[22]

All three men were severely beaten and left for dead. While Lee never recovered from his injuries and died a few years later, Georgetown's James Lingan died on the spot. Legend has it that when they pulled Lingan out of his cell, Lingan ripped open his shirt to show the mobsters his bayonet wounds inflicted by the British during the Revolutionary War. Caught up in the moment, however, the mob didn't care about Lingan's former patriotic services. Someone pitched a stone at Lingan's chest, and, well, that was it.[23]

A month after the incident, Lingan's funeral service was held at Parrott's Woods. Hundreds of citizens and dignitaries, including Lingan's son, attended the event (Lingan's wife did not, as she was too emotionally broken). Presiding over the funeral was George Washington Parke Custis, stepson of the first president. Under a formal tent used on several occasions by Washington himself, Custis spoke out to the crowd, "Say ye who best can tell, was he [Lingan] not the kind indulgent parent? The good husband? The faithful friend? The upright honorable man?...SOLDIER of my COUNTRY! DEFENDER of her LIBERTIES—FAREWELL![24]

Upset over the incident himself, Custis believed that revenge over Lingan's murder would take its course in due time:

> Oh, MARYLAND! Would that the water of thy Chesapeake could wash this foul stain from thy character!—Oh MARYLAND! Would that the recording angel, who carries thy black deed to Heaven's chancery on high, could drop a tear upon it, and blot it out forever! But no! A voice cries from the tomb of the brave. It rises to the God of Nature and Humanity, and demands a vengeance on the murderer![25]

James Lingan's body was ultimately interred in Arlington National Cemetery. He has the distinction and honor of being the only Revolutionary War veteran to be buried there.[26]

JOSHUA PEIRCE, LINNAEAN HILL AND AFRICAN AMERICAN SLAVES
Waltzing Camellias and Human Bondage

On an isolated, forested bluff located about two and a half linear miles north of Montrose Park, just south of Peirce Mill and just west of Rock Creek, lies the park's only historic mansion. Referred to as Klingle Mansion and today serving as Rock Creek Park's administrative headquarters, the mansion is part of a historic property known as Linnaean Hill. The historic building and grounds has a horticultural and African American slave past.

The eighty-two-acre property was given to Joshua Peirce in the 1820s by his father, Isaac, the original owner of Peirce Mill and most prominent landowner of the time in the Rock Creek Valley. A well-educated individual who spent most of his childhood in the heart of Pennsylvania Quaker country and also married there, Joshua Peirce named his estate Linnaean Hill either out of respect for Swedish botanist Carl Von Linnaeus, who developed the Latin classification system for cataloging plants, or to tap into the success of the Linnaean Botanical Garden and Nurseries, run by William Prince on Long Island, or a combination of the two. Either way, Peirce then set about building an eleven-room mansion and outbuildings using locally quarried blue fieldstone. The owner constructed a greenhouse, nursery, large farmhouse made of stone, springhouse and unique system of curving drives designed to show off his picturesque landscape overlooking Rock Creek. He planted extensively, and Linnaean Hill became a thriving plant nursery.[27]

On his property, in addition to the farm staples of oats, rye, corn, potatoes, peas, beans and buckwheat, Peirce planted and cultivated many types of trees and flowering plants. He did this by collecting and then expanding native species; directly purchasing wholesale seedlings, primarily from nurseries in New England; and by using propagation and grafting techniques. D.C. historian and Friends of Peirce Mill program manager Steve Dryden notes in *Peirce Mill: Two Hundred Years in the Nation's Capital* that "Peirce's catalog of

Linnaean Hill, mansion and greenhouse remnants, circa 1900. *Library of Congress.*

1857 lists approximately 50 varieties of eating and cider apples, 40 kinds of peaches, seventy varieties of pears, thirty kinds of cherries, and 25 apricot hybrids." Additionally, Peirce had several rows of vineyards—in 1860, records indicate that Peirce produced sixty gallons of red wine. He also cultivated pawpaws, Balm of Gilead, white pine, Norway spruce, several types of fir trees and hemlock.[28]

Regarding decorative plants, Peirce cultivated various types of roses and white-flowering horse chestnut magnolias, in addition to English ivy. Today considered a highly invasive, nonnative plant species by park staff, English ivy was planted, sold and spread in the 1800s due to its evergreen character (for more on invasive plants, see Chapter 9). The ivy was also "planted on the north façade [of Peirce's mansion] to blend the architecture of the house into the landscape."[29]

Of everything he cultivated, Peirce cherished most his camellias, an Asian flowering plant that he helped popularize in the D.C. area. Purchased by area residents and officials for the high price of one dollar each (around thirty dollars today), Peirce's twelve varieties of camellias were sold to beautify public spaces throughout the capital. Linnaean Hill hosted many rows of camellias both outside in rows and inside the greenhouse, which was situated on the backside of the mansion. In the early 1900s, Peirce Shoemaker, a relative of Joshua, noted that this "most beautiful of cultivated flowers" was still alive and well on the historic property.[30]

Due to its exceptional view overlooking Rock Creek as well as its artistically arranged curving pathways, Linnaean Hill became a popular destination for early Rock Creek Valley tourists. Sunday picnickers were a common sight, and Peirce, in good social standing in D.C., often hosted his friends Henry Clay and John C. Calhoun on his estate.[31]

In his later years, Peirce caught a young group of boys—including Charles Carroll Glover, the future "father" of Rock Creek Park—snitching cherries from his property one Sunday. As the story goes, with Glover high up in the cherry tree, Peirce came out of his mansion with a shotgun, yelling, "You get down from there right now!" Embarrassed at being caught, the young Glover apologized and proposed paying for the cherries. After the incident, despite the age difference between them, the two became friends.[32]

Who cooked the meals for Joshua Peirce and his famous guests, and who harvested the crops and cultivated the plants? Joshua might have overseen his properties' daily workings and doings, but he undoubtedly left the vast majority of hands-on labor to his slaves. Indeed, like his father at Peirce Mill as well as many other European American landowners in the Rock Creek Valley at the time, Peirce was a slave owner and relied on this system of forced bondage for much of his success. Records show that in 1840, Peirce owned thirteen slaves, and at the time of D.C. emancipation in 1862, he owned nine. His slaves served as house workers, cooks, farmhands, nursery foremen and market salesmen and were highly regarded by Peirce.[33]

Indeed, although not justifying slavery by any means, the image of slave-whipping owner was not applicable to the owner of Linnaean Hill. Peirce actually placed a great deal of trust with his business endeavors in many of his slaves and also made "generous arrangements in his will for many of his former slaves." For instance, his oldest slaves, Jeremiah Gibson and Nancy Rhodes, were given a $48 stipend per year, while William H. Beckett was bequeathed $1,000. Peirce described Beckett, his favorite and most prized slave worker, as "foreman in my garden, greenhouse, and nursery." Interestingly, after emancipation and the Civil War, Peirce asked Beckett to come back, and Beckett, in fact went, back to work for his former master. Beckett also served as Peirce's caretaker and nurse during Peirce's ailing health and final days and was at his former master's bedside when he died.[34]

Unfortunately, the relationship between Linnaean Hill and Beckett soured shortly after Joshua Peirce's death. Peirce never had children, and when he died in 1869, his nephew Joshua Peirce Klingle inherited the estate. Klingle refused to pay Beckett the high monthly salary of one hundred dollars that Peirce had given him, and Beckett eventually left. Regarding other themes of the historic property, Klingle did not have as much of an interest in horticulture, nor did he live on the property as long as his uncle. Nevertheless, ironically, the mansion today is referred to as the Klingle Mansion rather than the (Joshua) Peirce Mansion.[35]

John Quincy Adams's Mill

"All the Labor of the Year Has Been Lost"

If Linnaean Hill was a highly successful property of the Rock Creek Valley in the mid-1800s, a property nearby that was owned by America's sixth president was most definitely not. John Quincy Adams purchased a gristmill along Rock Creek in 1823, and for the next two and a half decades, it caused him constant stress and heartache. The story of this long-lost Rock Creek mill sadly sheds light on the fact that Adams was not a good businessman, at least when it came to gristmills.

Originally built around 1800 and known as Columbia Mill in honor of the recently created District of Columbia, in 1812, it was purchased by Adams's wife's cousin George Johnson. Unfortunately, Johnson's business acumen was even worse than the president's. Within a year, the mill burned down. Within two years, Johnson was being sued due to the fact that when he rebuilt the mill, he constructed it in the automated style patented by New Jersey millwright Oliver Evans but did not compensate Evans. Johnson lost the case, and his woes continued.[36]

By 1823, when John Quincy Adams purchased the mill, Johnson had gone bankrupt, and the mill was in the hands of the Bank of Columbia. Whether Adams knew the backstory of the mill and Johnson's poor record of milling or not, Adams bought the mill from the bank, seeing it as a potential source of profit. This was a mistake, and an even worse error of Adams was his keeping Johnson as his mill manager. Naturally, the immorality and poor work standards of Johnson continued.[37]

As a result, the sales at the mill struggled. While the money Adams gave Johnson to successfully operate the mill was used by Johnson instead to pay off his personal debt, mill woes were exacerbated by the fact that the flour market itself was bottoming out. As a result, Adams lamented in his diary that "the first year has been a total and a severe disappointment; and I have no reason to expect anything better from the second." A few

Adams's mill on Rock Creek, circa 1900. *Library of Congress.*

months later, in another entry, Adams complained that "the business of the mill has been a losing concern. All the labor of the year has been lost; and instead of a resource for retirement, is likely to prove a heavy clog upon my affairs."[38]

Things were so bad that by 1826, at the end of Adams's single-term presidency, Johnson had left the mill operation. Whether he was asked to do so by the president remains unknown. Nevertheless, the flour market continued to fluctuate as a series of mill managers, including one of Adams's own sons, took up the post. Perhaps the only moneymaking year of Adams Mill was in 1830, when its grain was shipped to Boston, New York, Liverpool and Baltimore. Unfortunately, this success was short-lived, as Adams's son died the following year, and several components of the mill then continually broke down.[39]

Even with all the challenges that Adams's mill faced—corrupt managers, a flour market that was bottoming out, broken gadgets—the blame might go back to the president himself. Records show that Adams, regardless of who the mill manager was, constantly critiqued and questioned him, though he himself knew nothing about milling. Was America's sixth president a micromanager of his Rock Creek mill? While this might never be known for certain, undoubtedly, Adams made a poor decision in hiring George Johnson in the first place.

BLAGDEN MILL

Slaughterhouse Recycling

Just a mile and a half north of Adams's mill was Peirce Mill. The most successful gristmill along Rock Creek and dating from the 1820s, Peirce Mill is not featured heavily in this text due to the fact that a book has already been published on it. Furthermore, readers can easily visit the mill and learn about its history. However, just a half mile above Peirce Mill stood a lesser-known mill. This was Blagden Mill, also known as the Argyle Mill.

Built prior to 1850, Blagden Mill was actually two mills in one. Including both a gristmill and fertilizer mill, or bone mill, the structure, as well as over three hundred surrounding acres, was purchased by Thomas Blagden in 1853. Blagden then hired an able miller who turned the mill into a successful business venture for the next two decades. In 1860, the mill produced 4,200 barrels of flour valued at $24,000. A decade later, the mill's income had nearly doubled.[40]

Blagden Mill ruins, circa 1889. *National Park Service.*

Like all the mills along Rock Creek, the Blagden Mill used renewable energy, the water of Rock Creek, to operate. Above the mill, a headrace was set up, which fed creek water speedily toward the mill wheel. The mill wheel then turned due to the force of water running through it. The mill wheel connected to gadgets on the inside the mill, including the millstones, and made everything function.

While it might be relatively straightforward to understand that local farmers brought their wheat, rye and corn to be ground into flour by the millstones and then sold in Georgetown and federal city markets, the bone mill actually ground animal bones from local slaughterhouses and farms. The finished product was then used as soil fertilizer.[41]

After good runs, some of the mills along Rock Creek began struggling by the 1880s as more modern processing methods, advancing technology and rail transportation developed. The nail in the coffin occurred for Blagden Mill in 1889 when the storm system that caused the tragic Johnstown flood, which killed over five thousand residents in the Pennsylvania town, hit the D.C. area. Blagden Mill was destroyed beyond repair with Rock Creek floodwaters, and during the initial construction of Beach Drive a decade later, the mill ruins were removed.[42]

Nevertheless, just below Boulder Bridge, remnants of Blagden Mill remain as silent reminders of Rock Creek Park's past. Part of the original millrace is visible, resembling a narrow gully. Across the creek, remnants of the Blagden Mill Road, as well as its bridge and footbridge—both washed out during the 1889 flood—can be seen.[43]

GODEY'S LIMEKILNS

Quicklime, Anyone?

Along the Rock Creek and Potomac Parkway, just a few feet north of the K Street overpass and across from mile marker zero of the Chesapeake and Ohio Canal, lie the two remaining kilns of William H. Godey's historic limekiln business. These are the only limekilns left in the District of Columbia, and they represent an important business of a bygone era. Godey's kilns operated between the 1860s and 1907.[44] Quicklime, the finished product of the limekiln, was used during the time as a type of industrial glue, specifically for sealing bricks and stones together to finish a building wall.

The process in which Godey, his family and staff made the quicklime was labor intensive. The first step involved quarrying the mineral, which was done most often in the hills above Harpers Ferry, West Virginia.[45] After this initial step, a canal boat would be used to transport the stones directly down the canal to Godey's kilns. Next came the process of felling trees for firewood. The fire needed to burn in the kiln for three days and three nights, so much deforesting occurred around Godey's property for the expressed purpose.[46]

After the limestone was placed in the kilns came the most dangerous work. With fire blazing on the bottom of the kilns, the limestone slowly melted above. The kiln doors were kept generally closed throughout the entire process, except for when the worker needed to check the fire pressure. When he did open up the doors, Godey and company had to be extremely careful not to get burned from the 1,500-degree heat when they added more wood. If done right, after the three days and nights, the lime would be melted down into the toothpaste-like substance of quicklime.[47]

Godey built and then operated the kilns between 1864 and 1873. When he passed away, his widow and sons took over the operation. Known as the

Godey's limekiln property, circa 1900. Three of the four limekilns are visible in the background. *Library of Congress.*

Godey's limekilns after construction of the Whitehurst Freeway, circa 1965. *Library of Congress.*

Washington Limekilns, one of the sons, Edward Godey, boasted that the business included twenty-five workers and could produce two thousand barrels of wood-burnt lime per week. Historians say this was most likely a bending of the truth, however, as probably only the more efficient coal-burning limekilns of the time could burn at this rate. Indeed, the Godey's sold the kilns into private hands in the late 1800s, and the kiln was outcompeted by the more efficient coal process by 1907, when it ceased operation altogether.[48]

JOAQUIN MILLER AND HIS CABIN

America's Most Bizarre Poet Has a Cabin in the Woods

Just north of picnic grove six on Beach Drive stands an unassuming, seemingly out-of-place log cabin. This is Miller Cabin, the mid-1880s home of the self-described "Poet of the Sierras" and "Byron of the Rockies,"

Joaquin Miller. The eccentric poet built and lived in the cabin originally on Meridian Hill, but when plans were laid out for a formal Meridian Hill Park in the early 1900s, developers needed to move the cabin to a new location. Despite objections by early park management, the Miller Cabin was moved to Rock Creek Park. Yet the story is not so much about the cabin itself as it is the man who lived in the cabin.

Joaquin Miller (1837–1913) was a lot of things to a lot of people. He was a playwright, journalist, editor and novelist; cowhand, horse thief, gold miner and pony express rider; county judge and candidate for both the U.S. Senate and Supreme Court; and conservationist. Miller traveled the Oregon Trail ("My cradle was a covered wagon, headed west," he said), lived among the Shasta Indians, wrote an extremely successful Broadway play on Mormon history and was one of the first of the American literati to gain success and fame in Europe. Most notable of all his careers and endeavors, though, Miller was known as a poet and poseur who often bent the truth in order to make himself seem more significant than he really was—"I don't lie; I simply exaggerate the truth," he once said.[49]

Miller had myriad experiences and travels before settling in his cabin now administered by Rock Creek Park. Born in Indiana as Cincinnatus Hiner Miller "in the year of our Lord 1837 on the 8th day of September," the poet later in life always told people that he was born in 1842 in order to seem five years younger.[50] At any rate, he did in fact begin reading and writing poetry at a young age, and traveled westward on the Oregon Trail with his family at age fifteen. But after farming and homesteading for only a year or two in Oregon Territory's Willamette Valley, Miller got gold fever and ran away to the Sierra Nevada foothills.

For the next decade, the young Miller tried his hand at various careers. While gold mining didn't pan out, he served as a gold camp cook for several months, noting that "I cooked all winter for twenty-seven men and [somehow] every man was alive in the spring." He then lived among the Shasta Indians for a time, becoming companion to and bedfellow of an American Indian woman named Paquita and thus fathering a child they named Cali-Shasta. Ironically, in the middle of this "gone Native" stint, the poet actually left to fight neighboring Indians in the Modoc War. Unfortunately, "Miller was a failure as a father and husband," notes a biographer, and Miller eventually left Paquita and his baby girl.[51]

The vagabond poet then got in trouble with the law, escaped from prison, went to college and served as a pony express rider between central Oregon and Idaho. At some point during this time, Cincinnatus Hiner Miller became

Joaquin Miller, the poet changing his name in order to sound catchy and also to honor Mexican Robin Hood–type bandit Joaquín Murietta.

While it is unknown when exactly he changed his name, it is known that from 1866 to 1870, Miller served as county judge for Grant County, Oregon. Apparently hardworking with his head in the law books, Miller published poetry for the first time during these years, but to little fanfare and notice. He also quickly fell in love and married again during his Oregon years but felt compelled to leave after his second wife humiliated him with a public, tell-all divorce.[52]

A chronic traveler, after a stint in San Francisco, Miller created a career for himself in England by posing as a mountain man and playing into cowboy stereotypes. Walking down the streets of London wearing animal fur and wooing the British press with his tall-tale life stories, the poet's books became much more successful abroad than at home. Historian Walt Curtis notes that all of Miller's friends, including "Walt Whitman, Oscar Wilde, Lily Langtry, the English literati, the Bierce brothers, Mark Twain, Bret Harte and yes even his critics[,] recognized his 'genius.' What was it? His greatest achievement may well have been the manufacture of his own career."[53]

Miller, never one to stay anywhere for a long period of time, rode his England wave of success back to New York City, where he "settled down" in the late 1870s and wrote *The Danites*, "an immediate and tremendous hit" chronicling the Mormon Church's secret police branch. The play remained on Broadway for seven weeks, according to Miller biographer M.M. Marberry.[54]

Though he never lived in the Rocky Mountains, the self-described "Byron of the Rockies" grew tired of his setting after a few years and moved with another wife to Washington, D.C. Conveniently, after Miller decided that the residence in downtown was not working out due to the fact that he wanted peace and quiet away from civilization, his wife fled, thus enabling the poet to move onto what he described as "a little edge of God's rest" on top of Meridian Hill. Here he built a humble, two-room log cabin—the one that today stands silently in Rock Creek Park:

> *The cabin nestled in a circle of huge oak trees, whose branches interlaced over the roof, and it stood far back from the road. There was no path leading to the door, as Joaquin preferred to let the grass grow wild everywhere. In the side yard, the long awkward arm of an old-fashioned sweep dipped picturesquely down into a deep park well…The logs of the cabin were peeled of bark and unadorned with paint or whitewash.*

Joaquin Miller's cabin on Meridian Hill, circa 1890. In 1911, the cabin was moved to Rock Creek Park. It sits just north of picnic grove six on Beach Drive today. *National Park Service.*

Miller Cabin at present location in Rock Creek Park, circa 1960. Joaquin's niece, Pherne Miller, leased the cabin, conducted art classes in it and sold soft drinks and candy there from the 1930s to the 1950s. More recently, the Joaquin Miller Poetry Series, hosted by the Word Works, was held outside the cabin in the summer. *National Park Service photo.*

On the outside walls Joaquin hung elk skins and bows and arrows. Inside, there were two small rooms, both unplastered [sic], with gaping chinks showing between the logs…The front room contained a writing table, a few chairs, a stove in the corner, a bearskin on the floor, a vase always filled with wild flowers, but little else. The room in the rear was barely large enough to hold a bed. For a blanket, Joaquin used the hides of wild animals. Some people thought the new home was on the primitive side. The poet pronounced it perfect.[55]

Because he chose to live in the primitive fashion on the outskirts of a major city, Miller and his cabin became a tourist attraction. Similar to what he did in London, Miller posed for these tourists. Upon seeing tourists approach his cabin, the poet would throw on a coonskin cap and bearskin and then stand at the door waiting for them. Then he would commence telling visitors the tales of his life, not much distinguishing between truth and fiction. Kathy Morrison Taylor, president of the Word Works Association that hosts the annual Joaquin Miller Poetry Series in Rock Creek Park, notes his storytelling style:

His voice is mesmerizing. He tells you of his life among the Modocs in California and the Indian wars, when a near-fatal arrow pierced his jaw. In the next breath, he tells you of his travels to England and introductions to Alfred, Lord Tennyson, Anthony Trollope and Edward John Trelawney, his friendship with Dante Gabriel Rossetti and others of the Pre-Raphaelite brotherhood, and a fantastic story of a reception in a castle with the Queen herself.[56]

After only a few years in Washington, Miller, as he had done in London, New York and places out west beforehand, continued his worldly travels. In Alaska for a short time, he served as a newspaper journalist and coaxed gold-seekers northward with false claims promoting how easy it was to get rich. He also continued to write poetry.

For the dozens of poems Miller wrote on topics of love, his personal experiences and history as he saw it, only one gained major success. This poem was "Columbus," which he was commissioned to write in 1892 in honor of the 500th anniversary of the famous explorer's voyage to the Americas. With its repetition of the words "Sail on, sail on, sail on," the poem was recited by elementary school children on Columbus Day for decades.[57]

During his "retirement years," although Miller continued to travel as a journalist to places such as Hawaii and even China to cover the Boxer Rebellion, the poet ultimately settled down in the Oakland hills of the San Francisco Bay area. In this last stage of his life, Miller became a conservationist. He planted thousands of trees on his property and also

COLUMBUS

By Joaquin Miller

Behind him lay the gray Azores,
Behind the Gates of Hercules;
Before him not the ghost of shores,
Before him only shoreless seas.
The good mate said: "Now we must pray,
For lo! the very stars are gone.
Brave Admiral, speak, what shall I say?"
"Why, say, 'Sail on! sail on! and on!'"

"My men grow mutinous day by day;
My men grow ghastly wan and weak."
The stout mate thought of home; a spray
Of salt wave washed his swarthy cheek.
"What shall I say, brave Admiral, say,
If we sight naught but seas at dawn?"
"Why, you shall say at break of day,
'Sail on! sail on! and on!'"

They sailed and sailed, as winds might blow,
Until at last the blanched mate said:
"Why, now not even God would know
Should I and all my men fall dead.

These very winds forget their way,
For God from these dead seas is gone.
Now speak, brave Admiral, speak and say"
—He said, "Sail on! sail on! and on!"

They sailed. They sailed. Then spake the mate:
"This mad sea shows his teeth tonight.
He curls his lip, he lies in wait,
With lifted teeth, as if to bite!
Brave Admiral, say but one good word:
What shall we do when hope is gone?"
The words leapt like a leaping sword:
"Sail on! sail on! sail on! and on!"

Then pale and worn, he kept his deck,
And peered through darkness. Ah, that night
Of all dark nights! And then a speck
—A light! a light! at last a light!
It grew, a starlit flag unfurled!
It grew to be Time's burst of dawn.
He gained a world; he gave that world
Its grandest lesson: "On! sail on!"

became a staunch wilderness supporter over fifty years prior to the passage of the Wilderness Act. As a conservationist, Miller wrote passionately against a rim drive around Crater Lake National Park. Miller had fallen in love with the region earlier in his life when he had spent five days camping there at the invitation of William Gladstone Steele, the "father" of the park. But when Steele drew up plans for a Rim Drive around the lake, Miller firmly opposed it. Before he passed away in 1913, Miller wrote, impressively for a poseur who most considered had poor prose:

Joaquin Miller, circa 1875. Described as extremely handsome at middle age, later in life Miller appeared unkempt and sported a long white beard and hair. *Library of Congress.*

This noblest natural park in the Republic, and the most unique park under the path of the sun. It took such hold of my heart…that I love it almost like one of my own family. The thousand and one "best points of view" from the rim of the crater keep you busy from morning to night. The plan is now to build…a drive around the lake, so that all these points may be considered

43

in a single day from a carriage…And a great hotel is planned!…Well, so be it, if you must so mock nature and break this hush and silence of a thousand centuries, but I shall not be here. No hotel or house or road of any sort should ever be built near this Sea of Silence. All our other parks have been surrendered to hotels and railroads. Let us keep this last and best sacred in to silence and nature. That which is not worth climbing to see is not worth seeing.[58]

In California, the Joaquin Miller Elementary School in Burbank, Joaquin Miller Middle School in San Jose and five-hundred-acre Joaquin Miller Park in the Oakland Hills, located on his former property, are named in the eccentric poet's honor, as is Rock Creek Park's cobweb-collecting Miller Cabin, although there is not a single sign or wayside exhibit out front explaining it as such.

2

THE CIVIL WAR IN ROCK CREEK PARK

Continuing the discussion of the pre-park era, the Civil War had a profound effect on Washington, including the land in and around the Rock Creek Valley. Forests were felled, private property was ignored due to "military necessity" and soldiers' lives were changed forever, especially for the nine hundred killed or wounded during D.C.'s only Civil War battle, which took place inside present-day Rock Creek Park. There are other sides to the park's Civil War story though. As the "peculiar institution" of slavery finally began crumbling in the 1860s, African Americans escaped bondage and fled to the safe haven of the Union capital in record numbers. Some of these new residents found work on hilltop fortresses. This chapter seeks to interpret the complex, multifaceted face of the Civil War in Rock Creek Park, beginning with the controversial eve-of-war president whose memorial is located bizarrely in Meridian Hill Park.

PRESIDENT JAMES BUCHANAN AND HIS MEMORIAL

Challenges of the Chief

In the southeast corner of Meridian Hill Park lies a formal bronze-and-granite memorial to President James Buchanan, America's fifteenth commander in chief. At the site, a bronze statue of Buchanan is framed by two allegorical figures depicting law and diplomacy, representing the president's rise to power and his background. Engraved in granite is a quote from one of Buchanan's cabinet members that reads, "The incorruptible statesman whose walk was upon the mountain ranges of the law."

There is some irony to the memorial, though, as Buchanan is regarded in practically every presidential ranking as one of the worst, if not the worst, presidents in U.S. history. Not knowing where to put the memorial but most definitely not wanting to put it on the prestigious National Mall, Congress stalled for as long as possible in accepting the donation for it, which had been bequeathed by the president's niece, Harriet Lane Johnston.[59] In a nation that perhaps overemphasizes the successes of Jefferson, Washington and Lincoln, there might be things to learn from studying the opposite side of the highest office—presidential failures.

The last president to be born in the 1700s, Buchanan was born into a well-off Pennsylvanian family in 1791. Described as "tall, stately, [and] stiffly formal in the high stock he wore around his jowls," the young Buchanan studied law in college and was highly noted as a debater and orator. He eventually opened up a successful law firm before turning to politics. His ascendancy to the presidency was a long one, and probably no other commander in chief has ever had a stronger résumé upon entering office. Buchanan was elected five times to the House of Representatives, served for an interlude as minister to Russia, served for a decade in the U.S. Senate, became Polk's secretary of state and, finally, was Pierce's minister to Great Britain.[60]

This final diplomatic post to London in the mid-1850s improved Buchanan's stature significantly in the United States. Back home, Northern and Southern states were debating fiercely over the issue of slavery. But since he was away, citizens began seeing Buchanan as one above the fray. Ironically, one particular incident that escalated Buchanan's standing in the United States was a "dinner clothing controversy" involving his appearance in front of the queen. Always one to abide by the law, Buchanan found his orders contradicting each other when he was invited while in London to dine with her majesty. British common law made it strict protocol to dress formally and professionally when seeing the queen, especially at estate dinners. However, Buchanan had received a written memorandum by the U.S. secretary of state stating that all foreign diplomats were to dress in "regular American attire" overseas. After debating in his head which clothing he'd wear, Buchanan shocked the British press by wearing slightly less formal American attire to dinner. As a result, English newspaper tabloids

Right: James Buchanan was U.S. president from 1857 to 1861. *Library of Congress.*

Below: Dedication of Buchanan Memorial in Meridian Hill Park, 1931. *National Park Service.*

criticized Buchanan as disrespectful and distasteful, while back home, U.S. newspapers proclaimed Buchanan a hero, sticking it to the British monarch and telling them nonverbally that America was all about the common folk, not aristocracy.[61]

And so James Buchanan, the only bachelor president, was catapulted to the highest office in the land. Sadly, however, four years later, the Pennsylvania native would leave the presidency with the country in shambles and his tail between his legs. President at a difficult time in history, Buchanan's administration struggled due to several factors. First, although claiming he was against slavery on paper, the president's pro-Southern and hence proslavery policies enraged the North, especially his attempts to turn Kansas into a slave state. Second, members of Buchanan's own cabinet backstabbed him and were "among the most corrupt in history," according to Buchanan biographer Jean H. Baker.[62] Third, the panic of 1857 and resulting stock market crash did not help things—when the economy struggles, people always look for a scapegoat.

The final two factors spotlighting why Buchanan failed as commander in chief are more complex. One involves the fact that he did not have a single close companion or family member to talk things over with or vent to while serving as president. Buchanan never married, and Harriet Lane Johnson, his niece, served as first lady. Though she was highly regarded by both the president and the public, Buchanan kept things formal between them and did not discuss politics with her.

Perhaps the only person in his life that Buchanan shared everything with was fellow politician William King. The two were best friends for decades, living with each other at various points and writing to each other often. Both men were said to be effeminate. Due to these factors, in addition to Buchanan never really dating or courting women, the deplorable Andrew Jackson once called Buchanan an "Aunt Nancy," and an additional congressman referred to the two men as "Buchanan and his wife." Whether Buchanan needs to be celebrated as America's first gay president we will probably never know for certain. What we do know is that King died just before Buchanan would need him the most. King died in 1853 just after becoming vice president, thus unfortunately becoming the shortest serving vice president in U.S. history.[63]

The primary reason why most historians see Buchanan as a failure is due to his part in the election of Abraham Lincoln and subsequent succession of Southern states. Indeed, Buchanan's policies and politics were the reason why Northern Republicans divided rather than united during the 1860 election, thus enabling the U.S. senator from Illinois to win. Even worse in the eyes of many, though, was that when Southern states began breaking away from the Union, for weeks, Buchanan did absolutely nothing. Confused and depressed at the predicament before him, Buchanan believed that it was not a legal right for states to secede. At the same time, the president believed that neither he nor Congress had the legal power to stop them. Buchanan's inaction allowed the South to mobilize for war months before the North could begin this process.[64]

Although just before leaving office Buchanan did, in fact, authorize a warship to send reinforcements to the Federally owned Fort Sumter in South Carolina, most historians see this action as too little, too late. "Buchanan was significant in presidential annals for what he did not do and for how slowly he did what he did do," writes Baker.[65]

Riding with president-elect Lincoln in a carriage on inauguration day, Buchanan turned to the man in the top hat and supposedly said, "Sir, if you are as happy in entering the White House as I shall feel on returning to Wheatland [his estate], you are a happy man indeed." Within days of taking office, the United States found itself in a Civil War.

After Buchanan left office, he retired to his Pennsylvania estate and spent the final few years of his life defending his presidency and writing his memoirs. While he claimed that the war did not start during his administration, Buchanan failed to realize that his direct actions, or rather inactions, brought it to fruition. Baker claims that "by every measure except his own—whether that of his contemporaries or later historians—Buchanan was an abysmal failure as chief."[66] Buchanan died in 1868. His memorial has not died and stands alive and well in Meridian Hill Park.

FORT DERUSSY

Rock Creek Park's Smithsonian Institution

With President Buchanan out of office and newly elected Lincoln taking the reins, at the outbreak of the Civil War, many U.S. politicians and army generals believed the Confederate States of America would crumble quickly. But early Confederate victories, poor Union general leadership and enemy defenses built only miles from D.C. changed this belief. Washington officials began worrying that their own capital was poorly defended, and as a result, dozens of forts and batteries were built around the perimeter of the city, thus making Washington, D.C., by the middle of the war the most heavily fortified city in the world.[67] Today, Rock Creek Park administers seven of these Civil War Defenses of Washington, or Fort Circle Parks, including the only five forts that saw action during the lesser-known and mostly ignored Battle of Fort Stevens. Beginning with Fort DeRussy, a look back at the four-year histories of these forts, as well as associated sites and leaders, offers us a view into the environmental, social and warring history of the area.

The only Civil War fortress located within the main confines of Rock Creek Park, Fort DeRussy was named after Brigadier General Edward DeRussy, superintendent of the U.S. Military Academy from 1833 to 1838. The earthen fort was constructed to provide crossfire onto the Seventh Street Pike (today's Georgia Avenue) and to protect the Rock Creek Valley from a Confederate march into downtown Washington. Situated on the highest hilltop in the main stem of Rock Creek Park, Fort DeRussy and its nearby batteries commanded a broad view not only due to its geography but also due to the fact that thousands of trees were felled in the immediate area.[68]

Indeed, at least a fifty-six-acre area around the fort was deforested during the Civil War by Union troops. They butchered the trees to gain a clear view of the land, to create a perimeter of abatis (a wall of sharp wooden branches that would have made a Confederate charge up the hill to the fort difficult) and for building materials. They also felled trees and then left them in place to make a Confederate march to downtown Washington impossible. While the fort itself (its parapet and gun magazine) was composed of compacted dirt, the outbuildings—including barracks, mess halls, officers' quarters, stables and guardhouse—were built using the felled trees. A soldier involved in the timbering described the systematic process at the time:

> It was an interesting sight to witness the simultaneous falling of a whole hill-side of timber, the choppers would begin at the foot of the hill, the line extending for perhaps a mile, and cut only part way through the tree, and in this way work up to the crest, leaving the top row so that a single blow would bring down the tree—then, when all was ready, the bugle would sound as a signal, and the last stroke of the axe be given, which brought down the top row; these falling on those below would bring them down, and like the billow on the surface of the ocean, the forest would fall with a crash like mighty thunder.[69]

Other projects that soldiers worked on during the first few months included building batteries, or miniature forts designed for emplacement of heavy guns, nearby. Indeed, one such battery was just downhill from Fort DeRussy on Rock Creek. Troops also constructed Military Road. Connecting each fort from Fort Stevens clear down to Chain Bridge on the Potomac River, the road was an important supply line for shuffling troops and supplies. The roadway was built forty-five feet wide.[70]

During both work and downtime at camp, biting insects were apparently a major issue at Fort DeRussy. Most likely due to the fact that all the trees were removed, bugs turned to human flesh instead of wood for food. Private H.T. Chance, stationed at Fort DeRussy, quipped at the time that "some of the boys call our tent the Smithsonian Institute, on account of the variety of bugs and insects it contains. In reference to the proposed trip to Washington, one said there was no use to spend any time at the Smithsonian there, as we have all the specimens of ants, flies, bugs, and lizards, in our own quarters." A similarly comical yet annoying experience was relayed by another soldier. In a letter complaining both of bugs and a particular officer, Lieutenant DeWolf wrote:

> *Fort DeRussy, the headquarters of Company D, is situated two miles east of Tennallytown, upon a high knoll in the midst of farms cultivated with more than usual care. With a short amount of labor, guided by engineering talent of a high order, our camp was first laid out upon an adjacent knoll, tents pitched, floors leveled, trenches dug, everything in apple-pie order, when a one-armed gentleman of critical aspect, known as Colonel Haskin, of the Engineers, come round, and told us to move nearer the fort. Now it seemed to us that in case of attack we could get there at least as soon as the enemy could, but the colonel didn't think so, and somehow the minority rule prevailed. We now occupy a narrow terrace just under the walls, very strong, very stumpy, and rather buggy. Before many hours, however, the stones had been removed, the stumps transformed to seats and writing desks, and the bugs well, the bugs, the spiders, the lizards, et id omne genis, still roam through their accustomed haunts, the ants build catacombs beneath our beds, the mosquitoes hum playfully about our ears, the wood-ticks climb up the tent walls, and by the light of our solitary candle, gaze curiously upon our little group, selecting the most promising victim.*[71]

Even though they had to avoid wood ticks and mosquitoes, some soldiers relished being near the beauty of the thickly wooded Rock Creek Valley. "The scene before me is enchanting. This is the wildest and most romantic country you were ever in," one soldier wrote. During their off time, soldiers took advantage of being in the scenic area by hiking down to Rock Creek to swim, bathe and fish.[72]

Soldiers particularly enjoyed the waters of Crystal Springs, situated on the slope east of the present-day Rapids Bridge footbridge and west of the tennis stadium. Dry today, Crystal Springs was a series of springs known for its large quantity of water and beautiful surrounding. A hotel and resort had been constructed nearby to attract tourists to the site, and on one occasion, a small group of Union soldiers went to the resort. Marked as off limits on their map due to the springs being on private property, when the troops found the proprietor to be a Southern sympathizer and secessionist who was gone during their visit, they decided to liberate several cases of wine. The troops then went back to camp and told fellow soldiers about the beautiful "Champagne country" they had found.[73]

Other fun times at Fort DeRussy included regularly scheduled target practice in order to keep gunmanship sharp. Unfortunately for farmers and homesteaders nearby, many of the shells accidently dropped on their properties. "Many of the shells would fall short of the mark, and drop, or explode in the air, long before they had reached the target, which greatly endangered the lives and property of the people who were living in range of the fire," the *Washington Post* reported in an article a few years after the war. Homesteaders in the Rock Creek Valley were tested even more so in July 1864, when, depending on their location in the present-day park, their properties bore the brunt of stray bullets and cannonballs fired by Confederate soldiers, Union troops or both.[74]

During this battle, known as the Battle of Fort Stevens, fourteen thousand Confederate soldiers under the forces of General Jubal Early, known as "foul-mouthed Early" and "Old Jube," marched into the District of Columbia and skirmished and probed along the outskirts of the city, looking for a way into downtown. Fortunately, the steps that Union soldiers and engineers had taken to defend the area made the Rock Creek Valley illogical for Early's Confederates to attempt to pass through. "On the right was Rock Creek, running through a deep ravine which had been rendered impassible by the felling of timber on each side…every appliance of science and unlimited means had been used to render the fortifications of Washington as strong as possible," noted the general.[75]

Nevertheless, thanks to archaeological work completed in the early 2000s, we know that fighting did occur in the 1890 stem of Rock Creek Park. Both north and northeast of Fort DeRussy, Confederate sharpshooters stood behind trees, logs and earthen mounds to fire on the Union soldiers, while

Union troops in rifle trenches in front of and below the fort fired back at them. Furthermore, the historical record tells us that Fort DeRussy's big guns, including three one-hundred-pound Parrott rifles, fired at Confederate targets to the north on either side of Rock Creek. John Norris, captain of the Provisional Second Pennsylvania Heavy Artillery, wrote to his superior after the battle, noting that "ten 100-pounder shells were thrown at a house about 1,700 yards to the north and this side of Rock Creek for the purpose of firing it, as the enemy's sharpshooters were reported there in great numbers." East of Rock Creek and north of Fort Stevens, Norris identified "The body of one rebel…found at a distance of 2,600 yards in the direction of our firing badly mutilated by a piece of shell."[76]

The Battle of Fort Stevens was the climax of action for soldiers stationed at Fort DeRussy. Less than a year later, after the war ended, the fort disbanded, and all its items went up for public auction. However, Fort DeRussy is in a good state of preservation today due to the fact that, since 1890, it has been preserved as part of Rock Creek Park. As a result, trees eventually grew back

Fort DeRussy commemorative plaque and parapet, circa 1965. From the Rock Creek Park Nature Center, a hike to the historic fortress takes only ten to fifteen minutes. *National Park Service.*

over the fort and hillside. Trees, not soldiers, are now the ones that stand guard over the fort, holding together the soil that make up the earthen walls, battery magazine, dry moat and rifle pit in place.

FORT STEVENS AND THE BATTLE

Aunt Betty and Abe

Unlike Fort DeRussy, Fort Stevens today is surrounded by urbanity on all sides. Because of this, it might be hard to imagine that on July 11 and 12, 1864, Fort Stevens bore the brunt of the only Confederate attack on Washington, D.C. Horses, soldiers, smoke and cannon fire took the place of today's working-class homes and car traffic. In this battle, President Lincoln could have easily been killed. Here's the story of the District's most significant Civil War fortress.

When war clouds gathered in the early 1860s, they affected several homesteaders in the area, no one more so than Elizabeth Proctor Thomas. A free African American woman with a newborn and a family, Thomas, known fondly as "Aunt Betty" in her later years, lived on a large working farm. Her property included a two-and-a-half-story home complete with a cow barn, corn shed, chicken coup, stable and perimeter fence. This property, her property, would soon not be hers.[77]

Union troops first built the original Fort Stevens in 1861. When the fort was declared too small to fully defend the Seventh Street Pike (today's Georgia Avenue) by General John Gross Barnard of the U.S. Army Corps of Engineers, Barnard lobbied for additional funds to expand the fort. Thus, an extension was completed in 1862, which destroyed everything on Thomas's property. According to Thomas's personal testimony, while she watched soldiers remove furniture from her house, she was approached by a six-foot, four-inch figure in a black top hat. "It is hard, but you shall reap a great reward," said Abraham Lincoln to Thomas. However, if the reward Lincoln was referring to was being compensated for her property, Thomas never got it. What she might have gotten, though, was the satisfaction that her property became a fort that helped protect the Union capital.[78]

An earthen fort like Fort DeRussy but nearly twice the size, Fort Stevens was first named Fort Massachusetts after the soldier regiment that built it,

Elizabeth Thomas, the lone woman and African American in the photo, sits at the Lincoln Monument at Fort Stevens in 1911. *National Park Service.*

but when Brigadier General Isaac Stevens was killed in action in Virginia in 1862, the fort was renamed in his honor.[79]

Speaking of action, the Battle of Fort Stevens was ultimately set in motion during the spring of 1864 by Confederate general Robert E. Lee. With Ulysses S. Grant and his Union troops attacking Lee on the outskirts of Richmond, the Confederate capital, Lee sent a group of fourteen thousand soldiers on a "hail Mary" mission, similar to a football quarterback's last pass attempt to try to somehow win the game when his back is to the wall. Led by the foul-mouthed, hard-drinking General Jubal Anderson Early, one of Lee's right-hand men, Confederate troops were tasked with marching up the Shenandoah Valley, arcing around Harpers Ferry and then attacking the Union capital. Lee believed that, if Confederates attacked Washington, Grant would be required to give up his stronghold in Virginia by sending troops back to the capital to aid in the Union capital's defense.[80]

From the Union's perspective, although Washington had a strong defensive ring of forts, in order for Grant to seize Richmond in the first place, thousands of soldiers and a disproportionately high number of

Union troops at Fort Stevens in 1864. Notice the wall of sharp tree branches. Known as abatis, this was a common defense system put in place in front of most of the forts. *Library of Congress.*

officers from the capital had to be brought down. Twenty-three thousand Union soldiers protecting the capital's defenses in 1863 dwindled to nine thousand a year later.[81] In Washington, Barnard wrote to one of Grant's officers at the time, noting that the Union troops "are very much reduced in numbers, and through loss of field officers and numerical weakness very much injured in efficiency."[82] Indeed, when it became clear that Early had Washington in mind, just like Lee had hoped, thousands of Union soldiers were forced to hotfoot it back up to the capital. In the meantime, injured soldiers healing in one of Washington's many temporary army hospitals, U.S. Army Corps of Engineers employees—all trained as architects and in mapmaking rather than in combat—and temporary "100-day soldiers" were called to the front line of Fort Stevens and other nearby forts such as Fort Slocum.[83]

And so, the morning of July 11 witnessed Confederate troops marching into the District from the north while simultaneously, six miles south, Union troops offloaded boats en route from Richmond. President Lincoln came down from his "cottage" near Fort Totten to greet the troops and, with characteristic humor, told them, "You can't be late if you want to attack [General] Early!"—a lighter note in an otherwise intense moment. The soldiers then marched quickly through town to support Fort Stevens. Along the way, District residents showed their support by lining the street with fresh food and trinkets for the soldiers.[84]

Early's soldiers arrived just north of the battlefield around noon. With Union troops marching northward from the river, Confederate troops claimed area trees, barns and ravines for sharpshooting purposes. Although some light skirmishing occurred, Early's troops were exhausted from a long morning march under the hot summer sun, enduring temperatures in the mid-nineties, and also from a recent victory at Monocacy Creek, and he decided not to press.[85]

That night, Early held council with his advisers and fellow officers in the upscale Silver Spring residence of Postmaster General Montgomery Blair, a member of Lincoln's cabinet. Due to the Confederates' occupying his home and town, Blair was stuck in downtown that night, and Early and company "liberated" myriad alcoholic beverages from Blair's collection. The Confederate officers and their commanding general were giddy about being inside the District of Columbia. Nevertheless, they all probably knew that trying to conquer Washington in the face of the Union's "strong defensive positions" would result in massive casualties. And when Early looked out through his field glasses at dawn the next morning, he knew that any chance of a full-out attack on Fort Stevens had been lost, as additional Union replacements had come in during the night.[86]

Not wanting to risk major fatalities, Early nevertheless decided not to leave the scene. And so a second day of probing, skirmishing and sharpshooting inside the Union capital occurred. Toward the afternoon of this second day, July 12, Abraham and Mary Todd Lincoln visited Fort Stevens. Wanting to see the action, the president stood atop the parapet, thus becoming the only sitting U.S. president to come under enemy fire. As this was not the smartest thing to do for a tall man in a top hat with Confederate sharpshooters firing all around, an officer standing just three feet away legendarily yelled, "Get down, you fool!" When an officer was mortally wounded near Lincoln just seconds later, Lincoln finally realized the danger and decided to get down.[87]

Possibly to show off for Lincoln, Brigadier General Frank Wheaton commanded Union troops in a short but bloody battle at dusk at Fort Stevens, during which the troops got out in front of the fort and attacked a Confederate line of soldiers. A total of 59 Union soldiers were killed and

Commemorative plaque at Fort Stevens showing President Lincoln under fire. *Author's collection.*

145 wounded during this charge, making it the bloodiest part of the Battle of Fort Stevens. However, the attack might have encouraged Early to retreat that night before more action took place.[88]

"We might not have taken Washington, but we scared Lincoln like hell," mused the Confederate general.[89] But Lincoln in particular and the capital in general had kept calm during the episode, even though Secretary of War Stanton had ordered ready an escape boat to evacuate the president should the worst occur. The Civil War Defenses of Washington had been tested, and they had stood strong. More significantly, although thousands of Grant's soldiers from Virginia had been forced back up to the capital, Grant himself and most of his troops remained behind in their stronghold outside Richmond. Due to this, Lee was unable to get Union troops off his back in Richmond and, less than a year later, was forced to surrender at Appomattox Court House.

Battleground National Cemetery

Tombstone Mysteries

After Confederate troops retreated back toward Virginia came the solemn duty for Union troops of burying their war dead. Forty Union soldiers who fell during the Battle of Fort Stevens are permanently interred at Battleground National Cemetery off Georgia Avenue. At only two acres in size, the cemetery is one of the smallest national cemeteries in the nation. As small as it is, however, the cemetery's two mysteries, as well as its association with a renowned engineer, make its story much larger.

Quartermaster General Montgomery C. Meigs of the U.S. Army Corps of Engineers chose the location for Battleground National Cemetery near Fort Stevens, undoubtedly knowing that the much larger Arlington National Cemetery he had helped design was full to capacity. Designer of the picturesque brick buildings that are currently referred to as the Smithsonian Arts and Industries Building (closed for some years now) and National Building Museum, Meigs was the officer who oversaw the design and layout of almost all military cemeteries in the 1860s and '70s. With two circular rows of graves and eventually a flagpole, superintendent's lodge and stately trees scattered throughout, Battleground National Cemetery was made in classic Meigs style.[90]

Another famous American associated with Battleground National Cemetery is Abraham Lincoln. However, while it has been said for decades that Lincoln formally dedicated the cemetery just after the Battle of Fort Stevens, evidence from at least one soldier who actually helped build the cemetery claims otherwise. In his book entitled *Three Years in the Sixth Corps*, Battle of Fort Stevens veteran George T. Stevens notes that he felt it was incredibly disrespectful and somewhat ironic that neither Lincoln nor any officer attended the dedication:

> *We gathered our dead comrades from the field where they had fallen, and gave them the rude burial of soldiers on the common near Fort Stevens. None of those high in authority, who had come out to see them give up their lives for their country, were present to pay the last honors to the dead heroes. No officer of state, no lady of wealth, no citizen of Washington was there; but we laid them in their graves within sight of the capital, without coffins, with only their gory garments and their blankets around them. With the rude tenderness of soldiers, we covered them in the earth; we marked their names with our pencils on the little boards of pine, and turned sadly away to other scenes.*[91]

While we might never know whether or not Lincoln dedicated the cemetery, an even more pressing mystery surfaced in 2006 due to the extensive research of former Rock Creek Park interpretive park ranger Ron Harvey. While cleaning headstones in 2006, Harvey and other National Park Service staff discovered the names of soldiers on the underside of the tombstones. "This provided sufficient evidence that the headstones had been recycled from previously made/used headstones designated for other soldiers for other cemeteries. It is unclear why these headstones were not used for the originally intended soldiers and documentary evidence has not provided any clues," notes Harvey.[92]

Conducting further research, Harvey uncovered the fact that five of the "double-labeled" tombstones were, in fact, misidentified on the front side in their naming of fallen soldiers from the Battle of Fort Stevens— for over one hundred years, the tombstones had been honoring fictional soldiers. Essentially, this was due to sloppiness in regards to at least a couple cemetery superintendents, or overseers. George T. Stevens noted that after burying the bodies, "we marked their names with our pencils on the little board of pine." Unfortunately, in just a few years, some of these scribbled names written in lead had been washed out by weathering. As a result, by

THE STORY OF EDWARD CAMPBELL

While forty Union troops that died during the Battle of Fort Stevens are buried at Battleground National Cemetery, there are actually forty-one troops interred at the site. The forty-first soldier of the cemetery is Edward Campbell. A Takoma Park resident, Campbell died at age ninety-two in 1936 and is the only veteran of the Battle of Fort Stevens to be buried at Battleground National Cemetery, albeit over seventy-one years after the battle. Born and raised in Vermont, Campbell fought for the Union all four years of the Civil War and saw action at Gettysburg and other key battles. Lucky to never get wounded, he eventually settled on a forty-year career with the U.S. Pension Bureau in Montgomery Meig's unique downtown D.C. building. Until his death, he was a regular visitor to Battleground National Cemetery, paying respects to his fallen comrades the final time only a few months before he himself died.[94]

1871, when the wooden boards were replaced with today's marble tombstones, the names were hard to decipher. Furthermore, in 1869, interment listings were formally completed for Battleground National Cemetery, and Harvey notes that careless errors were made in regards to the copying and spelling of soldiers' names. Due to these factors, Wilhelm Frei's name was adulterated to read W.M. Tray on his marble tombstone, Edward Garvin's name switched to Geo Garvin, Richard Castle's to Mark Stoneham and Thomas McIntyre's to H. McIntire. The real name of the fifth soldier, labeled as E.S. Bavett, remains unknown.[93]

If cemetery superintendents had better documented soldier names in the few years immediately after their interments, the mislabeling would probably not have occurred. "For those who looked after the cemetery as well as the veterans of the Battle of Fort Stevens, the idea of having one of their fallen comrades being accidently mislabeled was unconscionable and completely unacceptable," Harvey believes.[95] Furthermore, considering that Battleground National Cemetery is tiny compared to most others, if five of its forty tombstones were mislabeled, one must wonder how many other Civil War grave sites scattered around the country are also misidentified.

While these unacceptable misidentification mistakes of the past cannot be changed, Harvey's research has at least corrected the historical record for the future. A wayside exhibit at Battleground National Cemetery listing the soldiers interred on site now correctly labels four of the five formerly misidentified graves.

Battleground National Cemetery shortly after its creation. *National Park Service.*

JOSEPH TOTTEN AND JOHN GROSS BARNARD

They Didn't Believe in Retirement

Two of the easternmost park units administered by Rock Creek Park are Fort Totten and Barnard Hill Park. The parks are named after two high-ranking officials in the U.S. Army Corps of Engineers: Joseph Totten and John Gross Barnard. Both men were well-learned soldier-scientists, and Barnard in particular had a profound effect on the Civil War Defenses of Washington.

Fort Totten is named after Brigadier General and Chief Engineer Joseph Totten, who served in the army for a staggering sixty years. One of only a handful of soldiers to partake in both the War of 1812 and, fifty years later, the Civil War, Totten served as the head of the U.S. Army Corps of Engineers for a record twenty-six years, from 1838 until his death in 1864.[96]

A major advocate of a strong naval defense system, Totten is perhaps best known for designing a unique iron-reinforced shutter system at cannon windows of forts that protected soldiers from enemy fire. Referred to as "Totten shutters," upon firing a cannon, gases escaping from the muzzle would momentarily shove open the shutters, but the shutters were carefully balanced so that they would immediately swing shut.[97]

While records do not show Totten ever visiting his namesake fort, Fort Totten itself was similar to Fort DeRussy in that it provided artillery support during the Battle of Fort Stevens and also witnessed skirmishes out in front. As the fort was located less than a mile from Lincoln's summer retreat, now known as Lincoln's Cottage, the president often visited soldiers stationed at Fort Totten. Finally, a group of German Americans stationed at the fort were said to be rowdy, giving the officers there many headaches.[98]

South and east of Fort Totten is Barnard Hill Park, described by one D.C. blogger as "the best park you've never heard of." Ironically, Barnard Hill Park played no significance in the Civil War, but it's named after the father of the Civil War Defenses of Washington. A protégé of Totten, John Gross Barnard is described by historian Benjamin Cooling as "a capable, middle-aged…very dedicated soldier-scientist."[99] Hand-selected by Lincoln to replace Totten as chief engineer after Totten's death, Barnard declined the promotion for personal reasons. Nevertheless, Barnard served as "Chief Regular Army Engineers" until his retirement in 1881.[100]

Aside from designing the American defenses at Tampico during the Mexican-American War, the climax of Barnard's fifty-year career occurred during the Civil War. Among other capacities, Barnard served as the key architect and spokesman behind the Civil War Defenses of Washington. Throughout the war, he often went before Congress to lobby for additional funds to expand and improve the fort system. Barnard also lobbied, to no avail, for equal pay for African American soldiers. Due to his efforts in making sure the Union capital was well defended, by war's end, the ring of forts included sixty-eight forts and batteries, over nine hundred cannons, twenty miles of rifle trenches and thirty-two miles of military roads—an impressive feat.[101]

Besides his career in the Army Corps of Engineers, Barnard had an interest in science and the arts. He composed music, was one of the founding members of the National Academy of Sciences, published numerous books on engineering and wrote several articles for *Johnson's Universal Encyclopedia*, published in 1877, including "Aeronautics; Breakwater; Bridge; Bull Run, Battle of; Calculus; Gyroscope; Harbor; Imaginaries; Laplace's Coefficients;

Lighthouse Construction; Rotation; Tehuantepec; Variations, Calculus of; and Tides, Theories of."[102]

CONTRABANDS AND U.S. COLORED TROOPS

"The Defenses Would Not Have Been as Successful"

Soldiers stationed at Forts DeRussy, Stevens and Totten were primarily European American (white), but African Americans, despite major hardship, also played an active role in the construction and maintenance of the Civil War Defenses of Washington. Many found employment, specifically around Fort Slocum and Fort Reno.

Enslaved African Americans escaped to the Union capital in record numbers during the four years of war, primarily from neighboring Virginia and Maryland. Considered "contrabands," unemployed black men needed employment, and the fact that the Union army needed additional help in constructing and maintaining Washington's Civil War fortresses, roads and rifle trenches proved to be a win-win for both groups. Union officers began hiring "contrabands," and in 1863, President Lincoln formalized some African American soldiers by creating the U.S. Colored Troops, seen as extremely controversial at the time.103

Indeed, many European Americans did not see African Americans as their equals. As a result, black soldiers were often treated much poorer than their white counterparts. African American troops were most likely not permitted to fight in the Battle of Fort Stevens, were paid forty cents per day compared to the one dollar a day of white soldiers, had to wear second-hand uniforms and often bore the brunt of racist remarks.[104]

Despite all these challenges, African American troops serving Washington's defenses played important roles as day laborers and cooks. In general, they helped dig rifle trenches, construct roadways and repair the forts, which involved constantly adding new dirt to the earthen forts, especially after rainstorms eroded the parapets. Many also served as camp cooks. Behind most forts were large tent camps where soldiers slept and ate. Fort Reno's soldier camp was located just behind this largest of Washington fortresses, and many African Americans fed the troops there. Additionally, historic photos show Fort Slocum's soldier camp hosting the Fourth U.S. Colored Infantry for an undetermined amount of time, while

African American contrabands in the foreground at Camp Brightwood, located at the intersection of today's Georgia and Missouri Avenues. *Library of Congress.*

another photo shows black soldiers at Camp Brightwood, located just south of Fort Stevens. Civil engineer Edward Frost, a white soldier stationed in Washington at the time, wrote to his superior that "the contrabands were important to the construction and maintenance of the defenses of Washington and without the contrabands' numbers and labor, the defenses would not have been as successful."[105]

But what did the black troops say themselves? Unfortunately, we might never know. The vast majority of African Americans who served the Union cause were illiterate due to the fact that they were not permitted to read, write or gain an education while enslaved. Therefore, very few written records of African American Civil War soldiers exist. Rock Creek

Park Civil War interpretation volunteer John Hampton refers to this as the "granularity of history."[106]

Fort Reno and Wayland Seminary

The Failures and Successes of Reconstruction

After four years of warfare had altered the lives of and landscapes within the Federal capital, the Confederate States of America finally threw up the white flag in the spring of 1864. Lee's surrender on April 9 led to celebration among the troops stationed at Washington's forts. According to John Munro Longyear, a celebratory "wave" of cannon fire ensued. "The chain of forts around the city, and batteries of field artillery between, made a ring of cannons…which were fired in rotation for several hours. The line of cannon salutes running round and round the other always proceeded in the same direction, so that it went round and round the circuit 20 to 30 miles."[107] While the end of war is always a good thing, the African American experience in lands that became Rock Creek Park directly after the Civil War was ambiguous, being both good and bad.

Within days of the end of the war, almost all the Civil War Defenses of Washington were abandoned, and their items were put up for public auction. Thousands of white troops finally returned home, but to thousands of African Americans who had escaped slavery, Washington, D.C., was their new home. The reality was that there were now too many newcomers to the D.C. area, not enough jobs to support them and a lack of efficient government programs to house and feed them. The result of these factors involved Fort Reno and other defenses being used by the homeless: "Around the slopes of the fort…free negroes had built their cabins out of the wrecks of battery wagon and sentry-box, and down the paths that the cannoniers [*sic*] had made in the moist hill sides, negro men and women, with pails and bundles on their heads, went jogging steadily, as in the first listless experience of self-ownership," noted one observer in 1873.[108] Another firsthand account reported:

> *All the forts around or overlooking the city are dismantled, the guns taken out of them, the land resigned to its owners. Needy Negro squatters, living around the forts, have built themselves shanties of the officers' quarters,*

pulled out the abatis for firewood, made cord wood or joists out of the log platforms for the guns, and sawed up the great flag-staffs into quilting poles or bedstead posts.[109]

Sadly, this is what happens when the government does not provide for all its people. But ironically and also fortunately, amendments to the Constitution during this same time benefited African Americans. New freedoms—including the abolishment of slavery once and for all, equality under the law and voting rights for black males—gave African Americans unprecedented opportunity during the years directly after the Civil War. Unbeknownst to most Meridian Hill Park users today, one of these opportunities came in the form of the Wayland Seminary, an African American university situated in the northeast corner of the present-day park.[110]

Attended by Booker T. Washington in 1878, Wayland Seminary was constructed and opened in the late 1860s primarily thanks to charitable contributions from progressive D.C. citizens. The seminary was overseen by the American Baptist Home Mission Society, and according to an 1883 Baptist encyclopedia, although "the Bible holds, of course, the first place in the school," the society felt that it was important to "give attention to other branches of study" as well. The school's goal was to provide an uplifting education "for a race just…emancipated" at minimal cost. Many graduates of Wayland Seminary became teachers, while some became ministers. Just before the turn of the century, the college was incorporated into Virginia Union University in Richmond.[111]

The era of Reconstruction in Rock Creek Park, like much of the park's history, mirrored that of the larger nation. African Americans both benefitted and suffered from it.

3

THE ESTABLISHMENT OF ROCK CREEK PARK

Though beautiful in its human diversity, Washington's increase in population during and directly after the Civil War had some negative components. With urbanites living so close together, combined with an inadequate sewer system, waterborne diseases grew rampant. As a result, natural areas came to be seen by some as a healthier world away from the chaos of the inner city. New York City's Central Park was born, and two hundred miles south, the idea of a grand public park in the Rock Creek Valley was proposed. Would it come to fruition, and if so, when?

NATHANIEL MICHLER AND HIS 1867 REPORT

The First Official Proposal for a "Grand National Park"

Many visitors to Rock Creek Park don't realize that the park was originally supposed to serve both as a public park and presidential mansion. The reason why there is no high-security White House in the middle of the park is due to one individual: U.S. Army Corps of Engineer brigadier general Nathaniel Michler. Although there are some contrasts between his proposed park and the park landscape we see today, Michler (1827–1881) deserves a lot of credit for his foresight. Here's the story of the first official proposal for Rock Creek Park.

By the Civil War, as the Federal City was growing rapidly, so too was its stink. The area now known as the National Mall was perhaps the grossest locale of all. Out in front of the White House were the Potomac mud flats, in the middle of which was the Washington City Canal, a waterway where citizens regularly dumped their sewage. These unhealthy factors led to outbreaks of deadly diseases caused by dirty water. All this, in addition to the sultry summer heat, resulted in presidents of the 1850s and '60s often spending as much time as possible farther north in the District of Columbia in a rural estate now known as Lincoln's Cottage.[112]

At the same time, Washington citizens began calling for a public park in the area. In *Capital Engineers: The U.S. Army Corps of Engineers in the Development of Washington, D.C.*, Pamela Scott notes that serious citizen involvement in D.C.'s municipal affairs began when its residents began seeing what other municipalities were giving to their citizens. Famed landscape architect Frederick Law Olmsted had completed New York City's prized Central Park in 1857. Washingtonians wondered why the more prestigious national capital did not have a grand park of comparison.[113]

Due to this public pressure for a park, and also to protect the president from disease, Congress decided to kill two birds with one stone by tasking Secretary of War Edwin Stanton with providing recommendations for a site for a new presidential mansion and public park. Congress directed the secretary to find a site with "convenience of access, healthfulness, good water, and capability of adornment." Stanton detailed a forty-year-old, highly skilled army engineer named Nathaniel Michler to prepare a report.[114]

A career engineer, by the 1860s, mapping was not a new task for Michler. Brevetted brigadier general in the Civil War for distinguishing himself during the Battle of Petersburg, Michler had previous experience mapping the boundary between Virginia and Maryland as well as the U.S.-Mexico border after the Mexican-American War.[115]

During his years in Washington, Michler was highly regarded and provided several farsighted proposals. His proposal for Rock Creek Park was perhaps the most significant. Michler meticulously rode and walked the land in and around the Rock Creek Valley, studied old maps and looked at public records. In the report stating his findings, released in 1867, Michler made a key departure from what lawmakers had asked for: he separated the sites of the presidential mansion and park. Influenced by Olmsted and the city parks movement of the time, Michler did not believe that the two entities fit well together. And so in his report to Congress, Michler wrote absolutely nothing of a presidential home in the Rock Creek Valley and everything about "a grand national park" in the Rock Creek Valley:

> *In no place has nature been more bountiful of her charms than in this city and all can be found so near and accessible; the valley of the Rock Creek and its tributaries, the Broad and Piney branches, and the several minor rivulets, with the adjoining hills overlooking these beautiful streams, present the capital of the nation advantages not to be lightly disregarded in providing a park worthy of a great people. All the element[s] which constitute a public resort of the kind can be found in this wild and romantic tract of country.*[116]

Michler's proposal for the park was a passionate one, and Scott notes that his report had the tone of a "mid-nineteenth century romantic soul and not the stuff of a usual engineer's report to congress."[117]

Michler proposed both a 2,500-acre park and a smaller 1,700-acre park, "in case my [first] recommendation should be too extravagant." Interesting to note, Michler's larger park proposal included several of the present-day park's outlying Civil War sites, including Fort Stevens and Battleground National Cemetery. Michler claimed that the forts "have become historical, and from the parapets of which extensive views can be had." Although the cemetery and a part of Fort Stevens would ultimately come to be administered by Rock Creek Park, if Michler's larger proposal had won, a fully intact fortress and even part of the Battle of Fort Stevens's main battlefield would have been preserved in perpetuity.[118]

Michler's 1,700-acre park proposal was not the exact boundary of today's main stem of Rock Creek Park either. Both reports' northern boundaries were located at Military Road, while the valleys of "the Broad and Piney branches" were also included. And so neither park proposal included the northern section of today's park, but they did include a broader midsection continuing west of today's Broad Branch Road and east of Sixteenth Street.[119]

Although Michler's proposal was farsighted and the first of its kind, and although the "great nature" of the Rock Creek Valley was to serve as the backbone, he did propose several landscaping features that nature purists today might gawk at. Like Frederick Law Olmsted Jr. in his 1918 report for how to manage Rock Creek Park, Michler believed in landscape architecture rather than "letting nature rule supreme." Michler recommended damming the creek in select locations, "thus forming a series of lakes and ponds for useful and ornamental purposes." He also proposed spots "where observatories can be located, conservatories built for exotic plants, and geometrical flower-gardens planted...zoological and botanical gardens, grounds for play and parade, and many other useful purposes." Undoubtedly, if all these proposals had been implemented, the park would have looked much more like Golden Gate Park and Central Park, rather than the heavily natural area it is today.

At any rate, Michler urged Congress to pass a park bill on the grounds of public health and general civic well-being. Rock Creek Park was "the most economical and practical means of providing all, old and young, rich and poor, with that greatest of all needs, healthy exercise in open country," the engineer noted. Furthermore, Michler recommended that lawmakers "purchase at once a sufficient number of acres bordering on Rock Creek" before the area was bought up by realtors and made into "costly suburban villas," as this would then lead to soaring land values.[120]

After Michler's report came out in January 1867, U.S. senator Benjamin Gratz Brown of Missouri, chairman of the Senate Committee on Public Buildings and Grounds, introduced and lobbied for the passage of bill number S. 549. This bill, which created Michler's 2,500-acre park in the Rock Creek Valley, easily passed the Senate. However, it was tabled by the House of Representatives. Brown lost his reelection bid later that year, and no lawmaker would pick up the torch for another twenty-two years.[121]

In another report to Congress just one year later, Michler again recommended "a grand national park along the beautiful and romantic valley of Rock Creek." Again, though, Michler's Rock Creek Park proposal was ignored. Ironically, the nation and the city would pay significantly more taxpayer dollars for the park two decades later, when it was officially established. In 1890, when the park finally did come to fruition, land values in and around the Rock Creek Valley had increased substantially, much as Michler had warned.[122]

A few years later, Michler took an engineer assignment out west and left the capital, never to return. He died a few years after his fiftieth birthday with his wife by his side.

Rock Creek Reservoir Proposal
A Lakeside Park?

After Michler's report was ignored, the next call for a park in the Rock Creek Valley occurred in 1883. However, this report, released by Captain R.L. Hoxie, the engineer in charge of the District's water supply and underground sewer pipes, was much different. Hoxie proposed inundating the Rock Creek Valley from the northern reaches of Georgetown up past Broad Branch. Hoxie proposed a Rock Creek Reservoir:

> For Washington, an alternative line of supply, possessing peculiar advantages, is afforded by this valley of Rock Creek. A large reservoir can be constructed in the lower part of the valley, which will store the rainfall of about forty-five square miles, the area drained by Rock Creek, and will give to Washington from this source alone, in the dryest [sic] years, a daily supply of 26,000,000 gallons of water—rather more than the present consumption—at an elevation sufficient to secure the present pressure in the mains. A much larger supply could be drawn from this reservoir if delivered only to the lower levels of the city. The Rock Creek basin, is an admirable catchment area containing no manufactories, or other dangerous sources of water pollution which are common in the gathering ground for the water supply of nearly all larger cities. The close proximity of this reservoir to the city would obviate the necessity for long conduits of any description—the great factor of costs in all systems of water works.[123]

Indeed, it's hard to argue against the fact that a clean water supply is important, and a reservoir in the middle section of the Rock Creek Valley would have been cleaner than many other reservoirs at the time due to its forested location. Furthermore, construction projects seemed to be needed minimally outside building the dam itself, resulting in not much infrastructure and funds needed. But what would have been lost with a Rock Creek reservoir?

Fortunately for park admirers today, the 1883 report was shelved. In fact, due to the reservoir proposal, stronger requests to protect the forested bluffs and whitewater creek came filing in from influential citizens. But the park would need one key figure to ultimately be established.

Charles Carroll Glover and the Creation of Rock Creek Park

He Had "a Passion for Parks"

Numerous national park units might never have been established were it not for a single individual. Rock Creek Park's individual was Charles Carroll Glover (1846–1936). A prominent D.C. banker and philanthropist, Glover, according to a fellow businessman, was said to have a "passion for parks."[124]

Born in North Carolina, Glover was moved by his parents to D.C. at age eight for his education. He fell in love with the Rock Creek Valley as a child by exploring every nook and cranny of it. "When I was a little fellow, there were quite a number of boys who would walk all over the Rock Creek country. We would go out and play through what is now Rock Creek Park, and I became attached to almost every foot of it," he noted. "Peirce's Mill was operating at that time. We went up the creek, wading in it where we could not walk along the bank, as there were no roads of any kind whatsoever."[125]

After his formative years, Glover sought a career in banking, swiftly moving up the ranks of Riggs and Company. Glover became a partner at the downtown bank in 1873, and in 1896, Riggs National Bank was founded with Glover as its first president. With his banking business located across the street from the U.S. Treasury, Glover controversially secured a private office at the treasury building, thus enabling him to be the first banker to know about new banking policies and trends. Because of this, the Woodrow Wilson administration brought up charges of corruption against Glover. Fortunately for the banker, both Theodore Roosevelt and William Howard Taft personally testified to Glover's integrity and honesty, and a verdict of guilty was never reached.[126]

To be sure, Glover was ambitious and perhaps driven by the almighty dollar. However, a lot of that money went to the public good. He was a philanthropist, donating $75,000 for the start-up of the National Cathedral and giving eighty acres of land to the government in the area now known as Glover Archbold Park so that "it might be kept in its natural state for a bird sanctuary and for the enjoyment of the people." Glover also donated property that became part of the National Park Service–administered lands in the Anacostia hills and lobbied for the establishment of Potomac Park.[127]

Throughout his years of banking and philanthropy, though, Glover continued to enjoy the Rock Creek Valley in his free time. He often went horseback riding through the area with his famous friends, most notably

Charles Carroll Glover. A stern-looking businessman, Glover was in fact firm in his pushing for the establishment of Rock Creek Park. *Library of Congress.*

historian George Bancroft, who "took the most tremendous interest in the magnificent woodlands"; Randall Lee Gibson, U.S. senator from Louisiana; and A.R. Spofford, librarian of Congress. As years passed, however, Glover noted more and more on his rides that "we would witness the opening of a subdivision that would destroy a number of the old oaks and hickories and chestnuts. We would bewail the fact that all of this country would not be taken in as a national park."[128]

Indeed, by 1888, Rock Creek Park bills had been in the works for years, and Glover undoubtedly knew that they had all failed. On a now legendary ride with influential friends and business associates on Thanksgiving Day of the same year, while at a bluff overlooking the creek just above the present-day Boulder Bridge, Glover resolved with his group to lobby Congress for the park and see it through to fruition. He knew it would be a legislative battle—"it would take an avalanche of time" and was "one of the tasks of Hercules"—but he was determined to establish Rock Creek Park.[129]

Glover then went to U.S. senator John Sherman of Sherman Antitrust Act fame, who got on board with the park proposal immediately. However, the House of Representatives, like it had with Nathaniel Michler in 1867, rejected the park bill. Congressmen who disapproved of the bill did so primarily because they didn't think their distant constituents should have to pay for a "city" park. Many thought that Washingtonians should foot more of the bill, especially the wealthy Washingtonians whose estates bordered the park and stood to increase in value because of it. Many congressmen also felt the need for tighter control over District spending due to the fact that de facto city manager Alexander Boss Shepherd, a ruthless individual, had bankrupted the capital's treasury with an elaborate spending plan in the 1870s.[130]

Determined to establish the park before it was too late, Glover and Sherman worked together to create a new compromise bill that pleased all political factions. This new bill was, in fact, democratic and divided the cost of park acquisitions in three ways: the District and federal government would split the cost of the park, while landowners whose estates bordered the park would foot a higher portion of D.C.'s 50 percent.[131]

While the bill was being written and debated, Glover became the chairman of the Rock Creek Park Committee, made up of one hundred citizen-advocates. Many of the committee meetings took place at Glover's residence. Perhaps most important to getting the Rock Creek Park bill passed, though, was the fact that Glover personally met with dozens of congressmen. The late 1800s was a time known for the major influence of business tycoons and monopolies on the government. While some millionaires lobbied politicians or became them themselves to promote their interests and increase their personal profits, Glover used his private-sector power to push a public park.[132]

As a result, despite a name-change hiccup—one senator lobbied for a "Columbus Memorial Park" in the Rock Creek Valley to honor the upcoming 500th anniversary of Columbus's landing in the North America—Rock Creek Park was finally authorized by both houses of Congress on September 25, 1890. President Benjamin Harrison two days later wrote the park bill into law.

Rock Creek Park became the first federally managed urban nature park in the country, and it remains one of the largest to this day. It also became the national capital's first park and continues to be its largest. Furthermore, Rock Creek was established four days prior to Yosemite National Park, and

Plaque on Massachusetts Avenue Bridge over Rock Creek. *Author's collection.*

the bill authorizing its creation borrowed words from an even earlier park. Both Yellowstone National Park (the world's first national park) and Rock Creek Park were established for "the benefit and enjoyment of the people" as well as "to provide for the preservation from injury or spoliation of all timber, animals, or curiosities within said park."[133]

A couple days after the Rock Creek Park bill was passed, Congressman John J. Hemphill, chairman of the Committee of D.C., wrote a letter to Glover stating:

> *My dear Mr. Glover: The bill to establish Rock Creek Park, which has passed Congress only after the most strenuous efforts, has been approved by the President and is now law. As it was at your request that this bill was introduced setting aside this beautiful section of the country as a park for all time, I desire to congratulate you on the final approval of the measure, and to say that without your earnest, intelligent and untiring efforts during the entire contest, it would, in my judgment, have failed to become a law. Your valuable work in behalf of this great pleasure ground at the National Capital ought to be known and long remembered by the many thousands who shall hereafter enjoy it.*[134]

Today, the Glover Park neighborhood, Glover Archbold Park, the Massachusetts Avenue Bridge over Rock Creek and Glover Road in Rock Creek Park are named in honor of Charles Carroll Glover—not bad for a legacy.

Part II

THE EARLY PARK

4
MANAGING THE EARLY PARK

While Rock Creek Park was established on paper in 1890, there was technically no physical park. All the land that makes up the park today was private property; Uncle Sam had to purchase it using the laws of imminent domain. After this came the difficult task for early park managers and staff of opening up the park to visitors while at the same time receiving zero or minimal appropriations from Congress. Nevertheless, roads, bridges and fords—some that remain today and some that have gone the way of the Dodo bird—were built using innovative means and in a creative fashion.

LOUIS SHOEMAKER AGAINST THE UNITED STATES

Villain Turned Visionary

After the park was established on paper, Congress tasked a group of three individuals, known as the Rock Creek Park Commission, to purchase park inholdings using the laws of imminent domain. Many Rock Creek Valley residents were not happy about losing their lands, and many claimed they deserved more money. The most colorful of these individuals was Louis Shoemaker, a well-off real estate agent at the time and relative of the Peirce family of Peirce Mill fame. Arguing his case all the way to the U.S. Supreme Court, Shoemaker caused the commissioners many a migraine.

Shoemaker brought in his prominent lawyer for the court case, which made front-page news in the early 1890s. Stating that there was gold on his property, Shoemaker claimed he deserved more money for his land than the government was giving. When it became clear that he was going to lose his case, Shoemaker hacked down hundreds of trees on his property in protest, just days before it was to be turned into part of the nature park. Nevertheless, in *Shoemaker v. United States*, 147 U.S. 282 (1893), the Supreme Court upheld the ruling by lower courts: the federal government was giving Shoemaker fair market value for his property. No gold has ever been found on Shoemaker's land.[135]

That could have been the end of the Louis Shoemaker story in Rock Creek Park, but it most certainly was not. As Steve Dryden notes, Shoemaker "eventually swallowed his pride and became a major advocate for development of public facilities in the park."[136]

Shoemaker loved the park's natural character, as he had grown up exploring the Rock Creek Valley, but his primary interest was preserving the park's history, which his family had had a major role in over the years. In a presentation to the Columbia (D.C.) Historical Society in 1908, Shoemaker went on at length about the history of each mill and property. This document has proven invaluable for park staff and researchers over the years.

Shoemaker provided several farsighted ideas for the park during the presentation. Most notably, he recommended that Klingle Mansion (the current park headquarters building) be turned into a visitor center:

> *The main building is quite as good as it was when constructed 75 years ago. Why not utilize the grounds…and convert the buildings into a reception hall for the protection, advantage, and pleasure of the public, who would visit Rock Creek Park, if any effort were made to establish those attractive features found in other parks? Why not hang upon the wall a large map showing the outlines and shape of the park, its old and new roadways, its topography and relationship to Washington and the rest of the District? Why not have there also pictures of the gentlemen who at great sacrifice to their personal interest served the government for more than a year in the acquisition of the land, pictures of the lawyers employed by the government, pictures of the beautiful scenery and places of great natural beauty to be found in the park? And finally, why not have there a place where things of interest pertaining to the park, its past, present and future history could be preserved?[137]*

If Shoemaker's ideas had been implemented at the time, Rock Creek Park would have become home to most likely the first educational facility ever constructed in a federal park.

Another issue brought up during Shoemaker's lecture was his disapproval of the park's mill removal policy. During its early years, park managers ordered the razing of almost every mill and mill ruin along Rock Creek in order to beautify the park (the exception was Peirce Mill). Even so, the imminent domain battler turned passionate park enthusiast claimed that "commerce, trade, and business have disappeared from the banks of Rock Creek, but a most beautiful country remains."[138]

COLONEL LANSING BEACH, ROADS AND BRIDGES

Rock Creek Park's "Guardian Angel"

Once the court cases were completed and the land for the park had been purchased came the task of making the park accessible to the people without spoiling the natural scenery in the process. Overseen by the U.S. Army Corps of Engineers and D.C. commissioners, the Rock Creek Park Board of Control was established and given oversight of the park during its first few decades, and the man who led the board the first round of improvements was Colonel Lansing Beach.

A Dubuque, Iowa native and graduate of the U.S. Military Academy at West Point, Beach (1860–1945) was praised for his leadership in designing Rock Creek Park's early road system and rustic bridges. From 1894 to 1898, Beach served as assistant to the D.C. engineer commissioner. When the commissioner was called into action in Cuba during the Spanish-American War, Beach moved into the position and held it for three years. After engineering work in the Midwest, Beach's career would climax when he became chief of engineers, the head of the U.S. Army Corps of Engineers, in the early 1920s.[139]

Beach's influence on Rock Creek Park was profound. The park did not receive appropriations from Congress for several years after its establishment. And when it finally did receive maintenance funds, they were never steady but rather a roller coaster year after year. To partially remedy this, Beach creatively got the ball rolling by recruiting chain gangs. Indeed, under guard

Colonel Lansing Beach, namesake of Beach Drive. *Library of Congress Photo.*

supervision, many of the park's roads, including Ridge Road, Ross Drive and Grant Road, were first graded, laid out and macadamized by prisoners. In 1903, the *Evening Star* described these unique laborers at their staging ground for work in the park:

> *Every morning about 8 o'clock travelers down 14th Street will meet from two to three wagons filled with motley crews, all dressed with a similarity that*

is particularly striking. Their garments are late effects in stripes. Broad and black, these stripes have a horizontal direction and alternate with strata of white…Few visitors to the park realize how much these convicts have done here. They do not know that these same malefactors now doing penance in the way of municipal labor are engaged just now in clearing and cutting and grading what will be one of the most popular drives in the reservation.[140]

Beach's chain gangs also reconstructed and reopened Military Road, which had deteriorated since the Civil War; mowed grass in open areas of the park along roadways; and cleared trees and underbrush as a precursor to constructing additional roads, trails and bridges.[141]

Most of the roads that convicts constructed were winding and slow. As the automobile did not become a widespread middle-class household "appliance" until the 1920s, Rock Creek Park's early roads were not built for speed or commuting—the park road system's primary use today. Early roads were built for pleasure driving via horseback or horse-drawn carriage.[142] Ross Drive today is perhaps the best remnant of one of these winding, picturesque roadways.

Aside from recruiting nontraditional laborers, Beach oversaw the construction of the most technical road in the park, Rock Creek Drive. Graded from just north of Peirce Mill to Military Road at the turn of the century, the section of road that Beach and his workers completed parallels a section of the creek known as the fall zone, a geologic transition zone between the harder rock of the Piedmont Plateau and the softer, sedimentary rock of the Atlantic Coastal Plain. This fall zone results in the rapids along the mile-long section of Rock Creek. Beach carefully designed the roadway in this section so as to disturb the picturesque rapids, rocky outcroppings and scenery as little as possible.[143]

The roadway actually dropped seventy feet in elevation in the rapids area, but the D.C. Board of Trade, of which Charles Carroll Glover served as a prominent member, praised the road, noting in a report at the time that "it is climbed by such easy grades as to make it seem almost level." Some rock blasting did have to take place, but the blasting actually created the macadam, or small pebbles, that were then used on the gravel roadway.

As a result of this early construction, the board reported that "it is now possible to drive along Rock Creek, as it wildly dashes over falls and rapids, from the zoological park to Military Road." Beach was highly praised for his construction of the roadway, and in 1901, the U.S. Army Corps of Engineers changed the name of Rock Creek Drive to Beach

Left: Beach Drive across the creek from Peirce Mill. *Library of Congress.*

Opposite, top: Side view of Boulder Bridge with horseback rider. *Library of Congress.*

Opposite, bottom: Boulder Bridge over Rock Creek. *Library of Congress.*

Driveway in his honor. Over the years, "Driveway" has been shortened to "Drive."[144]

As early as the 1910s, Beach's roads began being widened and straightened to accommodate increasing traffic, most notably from the automobile. However, the engineer and his staff laid the foundation, both literally and figuratively, of Rock Creek Park's road system.[145]

Beach also left his mark on park bridges, and most of the rustic bridges still standing in Rock Creek Park today were designed under Beach's watchful eye. Perhaps the most famous is Boulder Bridge, and Beach was the one who suggested its unique boulder design and location. Completed in 1902, the final design chosen for Boulder Bridge was a "Melan reinforced concrete steel arch bridge with special boulder facing." Essentially, this means that the bridge was built with a metal arch with concrete covering. Picturesque boulders were then placed along the outside of the formation to make the bridge fit in with the natural environment.[146]

According to park lore, ironically, the boulders were actually supposed to be much smaller. The construction contract called for "man-sized stones, a technical term for stones light enough to be handled by a worker without machinery. However, the contractor of Boulder Bridge took the term man-size literally," notes historian Gail Spilsbury. When Beach arrived on the scene on the afternoon of the first day of construction, he saw the mistake, but he liked the way the large stones looked anyway and let the stonemasons continue.[147]

Other rustic-style bridges built at the turn of the century included a humble span over the Broad Branch tributary of Rock Creek at Ridge Road in 1898,

still there today but difficult to see, and a bridge with gneiss stone finish on Beach Drive over Piney Branch. Just north, perhaps the most picturesque bridge of all was built. Known as Pebble Dash Bridge, it was designed by D.C. architect Glenn Brown. Of the unique bridge design, National Park Service historian Timothy Davis notes:

> *Pebble Dash Bridge was a short span Melan arch concrete bridge faced with a sandy colored brushed concrete finish. The rough texture simulated a coarse, pebbled, rustic construction material. The "dash" designation stemmed from a regular row of small protuberances set a few inches below the top of the gracefully arched parapet. Additional ornamentation was supplied by a row of rectangular stones or bricks tracing a parallel arc at the level of the road surface.*[148]

One not so pleasant feature of Pebble Dash Bridge was its English ivy, planted around the base. The ivy's evergreen character was thought to beautify and further blend in the bridge to its natural surroundings. Planted commonly for decades, Rock Creek Park's natural resource managers and interpretation staff now consider English ivy an extremely harmful invasive, nonnative plant, prevalent throughout the park.[149]

As early as 1907, with Beach now gone, park managers moved away from the romantic, rustic style of architecture. During this year, a seemingly bland, modern cement span over Ross Drive was constructed, perhaps signaling a different, more modernistic style of construction to come. Indeed, two decades later, in the 1930s, Rock Creek Park would be criticized by National Park Service landscape architects as being "rustic in the worst sense of the word."[150]

Although manager of the park for less than ten years, Lansing Beach did a good job of balancing preservation of the park's scenery with the competing faction of visitor use. He was the individual who first opened up the park to the people via the construction of picturesque roadways. Perhaps rightly, a newspaper editorial of the time called Beach the "guardian angel of Rock Creek Park" and the "moving spirit" behind its early progress.[151]

CREEK FORDS

When the Best Way to Cross the Creek Was through the Creek

Many middle-aged visitors to Rock Creek Park recall an earlier era when, growing up, they forded the creek with their moms and dads. Indeed, Milkhouse Ford was open for decades, having just recently closed its gates in 1996. This and other fords were formalized in the early 1900s and were placed in the park at the time for visitor enjoyment, tradition and as a matter of practicality. Many of the crossings had been used for decades previously by millers, farmers, landowners and travelers and were placed where Rock Creek in general ran only inches deep.

Rebuilt in the first decade of the twenty-first century to allow for fish migration, Milkhouse Ford has the most extensive history of all Rock Creek fords. Prior to the adjacent road bridge, which was constructed in 1926, crossing Milkhouse Ford was the only way into the northern portion of Rock Creek Park. Used for centuries beforehand and previously referred to as Rock Creek Ford, workers paved Milkhouse Ford for the first time in 1904. They paved the rocky creek bottom with six to eight inches of concrete measuring twenty-four feet wide by seventy-four feet long. Granite benches were then constructed on both sides of the ford, and the entire project cost $800.[152]

In the early years of the park, at least two other road fords were paved and crossed Rock Creek south of Milkhouse Ford. Adjacent to Pebble Dash Bridge, Blagden Avenue Ford crossed the creek and connected to Broad Branch Road. Farther south, Klingle Road forded the creek at an area just below today's

A ford through Rock Creek with Pebble Dash Bridge in background. *National Park Service.*

modern Porter Street Bridge. Just south, technically on National Zoo property, were additional creek fords. Early visitors enjoyed wading and relaxing at the fords of Rock Creek, and one of the zoo fords was especially popular due to its numerous picturesque boulders strewn about.

Although enjoyed by generations of visitors, Rock Creek's fords were not without their challenges. Periodically, silt and sand pile-up had to be removed from these in-the-creek roadways. Furthermore, during and directly after storms, high water made fords extremely dangerous. Carriages and later cars sometimes got stuck during these storms. In 1911, a Rock Creek Park policeman pulled four people from the creek after their carriage overturned, while a decade later, Melvin (Micky) Coonin, a nine-year-old, although able to swim, mysteriously drowned while playing with a friend at the Blagden Avenue Ford.[153]

Hiking and Equestrian Trails
Over the Creek and Through the Woods

Park users very much approved of the early roadways, bridges and fords because they made Rock Creek Park more accessible. At the same time these features were being constructed, as much as appropriations would allow, footpaths for hiking and trails for horseback riding were established. The majority of trails used in the park today were constructed between 1900 and 1930.[154]

As Lansing Beach's right-hand man, assistant engineer William B. Richards was the primary planner and manager in the construction of Rock Creek Park's trail system. In December 1903, Richards recommended construction of the trail that would later be known as the Valley Trail:

> The main walk, like the main road, should be in the valley of Rock Creek and should be guided in its location and construction by the following considerations: First, to keep near the creek upon lines of fairly easy grade. Second, to keep the way as accessible and as easily traveled as possible. Third, to retain a rustic walk in harmony with its surroundings…Skirting the creek but located so as to cross the driveways at as few points as possible, and so as to be at some distance and not easily discernable from the main driveway along the creek.[155]

Richards recommended that cross trails be laid out to naturally guide visitors down to the creek trail. The assistant engineer also urged that instead of dirt, trails be constructed using broken stone or cinders so as to keep them less muddy and easily walkable year-round. While it is unknown whether these materials were used on early trails, most of Richards's other recommendations were implemented.[156]

In the early years of Rock Creek Park, when trails crossed the creek, they did so on bridges built in the rustic style with materials that were cheaper and more readily available than the concrete of today: wood. Historian Zack Spratt notes that eight wooden footbridges were utilized in the park by the early 1930s. Unfortunately, in a 1918 ice jam, some were destroyed and had to be replaced, while in 1934, each of the eight crumbled during a severe flood.[157]

Besides wooden footbridges, another difference from today regarding the early trail system was that equestrian trails and footpaths were established and operated distinctly from one another. Horse trails were built wider than footpaths to allow two riders to travel side by side. In the 1910s, the trails now known as the Western Ridge Trail and "Nature Center–Rapids Bridge Loop" were constructed, both being trails designated for horseback riding.[158]

TREE POLICY AND MANAGEMENT

"The Tragedy of the Cedars"

Rock Creek Park today is generally managed as a nature park, but this has not always been the case. Many park promoters over the years, most notably landscape architect Frederick Law Olmsted Jr., lobbied for a more formally landscaped park. Although subtle, in the early years of the park, this is how it was managed in many regards. As a result, select native trees were killed off, both by choice and by accident, while dozens of nonnative trees were introduced into the park as part of the U.S. Forest Service's experimental forest (a precursor to the National Aboretum). Here is the history of trees in Rock Creek Park.

Some contemporary park literature notes that Virginia pine, or scrub pine, was a dominant tree species in Rock Creek Park of yesteryear but that it died out due to natural forest succession. While this is partially true, it's also true that early park policy involved systematically removing this native species. Seen as unattractive and slow-growing by Olmsted Jr., hundreds of Virginia pines were felled to the protest of perhaps only one individual—of all people, U.S. president Woodrow Wilson (see next chapter).[159]

Managing the forest in other ways, staff during the first few decades of the park's existence spent the majority of time each winter removing downed trees. It was park policy to remove downed trees as much as possible in order to beautify the park and decrease the fire threat (the ecological benefits of downed trees was not widely understood at the time). Although park funds, then as today, ebbed and flowed due to partisan politics, Henry Cabot Lodge, influential U.S. senator from Massachusetts, orchestrated an uptick in appropriations for the express purpose of tree removal in 1914 and 1915. In perhaps the only discussion on the floor of the U.S. Senate dedicated to downed trees, Lodge stated:

> *For many years I have been in the habit of riding and walking constantly through Rock Creek Park. I have seen most of the parks of the great cities of the world, and I think that for natural beauty this is the most beautiful park I know. For a long time I have noticed in going through all the bridle paths and foot paths the great injury that is being done by the dead and down or partially down timber. Even along the main highways there are great dead trees standing that have been there for years, gaunt, disfiguring, ugly things…That great gale or cyclone last summer caused immense destruction, and the condition is now becoming a very serious thing. All through the woods in the region where the gale was most violent trees are down, and many of them have fallen only partially and are supported by and are crushing out the undergrowth; they are crushing out the dogwood and the laurel and the rhododendrons, which form the great beauty of the park in the spring and which are very important….Now, it is really very important for the woods in Rock Creek Park, and for the condition of the park, to get that dead and down timber out, and therefore I suggest this amendment.*[160]

While scrub pine and fallen trees were systematically removed, eastern red cedar became a dominant tree species in the first few decades of the park's existence but then began to die off quickly. One of the first trees to grow in fallow farm fields and open spaces, after Rock Creek Valley homesteaders and farmers abandoned their properties for the creation of the park, the cedar population increased. Old photos of Rock Creek Park attest to this. At the same time, however, Japanese honeysuckle, a highly invasive, nonnative plant species that spreads like wildfire, was planted along park stream banks to stabilize erosion. Unfortunately, in attempting to solve one environmental problem, park staff created another. The honeysuckle began killing off some of the park's native plants, most susceptible of which was perhaps the cedar.[161]

The U.S. Commission of Fine Arts, an environmental watchdog agency of sorts established by Congress to provide recommendations regarding management of D.C.'s public lands and buildings, noted this problem in the early 1920s. In a letter to Colonel Ridley of the Rock Creek Park Board of Control, fine arts commissioner John Greenleaf complained that "there is a hillside at a western entrance to Rock Creek, with its cedars rising against the sky was reminiscent of an Italian hillside. When I saw it three years ago, these cedars were shrieking under the throttling grasp of wild honeysuckle and tree weeds. Now as one passes he hears only a smothered moan. I call this 'The Tragedy of the Cedars.'" While it must be noted that some cedars died off naturally due to forest succession, many undoubtedly died from invasive plants.[162]

In a situation different from the cedar's, park staff were forced to remove a historically dominant mid-Atlantic region tree species, the American chestnut, in the 1920s and '30s. Once found relatively commonly in Rock Creek Park, the ultimate demise of this large, celebrated tree came in the form of a parasitic fungus accidently imported from a Japanese chestnut nursery around 1900. The fungus was unstoppable and spread rapidly from New England to the Deep South. It first entered the tree through cavities and wounds in the bark and, once inside, acted like a poison in the bloodstream. Once dead, these large trees were deemed dangerous hazards if near a park road or trail and therefore removed.[163]

It might have been an unhealthy American chestnut that almost killed a famous visitor to the park. During the Theodore Roosevelt administration, Admiral George Dewey, famous for his sacking of the Spanish flotilla in Manila Bay in the Philippines, wrote the park manager about a tree just feet and seconds away from smashing him and his car. "There came very near being a vacancy in the Admiral's grade yesterday," Dewey wrote. "I was driving in Rock Creek Park, near the Military Road, having just turned at that Road and started back, when a large tree, which I had passed a minute before, fell not a hundred feet in front of me directly across the road, breaking into three pieces. I think in ten seconds more I would have been under it!"[164]

At the same time that many trees were being removed or dying, redwoods and other nonnative species were being planted. Park managers permitted the U.S. Forest Service to develop an experimental forestry plot in the northern confines of the park from 1911 to 1921. National Park Service historian Barry Mackintosh notes that the board of control permitted the practice on the grounds that "the trees be set in irregular patterns to avoid

Exotic Animals

In addition to exotic trees, one day during the summer of 1916, Rock Creek was the location of two exotic animals. "It would be a great relief to the keepers of the park if they could fathom the mystery of how two full-sized alligators came to be sunning themselves along Rock Creek," noted the Washington Post. *The article continued:*

One of the keepers at the "Zoo" went for a stroll early yesterday, and was astonished to see an alligator sitting on the bank of the creek. He hurried back to the alligator quarters of the gardens, and found none of the regular specimens missing. Then he ran to the creek bank again. The alligator was still there.

The keeper organized an alligator hunting party, and after much maneuvering, managed to capture the animal in a net, taking him to the alligator house and depositing him with the regular specimens. With the new arrival safely locked up, the keeper started out again to see how the animal got on the creek bank.

As he neared the scene of the discovery he stopped short. He rubbed his eyes and pinched himself. Behold! There on the bank sat another alligator…The hunting party again was organized. The members crept up quietly, but when they were ready to toss the net the alligator slipped into the water and swam away…Where the alligators came from nobody knows. The supposition is that they are private pets which left their homes for a frolic in the park.[166]

Fortunately, this seemed to be an isolated, if not comical, incident. Nonnative alligators are not a factor in Rock Creek today.

the appearance of artificial cultivation." By 1920, the Forest Service had planted over 2,000 trees including over 170 species.[165]

While some trees fared well, others, specifically the California coastal redwood, being away from its native environment and its much-needed year-round precipitation in the form of fog and rain, struggled. Nevertheless, the Forest Service was intent at the time to plant additional trees from all around the world. Furthermore, the Forest Service expressed interest in formalizing its Rock Creek Park test plot and turning it into the U.S. Botanical Gardens and National Arboretum. Reasons for placing these features in the park included the park's large, picturesque appearance as well as the fact that no funds would be needed to purchase the land—it was already in custody of the government.[167]

The D.C. Commission of Fine Arts rejected this proposal. "The idea is in its very essence so full of danger to the fundamental purposes of the park," noted fine arts commissioner Frederick Law Olmsted Jr. in 1918. Another commissioner wrote to Congress, stating that "if the Botanic Garden is established in Rock Creek Park the inevitable result will be the gradual frittering away of a priceless and self-consistent piece of natural scenery…this piece of ground was set apart by Congress for the preservation of its scenery."[168]

Eventually this view won out. Neither the U.S. Arboretum nor the Botanical Garden was formalized in Rock Creek Park, and only a decade after they were started, the U.S. Forest Service plantings were terminated and all trees removed. Today, there is not a trace of the old tree farm, only memories. There are also, with the exception of perhaps a lone seedling here or there, essentially no American chestnuts in the park. Few Virginia pines and cedars remain, but downed trees can certainly still be found, which would not please Henry Cabot Lodge.

PRESERVATION VERSUS USE

Sixteenth Street Reservoir and the "State Monuments" Proposal

The biggest challenge for park managers and staff of any nature park is to protect the park's scenery and natural resources while at the same time providing for public use and enjoyment. These two management policies, preservation at one end and use on the other, have always and will always compete with and challenge each other. While Yosemite National Park's Hetch Hetchy Valley controversy might be the most recognizable historic example of a preservation versus use battle in which use won out (to supply the San Francisco Bay area with a steady supply of water, the scenic Hetch Hetchy Valley, which famous naturalist John Muir said rivaled Yosemite Valley itself, was turned into a reservoir), Rock Creek Park has had several preservation versus use controversies as well. A quick look back at two of these controversies in early Rock Creek Park, as well as their end results, will shed light on this recurring management challenge.

First, a win for use. Rock Creek Park was set aside by Congress in 1890 for both "the benefit and enjoyment of the people" as well as "for the preservation of all timber, animals, and curiosities." While early park managers saw the word "benefit" to mean "benefit park visitors," the District of Columbia Water Department apparently saw the word to mean "benefit D.C. residents," a big distinction. This debate played out in an 1897 water department proposal for a reservoir in the park bordering Sixteenth Street. Objecting to this proposal on the grounds that such development was not permitted under the park's enabling legislation, the Rock Creek Park Board of Control brought the debate to U.S. attorney general Joseph McKenna. Although McKenna sided with the board, the water department then lobbied Congress to authorize new legislation that would enable it to construct the reservoir in the park. Ultimately, realizing that the legislation would be authorized, the board of control submitted a compromise. As Barry Mackintosh notes:

> *The park boundary in the vicinity of the desired reservoir site, north of Blagden Avenue and west of 16th Street, was uneven. If the Water Department would purchase certain tracts, the board would exchange an equal or lesser amount of parkland for them so as to leave the department with an adequate reservoir site and the park with a straightened boundary.*[169]

This is exactly what happened, and the reservoir was built twenty-two-feet deep with a capacity to store fifteen thousand gallons of water.[170] Known as Brightwood Reservoir, or Sixteenth Street Reservoir, the reservoir was located for forty years in what is now the tennis center area of Rock Creek Park. Brightwood Reservoir was seen by some later historians as the "first major incursion into the park." It also set the stage for later development in the area. "If you've wondered why today there is a tennis stadium, an amphitheater and ball fields [not to mention a golf course] just north of Crestwood in Rock Creek Park, you can blame (or credit) the District Water Department," notes neighborhood historian David Swerdloff. "While nearly the entire park is preserved in its natural state, this parcel was developed because of a precedent set by a D.C. Water facility at the turn of the 20th Century."[171]

Nevertheless, most people at the time didn't see the reservoir as a controversy but rather a place to recreate. The land around the artificial lake was cleared due to the construction and then afterward became a popular area for horse shows and racing.

While Brightwood Reservoir was completed in 1899, just one year prior, a seemingly bizarre bill for "State Exhibition Buildings in Rock Creek Park, District of Columbia" was being promoted by select congressmen. The bill called for each state in the nation to claim one to six acres of land in the park on which to erect museums to promote the specific state. The idea was that each state building could be used for "any and all articles or things connected with its natural or industrial resources or evidencing its social, scientific, or artistic progress and development."[172]

Once again, the Rock Creek Park Board of Control opposed the bill on several grounds. Besides the fact that the state buildings did not correspond to the park's purpose, the survey noted that there were few places of level ground in Rock Creek Park suitable for large buildings. The board also believed that "these buildings would be much better accomplished by attaching their exhibits to the National Museum [located on the National Mall] instead of placing them in a remote corner of the District" away from tourists.[173] Ultimately, in this instance, the board of control won the battle on the side of preservation. Rock Creek Park is not home to fifty large buildings spotlighting every state in the union.

5

VISITOR RECREATION
AND ENJOYMENT

E arly recreation in Rock Creek Park was much different than today. Due to the fact that the park was beyond the reach of most electric trolley lines and thus beyond the reach of most citizens, it was much quieter than it is today during its first few decades. Furthermore, the national capital as a city had not filled out with development to its boundary yet. "When our children were little, we were for several winters in Washington, and each Sunday afternoon the whole family spent in Rock Creek Park, which was then very real country indeed," wrote Theodore Roosevelt at the time.[174] This "very real country" hosted foxhunting, a restaurant at Peirce Mill and even an overnight summer camp for low-income white children. Visitors might also be interested to know that on hot, sticky summer days, there once was a time where swimming and wading in Rock Creek was permissible. This chapter focuses on visitor enjoyment and recreation in the early years of Rock Creek Park.

FOXHUNTING AND HORSE RACING

Fun, Fun, Fun...But Now Maybe Illegal!

Horseback riding, perhaps the Rock Creek Valley's oldest form of recreation still in existence today, has a long history, and some forms of this equestrian fun might surprise you. Such was the scene at Peirce Mill in 1912:

To the bay of hounds and clatter of hoofs, more than 30 young society men and women and prominent army officers dashed through Rock Creek Park yesterday afternoon on the largest and most successful drag [fox] hunt ever held in the District…After a few minutes the riders had assembled at the mill, the dogs were set loose, and the chase was on. A few of the dogs went wrong, but the main pack took to the scent well and followed it to the end. The jumps were taken in fine style by most riders.[175]

The particular outing was led by the Rock Creek Hunt Club, a group of upper-class urbanites. Twenty-six hounds and approximately fifty riders were on the chase for a red fox. Starting at Peirce Mill, they raced through the park up to the Walter Reed Army Medical Center. One wonders how the chaos affected other park users![176]

Even prior to foxhunting, horse racing was popular at a site known as the Crystal Springs Raceway. Named after the largest and most picturesque spring flowing into Rock Creek, the raceway was located in the area now bordering the Rock Creek Park tennis stadium. When the raceway closed due to the expansion of Sixteenth Street to the D.C. boundary, similar horse events moved nearby to an area just inside the

Members of the Rock Creek Hunt Club just before a fox hunt in Rock Creek Park, circa 1915. *Library of Congress.*

Horse show in Rock Creek Park, May 15, 1938. The photo was taken near the site of the present tennis stadium and sports fields; the area was historically farmland. *Library of Congress.*

park adjacent to Brightwood Reservoir. (Reservoir construction in 1899 had created an open space.)

Rock Creek Park's horse racing events were large and attracted thousands of visitors. They remained popular annual events for decades. A *Washington Post* article noted in 1915 that fifteen thousand persons were in attendance for a horse show that included sixteen events, and "every event of the sixteen was of engrossing interest, from the mile-long work-horse parade with which the tournament opened, to the steeplechase at its conclusion."[177] Over twenty years later, in 1938, competitions included children's saddle ponies, junior horsemanship, three-foot jumping, bridle path racing and four-foot jumping. Horses entered in the competitions included Laura, Jeremiah, Timber Queen and Easy Money.[178]

During World War II, the horse racing area of the park was used by the U.S. Army as a de facto parking lot for excess tanks and military vehicles. Smaller-scale horse shows were then begun at the Equitation Field just south of the present-day Horse Center and Nature Center, a tradition which today has petered out.

Peirce Mill Teahouse

It's Time for Lunch!

"Is there a good place in the park to grab a bite?" This is a question Nature Center staff often hear from visitors, and unfortunately, they have to send them back out to Connecticut Avenue, the nearest roadway with substantial restaurants and grocery stores. Hungry visitors would have been in luck from 1905 to 1933, however. During this time, the last surviving gristmill along Rock Creek served as a teahouse and restaurant.

Peirce Mill Teahouse guests were able to choose from a variety of menu items, including salads, sandwiches, cheeses, beverages (nonalcoholic) and desserts. Favorite dishes included the "Tutti Fruitti Salad," chicken salad sandwich and homemade ice cream. Of course, the beverage of choice was tea.[179]

During the teahouse years, a screened-in, wood-framed porch was added to the side of the mill so that guests could relax while eating and enjoying the view out to Rock Creek. Out in front of the teahouse at the time, a dam was constructed along Rock Creek for visitors to enjoy the sound of falling

Peirce Mill Teahouse in 1934, just before demolition of its screened-in porch. *National Park Service.*

water. This was an early park beautification project. One prominent user of the teahouse who enjoyed the view was President and later Chief Justice William Howard Taft.[180]

With the exception of an owner in 1919 who provided poor service and was given the boot, the teahouse operated successfully as a park concessioner until 1920. But during this year, in racial stereotypes of the time, a distant relative of the Peirce family did not like the fact that Hattie L. Sewell, an African American woman, obtained the contract for the restaurant. E.S. Newman, who lived just outside the park boundary, wrote to Clarence Sherrill, park manager at the time, complaining that she didn't want the area becoming "a rendezvous for colored people, soon developing into a nuisance." Sherrill told Newman that Sewall had been operating the teahouse satisfactorily and that business had actually increased. Unfortunately, Newman persisted, and Sherrill was forced to terminate Sewall's contract in order to please park neighbors.[181]

Sherrill then gave the contract to the Girl Scouts Association of the District of Columbia, who operated the teahouse until 1922. A special dish the teahouse served at the time were Harding Waffles in honor of the incumbent president, apparently before his administration became largely known for corruption.[182] "A delightful air of hospitality will be found always in evidence at the tea house," Colonel Sherrill noted in a 1921 press release. "The management is directly under a large committee of ladies prominent in Washington society and there will be some one of these actively in charge each day."[183]

After the Girl Scouts Association, the Welfare and Recreational Association of Public Buildings and Grounds became manager of the teahouse. When it was decided that the mill would be historically renovated as part of a New Deal project in the 1930s, though, the era of the Peirce Mill Teahouse ended. Rock Creek Park hasn't had a restaurant since the mid-1930s.

CAMP GOODWILL

Free Rest and Relaxation for Those in Need

During the same time of the Peirce Mill Teahouse, from 1904 to the mid-1930s, a Catholic charity operated the first and only nonprofit overnight camping facility in Rock Creek Park. Camp Goodwill was located initially in the area of what is now the golf course off Sixteenth Street. In the 1920s, it moved to an area just north of Fort DeRussy. The camp offered low-income white children and their mothers free two-week-long summer vacations in the park. It hosted 150 campers at a time.

During its heyday, Camp Goodwill included an administration building, a dining hall, a nursery, two picnic pavilions, two bathhouses, three dozen tent platforms, a ball field and, perhaps most importantly, a swimming pool. Campers enjoyed free room and board in the form of hearty meals and rustic tents. They also played games, swam under the warm summer sun and enjoyed spending time in the great outdoors. Malnourished children were treated at the nursery with professional staff, as were newborns and infants. Mothers were trained in childcare, feeding and other "healthy baby" practices. A 1914 newspaper article described the camp scene:

> *The two months of the summer bring many visitors, all of whom exclaim over the beauty of the spot, and one cannot wonder for it is indeed a charming sight. The old rambling, white-painted farmhouse, with its white-outbuildings set among beautiful trees; the white canvas tents*

Camp Goodwill, 1924. *Library of Congress.*

glistening in the sunlight, the croquet grounds, see-saws, swings, tetherpole [sic], sandboxes, and baseball grounds, all occupied by happy children, while in the shade of splendid old trees, rocking, resting, sewing, or talking happily, are the mothers with their babies.[184]

When not in use for the traditional two-week camps, Camp Goodwill sometimes was used for Scout jamborees, especially in its later years. In 1936, one jamboree, or rather "camporee," included five hundred area Boy Scouts. The twelve- to fifteen-year-old adolescents camped overnight and had freedom as to what they cooked for their meals and how they set up their tents, though counselors advised campers not to "mix milk with pickles." Beyond bad taste, there was another incentive to eat well and keep a tidy tent: awards. By night, the mass of Scouts gathered around campfires to hear ghost stories and sing.[185]

They were all white Scouts, as were all the lower-income vacationers at Camp Goodwill. The early 1900s was the time of segregation, and Camp Goodwill was white only. However, the same charity, the Associated Charities of Washington, D.C., opened up Camp Pleasant for African American children in Prince George's County. Both camps moved to Prince William Forest Park, another unit of the National Park System, in the late 1930s and desegregated in 1954 when the Supreme Court issued its decision making "separate but equal" illegal. The multiracial camp continues today out at Camp Moss Hollow, a four-hundred-acre site in northern Virginia.

SWIMMING AND WADING

"Come on in Boys, the Water Is Fine"

Although wading and swimming in the creek has been illegal for decades due to poor water quality caused by stormwater runoff, raw sewage and illegal dumping (see Chapter Nine), in the early years of Rock Creek Park, when the water was cleaner, it was permitted. This resulted in the fact that on hot, sticky summer days in the nation's capital, hundreds of youth and adults alike would seek respite in the cool, shaded waters of Rock Creek.

Although not horribly deep or large, there were, in fact, swimming holes. Little Rock Swimming Hole was located just above Klingle Road, while perhaps the most popular, Sycamore Swimming Hole, was just below Boulder Bridge. Snaky Bottom Swimming Hole was located at an unidentified location.[186]

Fords were popular spots for wading, as their smooth cement bottoms were easier on a child's or teenager's feet than sharp pebbles and rocks. And by the Roaring Twenties, with automobiles being affordable to middle-class Americans, a new form of water recreation began at the fords: car washing. With the uptick in automobile usage, traffic became commonplace in the park, specifically around the creek fords, for the first time ever. Many cars would stop in the middle of the narrow fords. With the driver and family jumping out to wash their car or have a quick splash, cars behind would be forced to wait. Nevertheless, people were generally on good behavior.

Sometimes, however, boys will be boys. In 1913, a visitor complained about a group of youngsters in the park wading inappropriately: "These boys and young men commit all kinds of nuisances, such as exposing their persons to passersby, profanity, in its worst form, fighting, throwing stones…" Fortunately this seemed to be an isolated, if not comical, incident.[187]

Young visitors enjoying the cool waters of the creek in Rock Creek Park during a heat wave in 1922. Notice the one boy completely submerged in water! *Library of Congress.*

Farther down Rock Creek in Georgetown, youngsters waded appropriately "in the eyes of the lord." Historic photos depict Georgetown African American church congregations in mass baptisms in Rock Creek. Earlier in Georgetown history, in the 1800s, the Herring Hill subdistrict was founded along the banks of Rock Creek. The predominantly African American community, made up of both enslaved and free peoples, fished for herring in Rock Creek and bathed in its water. The creek baptisms occurred due to the fact that many white preachers refused to baptize African Americans in their churches.[188]

Although swimming, wading, car washing and even religious ceremonies were common creek activities for decades, by the 1930s, as Rock Creek grew increasingly polluted from its urban surrounding, public swimming pools became more popular.

Camping and Night Parking

"Deserves a Quiet Night"

Imagine yourself living in the national capital in July without air conditioning. Where would you go after work? Before the widespread use of artificial air conditioning in homes, visitors used the natural air conditioning of Rock Creek Park. Then, as today, it's always slightly cooler down by the creek because trees take the place of pavement and asphalt—there is no urban heat island effect. Visitors used to enjoy camping and night parking—relaxing in the park after dark—in Rock Creek Park.

During the park's camping heyday in the 1920s, it wasn't uncommon for park watchmen (staff precursor to U.S. Park Police) to observe five hundred cars per night parked along the roadsides and in the small picnic grove parking lots of Rock Creek Park. "The proliferation of fold-out beds and other devices for car-camping…made the conversion from touring car to outdoor bedroom relatively simple, though many people undoubtedly made do with regular car seats and makeshift expedients," notes National Park Service historian Timothy Davis. "Others just drove into the park in the evening to enjoy several hours of cool respite."[189]

Most of the nighttime park users were members of Washington's middle and working class who lived downtown. Some wealthy Washingtonians who, then as now, lived generally west of the park and enjoyed the slightly higher geography and its benefit of slightly cooling summer breezes frowned on this practice of night parking. And although most night parkers were appropriately relaxing in the park, a few spoilers undoubtedly partied and then left their trash in the park. Furthermore, at least one particular administrator did not approve of teenagers and others enjoying date nights in their cars in Rock Creek Park. Ulysses S. Grant III, grandson of the former U.S. president and Civil War general, declared a "war on necking."[190]

For these reasons, the superintendent of the park and his higher-ups terminated the policy of night parking "to protect the law-abiding public from nuisance and young girls from waywardness…It is the parties of young men and women, giving no thought of the beauties of the park, and who remain parked, sometimes without lights at midnight, whom we will remind of this regulation." However, so many protests came in from the new ruling that park managers were forced to backtrack.[191]

Because of the popularity of camping and night parking in the park, individuals—including park administrators, city planners and the general public—debated whether or not to construct a more formal camping facility. Not wanting to spoil the natural scenery of the park, it was ultimately decided to place a large campground resort a few miles south at the reclaimed mud flats at Hains Point in East Potomac Park. Rock Creek Park overnight campers began using the new campground facility when it opened, and the night parking era faded into memory.

Winter Sports in Rock Creek Park

Ice Sculptor Rivals Michelangelo

Significant snowfall in the nation's capital is relatively rare, but when it does happen, many residents have known exactly what to do: visit the winter wonderland of Rock Creek Park! Over the years, residents have traveled into the park by snowshoe, cross-country ski, snowboard and sleigh. They've gotten pounded with snowballs, enjoyed ice skating on Rock Creek Pond, listened to the sound of silence on backwoods trails and even created art comparable to Europe's finest.

In 1932, just three days prior to Christmas, the *Washington Post* reported holiday visitors to the park happily observing a nearly perfect, snow-sculpted "life-size replica of the Blessed Virgin with the infant Christ at her breast."

Located at the corner of Sherrill Drive and Beach Drive, the snow statue was constructed by a Catholic priest from New York City "in apparent winter street clothes…The placid features of the Madonna are reproduced with the facility of a master and the tiny Son of God nestles against the snowy breast of its immaculate mother with the same placidity delineated in the creations of a Michelangelo," noted the article.[192]

Farther south, technically located on National Zoo property, ice-skating was popular on Rock Creek Pond. During cold winters, the shallow water of the creek would freeze just enough for ice-skating escapades. Park administrators deemed two inches of ice sufficient for skating. Although it is unknown when this practice ended, ice-skating was particularly popular into the 1920s.[193]

On one additional note of interest regarding winter, Rock Creek Park actually holds the record for most snowfall in the District of Columbia. In 1922, during the now famous Knickerbocker Snowstorm, thirty-three inches of snow fell in the park, compared to twenty-six inches on top of the Knickerbocker Theater downtown. During the Friday night performance,

Skiing in Rock Creek Park. *Library of Congress.*

the roof collapsed due to the heavy snow, killing 98 patrons and injuring almost 150. Snowfall is much more tranquil in Rock Creek Park than most other urban locations.

Rock Creek Golf Course

"This Course Has Bite"

Not many national park units are home to an eighteen-hole golf course, a five-thousand-seat outdoor amphitheater and a professional tennis stadium. Rock Creek Park is. While Carter Barron Amphitheatre and the William H.G. Fitzgerald Tennis Stadium were built in the mid- and later half of the twentieth century, the golfing tradition in Rock Creek Park dates from 1905.

During this year, longtime park foreman Patrick Joyce, after whom Joyce Road is named, oversaw construction of a nine-hole course around the Sixteenth Street Reservoir. In 1923, the site was abandoned and the golf course relocated to its present location. The new course was designed by noted golf course architect William Flynn and constructed again under the supervision of Joyce. By 1926, the full eighteen-hole course was complete. On April 3 at 6:00 a.m., U.S. senator Wesley Jones of Washington State and U.S. congressman William Oliver of Alabama teed off against Superintendent of the Senate Press Gallery James Preston and Edwin Halsey of the U.S. Senate Sergeant of Arms Office. The game was on, and the Rock Creek Golf Course has been open to the public continuously ever since.[194]

The course is unique with its steep hills and has offered hundreds of thousands of golfers a challenge over the years. In the 1930s, the Rock Creek Open and turkey golf tournament were popular annual events attracting the national capital area's best golfers. The turkey tournament was played just before Thanksgiving with the grand prize being the centerpiece of Thanksgiving dinner! Most course visitors, though, have simply enjoyed playing a round of golf with their friends rather than in formal competition.[195]

While the once spacious golf course was severally shrunk with the modernization of Military Road and construction of Joyce Road in the late 1950s, its new reconfiguration remains popular, especially the back nine holes:

Aerial view of the Rock Creek Golf Course, circa 1960. *National Park Service.*

Rock Creek's short layout of par 3's and 4's might not look all that difficult on a scorecard but this course has bite. The front nine consists of short par 4's and medium to long par 3's; just enough to get you warmed up for the back. The back nine is a true test of accuracy and perseverance. Dense woods on either side of the narrow fairways will show how much confidence you have in your driver. Postage stamp greens and large elevation changes combine to force risk/reward decisions on every shot.[196]

6

FAMOUS VISITORS

While the park is largely ignored by commanders in chief today, U.S. presidents as well as key politicians and diplomats of yesteryear utilized it often for play. This series of four articles will spotlight four famous individuals that recreated in Rock Creek Park during its early years. One of these individuals, John Burroughs, did what many naturalists in the park do today two decades before the park was even established: he went birding.

JOHN BURROUGHS

Wildflowers and Warblers

A noted American writer and naturalist, John Burroughs (1837–1921) spent almost his entire life on his New York farm in the Catskill Mountains. But for a few years in the 1860s, the John Muir look-alike and good friend of Walt Whitman (the three men all sported long white beards) came down from his haunt to work and live in the nation's capital. The introverted, shy and reserved Burroughs countered his work in his office at the U.S. Treasury by getting away from downtown to study the flora and fauna of the capital's wilder side. Where was this wild, natural side? Then as now, it was the Rock Creek Valley. The famed naturalist often tromped through the area that later became Rock Creek Park, studying and admiring its

Outside of the city limits, the great point of interest to the rambler and lover of nature is the Rock Creek region. Rock Creek is a large, rough, rapid stream, which has its source in the interior of Maryland, and flows in to [sic] the Potomac between Washington and Georgetown. Its course, for five or six miles out of Washington, is marked by great diversity of scenery. Flowing in a deep valley, which now and then becomes a wild gorge with overhanging rocks and high precipitous headlands, for the most part wooded; here reposing in long, dark reaches, there sweeping and hurrying around a sudden bend or over a rocky bed; receiving at short intervals small runs and spring rivulets, which open up vistas and outlooks to the right and left, of the most charming description…Rock Creek has an abundance of all the elements that make up not only pleasing but wild and rugged scenery. There is perhaps, not another city in the Union that has on its very threshold so much natural beauty and grandeur, such as men seek for in remote forests and mountains.

—John Burroughs, 1868

unique flora and fauna. His writing on the region offers us an intimate look into its early natural history.

Burroughs's favorite area of the pre-park was where Piney Branch flowed into Rock Creek. "It is a small, noisy brook, flowing through a valley of great natural beauty and picturesqueness, shaded nearly all the way by woods of oak, chestnut, and beech, and abounding in dark recesses and hidden retreats," he wrote. In this locale, Burroughs noted many varieties of wildflowers. No longer common in the park due to encroaching invasive, nonnative plant species, the naturalist observed that skunk cabbage, which, as its name suggests, emits an unappealing smell when its leaves are rubbed, were widespread in, wet areas. Burroughs also noticed patches of spring beauties, a small, five-pedaled purplish-white flower that blooms for only a short time in spring. Another common spring flower was the white-and-yellow bloodroot, which Burroughs said was prevalent "at the foot of almost every warm slope in the Rock Creek woods." Burroughs knew the flowering plants of the park so well that he wrote what week in spring each species could be expected to bloom.[197]

He also studied the valley's migratory bird populations. Located on the Atlantic flyway between the warm tropics and summer breeding grounds of eastern Canada, Rock Creek Park serves as a highway rest stop in spring and fall for dozens of neotropical migrants. Of these migrants, Burroughs noted an abundance of warblers in early May. Species such as the "blue yellow-back, the chestnut-sided, and the Blackburnian [*sic*]" warblers inhabited "every branch and leaf, from the tallest tulip to the lowest spice-bush," he wrote. And they sang loudly and proudly.[198]

Regarding the population of year-round resident birds, Burroughs's favorite was probably the "most interesting, though quite rare" Kentucky warbler. He wrote of the bird's large size and unique coloring. Another year-round resident that Burroughs seemed to both love and hate was the yellow-breasted chat, which, as its name suggests, was quite vocal:

> *I seldom go the Rock Creek route without being amused and sometimes annoyed by the yellow-breasted chat…His voice is very loud and strong and quite uncanny…If one passes directly along, the bird may scarcely break the silence. But pause a while, or loiter quietly about, and your presence stimulates him to do his best. He peeps quizzically at you from beneath the branches, and gives a sharp feline mew. In a moment more he says very distinctly, who, who. Then in rapid succession follow notes the most discordant that ever broke the sylvan silence. Now he barks like a puppy, then quacks like a duck, then rattles like a kingfisher, then squalls like a fox, then caws like a crow, then mews like a cat…and so on till you are tired of listening.*[199]

Burroughs cherished the time he spent in the Rock Creek Valley in the 1860s. Decades later, he would explore the park again with Theodore Roosevelt before their trip to Yellowstone National Park, where he served as the expedition's journalist-in-chief. Indeed, the two men were quite different in physical ability and personality. At age forty-two, the youthful Roosevelt was the youngest president to ever take office. He had boundless energy and was a proud man. Burroughs, on the other hand, was over twenty years Roosevelt's senior and was more meek and humble. Nevertheless, the two were good friends.[200]

THEODORE ROOSEVELT

We Would Arrange for Point to Point Walks

The commander in chief who has spent the most time in Rock Creek Park is undoubtedly Theodore Roosevelt. America's twenty-sixth president could often be found in the park hiking, horseback riding, skinny-dipping, birding and picnicking with his family.

Roosevelt (1858–1919) was known for his boundless energy, and this showed on his fast-paced hikes: "We liked Rock Creek Park because we could do much scrambling and climbing along the cliffs," Roosevelt noted. "We would arrange for a point to point walk, not turning aside for anything—for instance, swimming Rock Creek…if it came in our way." Roosevelt often trekked through the park in winter and early spring "when the ice was floating thick upon" the creek.[201]

The president often went hiking with his good friend French ambassador Jean Jules Jusserand, who was about the only person that could keep up with him. Indeed, when naturalist John Burroughs trekked with Roosevelt through the park, Burroughs complained that "we saw no birds. They couldn't keep up with us. I haven't walked at such a pace in years."[202]

But Roosevelt did give time to the study of birds. When he wasn't rigorously hiking in nature, he was perhaps birding in nature. In Rock Creek Park, Roosevelt observed large quantities of wood thrush (today the District of Columbia's official bird) as well as redheaded woodpeckers. He also noted brown-headed cowbirds.[203]

One incident that made news headlines was in 1902 when Roosevelt lost a particularly valuable ring just below Boulder Bridge. The group he was with scoured the area searching for it but came up short. Supposedly, Roosevelt put an ad in the paper stating, "Golden ring lost near Boulder Bridge in Rock Creek Park. If found, return to 1600 Pennsylvania Ave. Ask for Teddy." The ring has never been found.[204]

Regarding horseback riding in the park, on at least one occasion President and Mrs. Roosevelt enjoyed a quiet Thanksgiving ride through the sylvan woods. Roosevelt also went horseback riding with members of his cabinet through Rock Creek Park, most notably Secretary of War Elihu Root. Roosevelt rode horseback through the park no matter what the weather, snowstorm included.[205]

With his passion for the great outdoors and exercise, many people think that Theodore Roosevelt established the National Park Service (NPS), but the NPS was established in 1916 after his presidency. Roosevelt did, however, protect more acres of federal land in the form of national forests, national monuments and national wildlife refuges than any other president in U.S. history. "Here is your country. Cherish these natural wonders, cherish the natural resources, cherish the history and romance as a sacred heritage, for your children and your children's children. Do not let selfish

Theodore Roosevelt, laughing. "I do not believe that anyone else has ever enjoyed the White House as much as I have," Roosevelt said. He also enjoyed Rock Creek Park. *Library of Congress.*

men or greedy interests skin your country of its beauty, its riches or its romance," he wrote.

Though Roosevelt's namesake memorial and grounds are not in great shape, Theodore Roosevelt Island, at the confluence of Rock Creek and the Potomac River in Georgetown, honors the life and legacy of our outdoorsy, conservation-minded president. The island is administered by George Washington Memorial Parkway. In Rock Creek Park proper, the Theodore Roosevelt Trail paralleling the Valley Trail just south of Pulpit Rock honors him as well.

Jean Jules Jusserand
Skinny-Dipping with the President

A single, subtle granite bench is often overlooked by joggers and commuters on Beach Drive and the adjacent multiuse trail just south of Peirce Mill. Etched on this old bench are the words "Jusserand: personal tribute of esteem and affection." This is the Jusserand Memorial, the first memorial dedicated to a foreign diplomat on U.S. public lands.

As Jean Jules Jusserand (1855–1932) was the longest-serving French ambassador to the United Sates, it's perhaps fitting that he has a memorial in the park because he often strolled, picnicked and relaxed with his wife here. Furthermore, as a member of President Theodore Roosevelt's informal "tennis cabinet," Jusserand and Roosevelt spent significant time in Rock Creek Park hiking together—Jusserand was about the only individual who could keep up with Roosevelt's boundless energy. In his personal memoirs, Jusserand noted that "President Roosevelt gave me that unique proof of trust and friendship: he asked me to a 'walk'…But what the President called a walk was a run: no stop, no breathing time, no slacking of speed, but a continuous race, careless of mud, thorns, and the rest…The Rock Creek walk usually ended at the cliff overhanging the river, near…the zoo."[206]

As mentioned, Roosevelt liked point-to-point hikes rather than staying on trails. As a result, on their first hike in the park together, when Jusserand and Roosevelt approached Rock Creek, the president immediately began taking off his clothes so as to not get them wet when they forded it. The French ambassador, placed in potentially a very awkward situation, took it all in stride. He later wrote of the incident, humorously, "I, too, for the honor of France removed my apparel, everything except my lavender kid gloves. The President cast an inquiring look at this as if they, too, must come off, but I quickly forestalled any remark by saying, 'With your permission, Mr. President, I will keep these on; otherwise it would be embarrassing if we should meet ladies.'"[207]

Known as the "biggest little man in the capital," Jusserand served as French ambassador to the United States from 1902 to 1925. As the words on his memorial suggest, he was a highly regarded diplomat in both the U.S. and France and strengthened the tie between the two countries significantly. He received the first Pulitzer Prize in history for a book discussing great Frenchman of U.S. history, and conversely, created an organization in France

Jusserand Memorial in Rock Creek Park. Jean Jules Jusserand was the longest-serving French ambassador to the United States in history. *National Park Service.*

Franklin and Eleanor Roosevelt and Sara Ann Roosevelt (FDR's mother) arrive at the dedication of the Jusserand Memorial in Rock Creek Park on November 7, 1936. *Library of Congress.*

honoring important Americans in French history. Jusserand also spoke at numerous formal engagements; attended the dedication of the Joan of Arc Statue in Meridian Hill Park, which is now administered by Rock Creek Park; and even married an American national named Elise. When the married couple was strolling around the capital or in Rock Creek Park, passersby that recognized them often proclaimed, "Vive le France!" Jusserand would then shout back, in his broken yet correctly phrased English, "Long live the United States!"[208]

After Jusserand's death, Franklin Delano Roosevelt presided over a formal dedication of the Jusserand Memorial in Rock Creek Park on November 7, 1936. Eleanor Roosevelt and the president's mother were in attendance, as was Mrs. Jusserand.

WOODROW WILSON

In Love

Woodrow Wilson (1856–1924), U.S. president from 1913 to 1921, was a romantic, and part of that romance took place in Rock Creek Park. When Wilson's first wife died in 1914, he became so depressed that he shied away from the spotlight and struggled to get his job done. An assistant saw this as a big problem and decided to set him up on a date with one Edith Bolling Galt to see if the two would click. They did.

The courtship between Woodrow and Edith was quick and controversial. A U.S. president had never courted another woman so quickly after his wife's death. The media followed the lovebirds closely, sometimes very critically. To escape this chaos, the duo often snuck off to the quiet locales of Rock Creek Park. Trying to remain anonymous, they would get dropped off on the heavily forested and secluded Ross Drive. Then, with only two security agents—one just out of site ahead of them and one just out of site behind them—Woodrow and Edith would walk the quiet trails of the park hand in hand. Romantics, Galt and Wilson regularly wrote poetry to each other. One can almost imagine them doing this on walks in Rock Creek Park.[209]

In addition to falling head over heels for Edith, Wilson fell deeply in love with the park. In poor health just after his presidency, the Washington resident came to despise construction projects that diminished the park's

Edith and Woodrow Wilson, circa 1914. The two lovebirds also loved Rock Creek Park. *Library of Congress.*

natural beauty. In fact, after a drive through the park where he noticed several trees being felled, Roosevelt wrote a letter to the park manager stating, "Couldn't you give the trees in Rock Creek Park a vacation? I have been distressed by the number I have seen cut down there." When Wilson received what he interpreted as an inadequate response, he wrote back again: "I do not profess to be a forester, but the great majority of trees that I have noticed laying [*sic*] prostrate in the park are certainly sound. I know a sound tree when I see it inside the park. Moreover, in one part of the park a whole plantation of young pines have been cut down and it made my heart ache to see it."[210]

In another instance, Wilson became appalled when he learned of plans for the formal golf course:

> *Is it possible that it is true that a golf course is to be laid out in Rock Creek Park? I am loath to believe that such an unforgivable piece of vandalism is even in contemplation, and therefore beg leave to enter my earnest and emphatic protest. That park is the most beautiful thing in the United States, and to mar its natural beauty for the sake of a sport would be to do an irretrievable thing which subsequent criticism and regret would never repair.*[211]

Apparently, being a former U.S. president was not enough to convince park management, and the golf course was created. Ironically, another president, Dwight Eisenhower, would enjoy playing on this very golf course thirty-five years later.

Part III

Evolving Park and Parklands

NEW ADDITIONS AND THE NEW DEAL

During the three and a half decades from 1907 to World War II, Rock Creek Park expanded outward in every direction. While unique stream valley parks were added to the east, west and north, a unique parkway was constructed in the lower portion of the Rock Creek Valley, albeit at a turtle-slow pace for many years. At the same time Rock Creek Park was expanding outward with new additions, it expanded "inward" with the completion of numerous new conservation- and recreation-based projects, courtesy of the New Deal.

PINEY BRANCH PARKWAY AND OTHER TRIBUTARIES

An Aging Archaeologist Joins in the Battle for Conservation

Soapstone Valley Park, Normanstone Parkway, Melvin C. Hazen Park, Piney Branch Parkway, Klingle Valley, the Pinehurst Tributary—looking on a map of Rock Creek Park today, these Rock Creek tributaries and their adjacent narrow belts of forest show up as green just like the park itself. Yet they were all established after Rock Creek Park was created in 1890 and for a different reason.

As the city expanded toward the District of Columbia boundary in the early to mid-1900s, Rock Creek tributaries and nearby lands began being filled over with pavement. As a result, many of the area's historic and prehistoric springs stopped flowing. Afraid that Rock Creek Park's namesake creek could possibly dry up, citizens and officials began moving to protect its flow by purchasing surrounding areas and tributaries that were still somewhat natural. At the same time, many wanted the tributaries purchased so that roads could be built to connect city neighborhoods to Rock Creek Park and Beach Drive. These two ideas formed the basis for the establishment of the tributary parklands, and perhaps the tributary with the most significant history is Piney Branch, the first to be protected.[212]

Excavated by archaeologist William Henry Holmes in the 1880s and cherished by naturalist John Burroughs in the 1860s, a small section of Piney Branch bordering Rock Creek Park was preserved in perpetuity by Congress in 1907. Throughout the next two decades, the narrow stream valley park was expanded on all sides. Aging and perhaps wanting to secure a legacy in the 1920s, Holmes himself lobbied for his quarry site to be included in the park. In a series of letters back and forth with park executive manager Colonel Clarence Sherrill in 1925, the archaeologist wrote:

> *To me this old quarry in the middle of the capital city is a sacred spot...My recent visit with you to Piney Branch has aroused anew the hope that this secluded little valley may yet be rescued, at least in large part, from the ruthless invasion of suburban improvement. This valley, as you know, deserves the city's attention not only on account of its romantic beauty and desirability as a park area, but especially for the reason that it bears on its forest covered slopes one of the most important historical sites east of the Allegheny Mountains,—the site on which for hundreds, possibly thousands of years the Indian tribes of the Potomac Valley quarried quartzite boulders from which they roughed out by fracture their implements of war and the chase.[213]*

Holmes succeeded in getting his Piney Branch quarry and adjacent stream valley preserved, but in the 1930s, New Deal workers replaced a narrow, dirt roadway through the parkland with a wider, paved roadway, thus altering the stream valley's feel forever after. "Piney Branch is now in a sad condition," noted a National Park Service landscape architect soon after Piney Branch Parkway was constructed. "The new road has narrowed the stream bed to such an extent that the flood waters from heavy rains above are forced into a small bed." The result has been widespread erosion over the years.[214]

Piney Branch Valley, prior to parkway development. *National Park Service.*

Other tributaries to Rock Creek remained free of roads, though. The National Capital Parks Commission was chartered by Congress in the 1920s "to preserve the flow of water in Rock Creek, to prevent pollution of water in Rock Creek…" and "to preserve the forests and natural scenery in and about Washington." The commission was made up of the heads of all the federal and District agencies involved with parks, engineering and public lands. Working together and with Congress, the commission established the Melvin C. Hazen, Pinehurst and Soapstone Valley tributary parks, which now host hiking trails rather than roadways through them.[215]

While today many of these tributary valleys offer trails into and out of Rock Creek Park for hikers and runners, every Rock Creek tributary valley's topography and overall environment have been severely degraded over the years by stormwater runoff, which causes major erosion. Furthermore, due to their proximity to urban streets and yards, many invasive plant species rule supreme. (The Melvin C. Hazen Park and its widespread English ivy ground cover is a prime example.) Nevertheless, they serve as narrow strips of green and provide the District of Columbia with oxygen-making trees.

THE ESTABLISHMENT OF ROCK CREEK PARK–MARYLAND

In 1913, British ambassador to the United States Lord James Bryce wrote that "I should like to go even further…and consecrate the whole of Rock Creek Valley for 10 or 12 miles above Washington to the public. It is a very beautiful valley…Some day or other such a piece of scenery will be of infinite value to the people of Washington, who want to refresh their souls with the charms of Nature."[216] Two decades later, Bryce's call for a Rock Creek Park–Maryland came to fruition.

Although most visitors probably don't notice any difference between D.C.'s Rock Creek Park and Maryland's park of the same name, Rock Creek Park–Maryland was actually established four decades after D.C.'s park. While the National Park Service has administered D.C.'s Rock Creek Park since 1933, Maryland's park has always been administered by the Maryland National Capital Parks and Planning Commission (MNCPPC).

Rock Creek Park–Maryland found its legislative beginning in the Capper-Cramton Act of 1930. A bold bill specifying federal funds for the extension of park systems beyond but near the District (George Washington Memorial Parkway, Sligo Creek Parkway and other stream corridors were authorized with this piece of legislation), the bill was written by Representative Louis C. Cramton of Michigan, an ardent supporter of the National Park System, and Senator Arthur Capper of Kansas.[217]

With District of Columbia officials working with their Maryland counterparts, the tract from Boundary Bridge to East–West Highway was purchased and opened to the public by the mid-1930s. Ultimately, Rock Creek Park–Maryland has grown to include 4,193 acres— over twice the size of D.C.'s Rock Creek Park. Although a narrower strip of parkland and not as hiker friendly as D.C.'s park, Rock Creek Park–Maryland has a paved multiuse trail that allows bicyclists to ride from the D.C. boundary all the way up to Lake Needwood in Rockville. Lake Needwood itself is popular among fisherman.

MARY FOOTE HENDERSON AND MERIDIAN HILL PARK

Eccentric Character and an Eccentric Park

During the same time that Holmes was lobbying for the preservation of Piney Branch, an eccentric woman living nearby had plans for her own on top of Meridian Hill. Mary Foote Henderson (1842–1931), a lifelong vegetarian, Prohibitionist and health enthusiast who lived in a castle, was perhaps most passionate about two things: money and civic improvements. Both of these factors helped establish Meridian Hill Park, an administrative unit of Rock Creek Park.

Born into a wealthy New York family, Mary eventually married John Brooks Henderson, a wealthy, single-term U.S. senator. In 1887, the couple moved to Meridian Hill, where they built an elaborate, Seneca sandstone mansion that came to be known as Boundary Castle and Henderson Castle. In the castle, they held formal dinners that were well publicized around town—this was the Gilded Age, and the Hendersons were at the era's forefront.[218]

Washington Post articles of the time commented not only on the grandeur of the house ("the mellow Moorish entrance hall, plush-lined picture gallery used as a ballroom, and grand oak-paneled dining room hung with oak-leaf embroidered tapestries") but also on the eccentric meals served. As local historian and author of the fun, informative Streets of Washington blog John DeFerrari notes:

> *A 1905 fête included a fruit soup, mock salmon in hollandaise sauce, broiled slices of pine-nut Protose* [Protose was a meat substitute made of peanut butter, wheat gluten and corn starch, among other things], *unfermented Catawba wine, iced fruit, and Kellogg Gelatine for dessert. As reported in the* Post, *the printed menu cards for this dinner included "figures corresponding to each item on the bill of fare, showing the number, kind, and proportion of the food units, or 'calories,' contained in each dish." Like all meals prepared by Mrs. Henderson's accomplished English chef, it was said that the uninitiated couldn't tell that they weren't eating meat or fish.*[219]

Outside hosting elaborate dinners and promoting and writing about vegetarianism and health, Henderson pushed to make the area outside her front doorsteps an elite, world-class neighborhood. With this in mind, Henderson bought up numerous parcels of land and erected stately mansions and buildings on them, inviting foreign countries to then move in and set up embassies. She also purchased the land across from her castle, which had been used in succession historically as a farm, Civil War encampment and African American college. On this parcel, she staunchly supported a number of seemingly bizarre proposals before it ultimately became Meridian Hill Park.[220]

Indeed, Henderson lobbied in 1900 for a proposal put forth for constructing a massive presidential mansion on the site to replace the White

Mary Foote
Henderson and
unidentified
children.
*Library of
Congress.*

The
Henderson
Castle,
elaborate
residence of
Mary Foote
Henderson.
Located across
the street from
Meridian Hill
Park, the castle
was razed in
the 1940s to
make way
for modern
apartments.
*Library of
Congress.*

JOAQUIN MILLER REVISITS HIS CABIN ON MERIDIAN HILL

Joaquin Miller, who had lived in his two-room log cabin on Meridian Hill for three years in the 1880s, was not pleased with the widening and expansion of Sixteenth Street and Mrs. Henderson's developing of the area. When he revisited the national capital in 1899, he lamented over his decaying home and property in a Washington Times *interview:*

Joaquin Miller—with his own picturesque peculiar attire, with his poetic photographic description of pilgrimages, with his venerable personality—is again in Washington after an absence of nearly thirteen years. The bard of snow, of wind, of pine, and of mountain has changed little since his last visit here. The long flowing hair is slightly tinged with gray, the strong face is more rugged and weather beaten. His beard is now snowy white. The old poet is attired in a suit of brown corded velvet, and wears a great slouched hat. From a waistcoat pocket hangs a quaint chain of colored Alaskan diamonds with a big gold nugget as a charm. The attire includes top boots, but the trousers are not tucked in as of yore.

"Yes, I find many changes in Washington," said Mr. Miller to a *Times* reporter last night. "But the greatest is that which has taken place in Meridian Hill, at the top of Sixteenth Street. This hill has been mutilated by the grading of the street, and a big slice has been taken out of it. Now when I lived on that hill it was a magnificent place. I built my cabin there because it was the highest point in Washington, and now they have destroyed it. Had I known that the hill was mutilated I would have kept away from Washington.

"Yes, everything is changed. My old cabin, where I spent three happy years, is now a ruin. It looks like a bird's nest beside former Representative Henderson's castle. Captain Du Bois, who is now stationed at the White House, has purchased my cabin and it is falling into decay.

"I went out to Meridian Hill today to visit my old home and I was greatly broken up over the way it has been cut up. I would need a ladder to get at my cabin. The hills of Rome and Athens are sacred. Why not save those in the capital. They have scalped my hill and I shall not soon forget."[221]

House. Next, after the park was authorized by Congress in 1910 and the land purchased from Henderson, architect John Russell Pope prepared designs for a grandiose Lincoln Memorial on Meridian Hill, with which the matriarch of the hill quickly jumped on board. Based on the ancient Greco-Roman temple at Paestum, Italy, Pope's memorial design would have been situated in the center of Sixteenth Street, with the street itself diverting around the park. Additional design concepts included a 100-foot-wide staircase leading from an open plaza to a platform 250 feet above the Potomac River level, thus the memorial would have been a dominant D.C. landmark. When Pope's design was rejected, Henderson commissioned her own architect to draw up plans. But the Lincoln Memorial was not ultimately placed at Meridian Hill.[222]

Perhaps an only slightly more successful idea was Henderson's push to change the name of Sixteenth Street to the Avenue of the Presidents. Her goal was to have a bronze bust of each president lining the street and to make the roadway a grand entry into the city, comparable to the Champs-Élysées in Paris. However, when the avenue's name grew unpopular, it was quickly changed back after only a year.[223]

With her myriad defeats, Henderson finally settled on and endorsed an already in-the-works plan for a formal, unique, Italian Renaissance park. Construction of Meridian Hill Park took place between 1914 and 1936, and primary landscape architects included George Burnap and Horace Peaslee. The elaborate planting plan for the park was led by Ferrucio Vitale. A member of the D.C. Fine Arts Commission, Vitale and the commission also served as watchdogs over the project.[224]

Similar to early appropriations for Rock Creek Park, funding for the construction of Meridian Hill Park fluctuated from year to year. Who got involved lobbying Congress for better appropriations? None other than Mary Foote Henderson. On one of these instances, though she was nearing age ninety, Henderson and Vitale traveled to the floors of Congress in 1928 asking for money to continue building the park.[225]

Construction of Meridian Hill Park's upper terrace during the 1920s. *Library of Congress.*

Meridian Hill Park's lower terrace and cascading fountain shortly after completion. *Library of Congress.*

Although it did take over two decades to complete, Meridian Hill Park would eventually include the largest cascading fountain in North America; formal statuaries to Joan of Arc, Dante and Serenity; a somewhat unwanted U.S. Presidential Memorial to James Buchanan (see Chapter Two); and unique concrete aggregate making the cement walks, walls, urns and obelisks somewhat resemble the bottom of a west-running brook. The planting plan and overall layout of the park was one of an Italian garden. Specifically, the stepped character of the park design was reminiscent of Italian king Victor Emmanuel III's gardens. Meridian Hill Park was a point of pride for urban planners, as gardens of this magnitude in Europe were generally reserved for aristocrats, but Meridian Hill was open to all.[226]

Only a few years before the park was formally opened, Mary Foote Henderson died in 1931. Upon her death, the Commission of Fine Arts honored her, saying, "Persistently she labored during four decades, persuading and convincing Senators and Representatives; single-handed and alone she appeared before committees of Congress to urge approval for the work of development. She won." For these reasons, the House of Representatives actually voted on a bill to change the name of the park to Henderson Park.[227]

However, this name change was staunchly opposed by some who had always seen Henderson as a money-hungry pest. Ulysses S. Grant III, head of D.C.'s park department and an eccentric (not to mention extremely racist) character himself, complained:

> *Mrs. Henderson did not donate any of the land or contribute in any way to the cost of this most expensive project. Her only connection with it has been in urging the project in Congress and assisting in the same way in getting appropriations for its execution. Her interest in it has naturally been largely in its beneficial effect on the value of her Sixteenth Street property.*[228]

These two ending quotations bring to light Henderson's two competing interests of civic improvement and increasing personal profit. Whichever of the two played a bigger role in her heart, it's difficult to talk about Meridian Hill Park's unique history without talking about Mary Foote Henderson.

PRESERVING THE CIVIL WAR FORTS
Fort Stevens–Lincoln National Military Park?

Three miles north of Meridian Hill, throughout the late 1800s and early 1900s, proposals were submitted and plans made to protect the Civil War fortresses that had battled the Confederacy in 1864. By this time, many veterans of the Battle of Fort Stevens were in their twilight years.

In the 1890s, wanting to protect and promote the history that they were a part of, many of these veterans formed themselves into a lobbying organization and then pushed to establish Fort Stevens–Lincoln National Military Park. The organization, known as the Fort Stevens–Lincoln National Military Park Association, proposed that a national military park be established on land in and around Fort Stevens, Battleground National Cemetery, Fort Slocum and Fort Totten. A veteran purchased much of the land that made up Fort Stevens for this purpose. The association proposed that after the park was formed, the secretary of war could appoint three commissioners, including two veterans, to oversee it.[229]

But Fort Stevens and environs is not a separate unit of the National Park System today, as Fort Stevens National Military Park was never established. This is largely due to Elihu Root, Theodore Roosevelt's influential secretary of war. Root derailed the plan with comments and a stance such as the following:

> *I think that if Congress considers it prudent to devote any more money for establishing battlefield parks, the places recommended in my Annual Report for 1899, which would include the battlefields of Fredericksburg, Salem Church, Chancellorsville, the Wilderness, and Spotsylvania Court House should be selected rather than Fort Stevens…The National Government cannot own and take care of all the spots of historic interest in the United States.*[230]

Despite the failure of the national military park bill, citizen action as well as a National Park Service (NPS) director with a passion for history took important steps to preserve part of Fort Stevens and adjacent fortresses. Patriotic organizations—including the Brightwood Avenue Citizens Association, the Grand Army of the Republic, the Loyal Legion of the United States and the Women's Relief Corps, among others—took part in ceremonies at Fort Stevens annually on Memorial Day, Flag Day and July 11 (the day commemorating the battle) to promote the fort's story. Most notably perhaps, on November 7, 1911, roughly 4,500 citizens attended a ceremony at the fort unveiling a stone monument at the site where President Abraham Lincoln stood on July 12, 1864. Eventually, due to these "patriotic promotionals," Forts Stevens, Slocum and Totten would be repurchased by Uncle Sam in the 1920s.[231]

After the land was purchased, NPS director Horace Albright was instrumental in transferring Washington's Civil War defenses to his agency as well as getting Fort Stevens restored as historically accurate as possible. This process began when Harold Ickes, FDR's secretary of the interior and new to Washington at the time, asked Albright to show him around the city and its environs on Sunday drives. Albright obliged, and the unique pair—Albright was twenty-five years Ickes's junior, and Ickes, a self-described "curmudgeon," was often difficult to get along with—became friends.[232]

Pushing his agenda, Albright took the opportunity during these field trips to discuss with the secretary his vision for all Department of War battlefield parks as well as the nation's capital park system to be transferred to the NPS for care, maintenance and visitor education. Notably, some of Albright's lobbying took place on the parapet of Fort Stevens. The director passionately explained the story of the Battle of Fort Stevens to Ickes while the two politicians and conservationists explored the fort itself one Sunday. Months later, in 1933, Ickes and FDR passed a major government reorganization meeting Albright's requests. With the reorganization, the NPS now administered the forts, not to mention the main stem of Rock Creek Park as well as the National Mall.[233]

Young men of the Civilian Conservation Corps work at reconstructing Fort Stevens on September 16, 1936. *National Park Service.*

Amphitheater at Fort Bunker Hill Park, circa 1960. The rustic amphitheater was constructed by the CCC. *National Park Service.*

Just before Albright resigned as NPS director to seek a long-sought-after career in the private sector, he orchestrated for the Civilian Conservation Corps to complete important work projects throughout the National Park System. As a result, CCC workers restored Fort Stevens as historically accurate as possible in the late 1930s. They heightened the fortress walls, re-dug the dry moat, rebuilt the battery magazine and placed cannons on top of the parapet. Instead of using logs for structural support as was done in the 1860s, CCC workers cemented the previously wooden features of the fort. The thought was that cement would last longer. They then painted the cement to look more rustic and wooden. Fort Stevens today continues to be primarily a product of this CCC reconstruction.[234]

THE LIFE AND DEATH OF
FORT BUNKER HILL PARK

Located on a square block of forested, hilly ground in the Brookland neighborhood of D.C., Fort Bunker Hill was a Civil War fortress that was also improved by the CCC in the 1930s. Opting to not historically restore the fort, however, workers turned Fort Bunker Hill into a recreation site. A series of trails were established, flowers and trees were planted and pipes and four water fountains were put up around the park. Picnic tables were also constructed and laid out on the park's highest promenade, with a view overlooking the area. Finally, an outdoor amphitheater was established in a natural bowl-like area with logs set into the hillside for seating.[235]

As a result of these improvements, from 1936 when it opened into the late 1970s, the amphitheater, which could accommodate roughly two hundred people, remained a popular summertime venue for ranger-naturalist programs put on by the National Park Service, musical performances and theatrical productions put on by local college students. The Catholic University Drama Department performed numerous plays at the site over the years, most notably Shakespeare's The Tempest. *The music group Earth, Wind & Fire also played at Fort Bunker Hill Park.[236]*

Unfortunately, though, in 1978, the year the drama department stopped performing at the amphitheater, Fort Bunker Hill began "a long, slow process of deterioration," according to a neighbor. With National Park Service resources pulled elsewhere, combined with not enough citizen interest to keep up the park, the picnic tables were eventually removed and water fountains eventually broke. When I visited Fort Bunker Hill Park in late February 2014, I noticed that the amphitheater itself is missing all its logs, and trees and nonnative vegetation rule supreme.[237]

Regarding the other sites of the once proposed Fort Stevens–Lincoln National Military Park, Fort Slocum would eventually come to be managed as a partially forested, partially green grass and picnic table park for neighborhood recreation. The earthen fort was razed after the Civil War and was never historically restored, but the forested Fort Totten, more by luck than anything, remains in a sufficient state of preservation to this day.

In addition to Rock Creek Park–administered fort sites, if you look on a comprehensive park map today, you'll see several narrow greenbelts connecting the various forts. Although these strips of grass do not much resemble a national park, most are, in fact, managed by Rock Creek Park.

This is due primarily to the numerous attempts of a comprehensive Fort Circle Drive. Although in the northeast sector of the city there is a roadway entitled Fort Circle Drive, the original vision of having the drive connect all the fortresses did not pan out. Nevertheless, we have greenbelts and additional fort-parks to thank for this.[238]

From the 1890s into the 1950s, continual proposals for this "fort-to-fort drive" were made. Initially planned as just a highway, later designs would call for adjacent land to be protected in greenbelts. The proposal got far along, as a 1937 *Washington Post* headline read, "One More Mile and the District Will Have a Driveway Linking Forts…Road to Pass Fortifications of Civil War…Will Run Along Rims of Hills That Make Saucer of City…Expected to Be One of Nation's Most Scenic and Historic." The federal government by this time had gained the right of way or purchased twenty-three and a half miles of roadway, and the ring road from Georgetown to Anacostia was nearly complete. However, due to politics, meager appropriations and ultimately the construction of the larger beltway thereafter, a full Fort Circle Drive never came to fruition.[239]

In 1968, the first-ever Fort Circle Parks General Management Plan was published. Admitting defeat of the unique roadway idea, the plan called for a paved multiuse trail to connect all the forts. The plan would have given bicyclists a twenty-three-mile trail system for exercise and recreation. Unfortunately, however, essentially not a single mile of this trail was ever constructed.[240]

Neither Fort Stevens–Lincoln National Military Park, Fort Circle Drive nor a paved trail system ultimately came to fruition. Nevertheless, because of the efforts to establish these features decades ago, Washington, D.C., remains the only city in the world with an extensive ring of forts turned public parks around its midsection. This heritage is unique.

ROCK CREEK AND POTOMAC PARKWAY

Not Your Normal Interstate

During morning rush hour, just south of the National Zoo, thousands of commuters seamlessly drive from the two-lane Beach Drive onto the four-lane Rock Creek and Potomac Parkway. Most don't know that these two entities are, in fact, two separate park units created at separate times. Authorized in

1913 and officially opened in 1936, the story of the Rock Creek and Potomac Parkway is more than just asphalt. Designed and constructed to connect the monumental core (National Mall area) with the National Zoo and Rock Creek Park and also to decrease pollution in the creek, the parkway story is ultimately one of controversy, debate, endurance, success and, well, traffic.

In the late 1800s and early 1900s, the lower section of Rock Creek between Georgetown and downtown was regarded as a cesspool of filth. Much of the area was a de facto dumpsite for construction companies, and raw sewage poured into the valley from adjacent buildings and pipes. A former District official at the time claimed of seeing a group of young swimmers in Rock Creek using the bloated body of a dead horse as a diving board.[241]

The unclean view of most of the area was widely shared. But a controversy involved the portrayal of the lower valley's working-class residents. While official reports from some business and government groups at the time claimed the housing areas were full of the "lowest type of population" living in slums and wooden shanties, photos of dwellings in select locations do not match the description. Though certainly working-class homes owned by working-class whites and African Americans, the houses were, in fact, decent, according to parkway historian Timothy Davis. Many of the yards included flower and vegetable gardens, while "one creek-side resident maintained an extensive set of beehives and advertised honey for sale." Nevertheless, when it came time for parkway construction, the working-class homes were razed and the residents evicted.[242]

After controversy comes debate. The authorization of the Rock Creek and Potomac Parkway in 1913 was the culmination of some heated arguments. If Georgetown businessmen had gotten their way, a closed valley plan would have been implemented involving Rock Creek being piped underground and the Rock Creek Valley filled in. To them, the steep valley blocked Washington shoppers from visiting Georgetown, thus leaving the once thriving port city turned neighborhood a lesser piece of the economic pie. On the other side of the spectrum, other area businessmen lobbied for the open valley plan in which the creek would remain in its original channel. Both proposals called for a formal promenade to carry carriages and horseback riders as well as a thin row of stately trees.[243]

The McMillan Commission, a select group of landscape architects and city planners tasked with coming up with a grand plan for the design of public parks and open spaces in the capital, in 1902, formally adopted the open valley plan "on grounds of economics, convenience, and beauty."[244] However, due to the ultimate rise of the automobile in the 1910s and '20s,

Trolley bridge over Rock Creek. The first task in constructing the Rock Creek and Potomac Parkway was removing thousands of tons of industrial debris and litter, such as the pile of rubble below the bridge. *National Park Service.*

as well as the slow pace of parkway construction, the approved parkway plan would change and evolve over the years to accommodate more fast-paced traffic.

The Rock Creek and Potomac Parkway was authorized in 1913 as the nation's first federal parkway project. However, *authorization* and *completion* are very different words. It ultimately took over two decades to finish. The process of condemning and purchasing inholdings took time, as legal settlements had to be made with the Chesapeake and Ohio Canal Company and other businesses in or bordering the valley. Perhaps the biggest issue though, once again, was limited appropriations from Congress, resulting in a slow initial construction phase. This was actually a source of great embarrassment for parkway contractors and planners.[245]

Because of this hodge-podge funding, architects took all the help they could get, including once from a British army tank. As part of a promotional scheme by the government to raise awareness and importance of World War I, the Department of War brought over Britannia, a state-of-the-art

British tank. During a special Liberty Loan Day holiday on April 26, 1918, established to benefit the wartime economy, thousands of Washingtonians observed this tank in action from atop the William Howard Taft Memorial Bridge over Rock Creek. About 150 feet below, Britannia was at work demonstrating its might: it mowed down decades-old trees and forded Rock Creek like it was a puddle.[246]

Bizarre demolition schemes aside, thanks to increasing funds courtesy of FDR and the New Deal, the parkway finally began being developed in earnest in the early 1930s. The process first involved removing thousands of tons of dirt, industrial waste and litter in order to clean and widen the creek valley, especially in the lower section toward the Potomac River. Next, Rock Creek was rechanneled in select locations in order to make way for the four-lane road and creek bed in the narrow corridor that engineers had to work with. Workers then graded the hillside, planted thousands of trees and shrubs to stabilize the hillsides from erosion and constructed the roadway itself.[247]

Although creek channeling and soil removal was necessary, the parkway design and ultimate construction proved vastly different than regular freeways and later interstate highways. The Rock Creek and Potomac Parkway was made to blend in with the landscape as much as possible.

In a sense, the two-and-a-half-mile parkway was constructed in two halves. Above P Street, the valley is deeper and wider. The hillsides were left forested along this corridor, making the parkway appear to be secluded from the city. In one particular section, the southbound and northbound lanes of the parkway were separated, and an island created "a relaxing, sylvan character that is enhanced by the leafy canopy where the trees meet overhead." This feature can be seen today where Waterside Drive enters the parkway.[248]

Along the lower part of the parkway, between Georgetown and Adams Morgan and then along the Potomac River, the urban surrounding is more viewable. This is due in part to the topography of the land, as the Rock Creek Valley broadens and is also not as deep. Also, the mouth of Rock Creek was more commercialized than the northern part of the parkway, leading to planners and workers constructing the parkway through a narrower space. Nevertheless, parkway builders worked some of the historic commercialization into the landscape. For instance, Godey's Limekilns were left intact, while just south, a rustic, stone-clad gas station was constructed that still stands (and sells perhaps the highest-priced gasoline in the District!) to this day.[249]

Speaking of narrow spaces and historic structures, a challenge parkway workers faced were overhead bridges. While some of the Rock Creek Valley bridges were built before the parkway was completed, some were erected during construction. The Pennsylvania Avenue Bridge, which had been designed initially by Battleground National Cemetery designer, renowned architect and quartermaster general of the U.S. Army Montgomery Meigs in the 1850s, was replaced in 1915. But Meigs's low-to-the-ground arches remained, which allowed just enough room for the parkway to go under it. For horseback riders on a parallel trail—later the paved multiuse trail accommodating bicyclists and joggers—this would prove to be an almost dangerous overhead.[250]

Despite these challenges, the Rock Creek and Potomac Parkway officially opened on June 4, 1936, with much fanfare. Commuters could now travel from Maryland to the Lincoln Memorial without ever having to see urban blight. The *Washington Evening Star* celebrated the completion, proclaiming that "motorists from the Chevy Chase–Bethesda area will have the privilege of riding downtown through a veritable fairyland, a natural setting for nature's own worship, and not so much as a traffic light to impede progress. There is, perhaps, no city in the world offering so much beauty for those going to work."[251]

However, if you build it, they will come. Practically from the moment it opened, the parkway became heavily congested with the almighty

The Rock Creek and Potomac Parkway near P Street. The parkway opened to traffic prior to landscaping completion. *Library of Congress.*

View of completed Rock Creek and Potomac Parkway and Taft (Connecticut Avenue) Bridge. *Library of Congress.*

automobile. To remedy this, in 1937, a rush-hour lane change was put into effect. All lanes of the parkway were to be used for southbound traffic during morning commute and northbound for late afternoon commute. This long-standing tradition continues today.

Also to decrease traffic, one final construction project was implemented between 1939 and 1941. Prior to this project's completion, the parkway shrunk from four lanes to two underneath Massachusetts Avenue, which crossed the valley in an "unsightly earthen causeway." This led to a major traffic bottleneck, and the parkway's two-lane culvert underneath the avenue was also said to be unsightly. In order to beautify the valley and increase traffic flow, a "single, soaring arch" bridge was constructed high above the earthen crossing. The old parkway culvert was then razed and the section of roadway widened into four lanes.[252]

What was initially planned as a scenic, recreational, winding drive into the monumental core of Washington is now a heavily used commuter corridor. Frustrated drivers along the parkway seem to be either stuck in traffic or racing well above the posted speed limit to get to work or home. Hopefully, though, commuters take a deep breath once in a while and appreciate the unique roadway they are on as well as its surrounding scenery.

BEATRIX FARRAND AND DUMBARTON OAKS PARK

"She Listened to the Light and Wind and Grade"

In 1940, Robert and Mildred Bliss donated and divided their ritzy Georgetown estate between the National Park Service and Harvard University. The formal part of the estate, now known as Dumbarton Oaks, was given to the university, while a thirty-three-acre, less developed area behind the formal estate was given to the National Park Service. This park became known as Dumbarton Oaks Park. While the entire estate was landscaped by Beatrix Farrand between 1921 and 1940, this brief article will focus on the Rock Creek Park–administered Dumbarton Oaks Park as well as the pioneering female landscape architect behind its construction.

Born in 1872 to a wealthy mother and father of the Gilded Age, Farrand ultimately chose a nontraditional career for such a family: landscape architecture, or as she preferred to call it, gardening. Whereas architecture involved industry and mathematics, gardening, to Farrand, was art that "must be treated in the impressionist manner."

As the first professional female landscape architect in the United States, Farrand's career spanned five decades. She completed over two hundred commissions, and among her most notable employers were Theodore Roosevelt, John D. Rockefeller Jr. and First Lady Ellen Wilson. She landscaped estates on Long Island, parts of Princeton and Yale Universities and Darlington Hall in Devon, England. Georgetown's Dumbarton Oaks, however, is considered Farrand's masterpiece.[253]

The well-off Blisses purchased the property in 1920 and quickly commissioned Farrand to landscape their estate. While the upper section of the property would formalize under the landscape architect's leadership to include statues, fountains, formal plantings, walkways and even a swimming pool, Farrand chose a different landscaping style in the lower section. Designed to complement the formal estate above, Farrand referred to the lower section as a wilderness landscape. In it, she combined the concepts of wild woods with formal gardens.[254]

In her wilderness landscape, today known as Dumbarton Oaks Park, Farrand was unique in creating outdoor spaces, or rooms. Many of these outdoor rooms focus on the use of water and plants near the small stream running through the park on its way to Rock Creek. In one area, for instance, Farrand designed a pool of stream water in the shape of a mountain laurel leaf and then planted mountain laurels around it. In another outdoor room, Farrand created a miniature waterfall by placing two-foot-tall stone walls in a select location of the brook. Estate guests could then enjoy the sound of trickling water, in addition to daffodils she planted alongside.[255]

Just off the streamside path and leading up to the formal estate, Farrand planted dozens of forsythia that light up the hillside in early spring with blooms of yellow. In a different area, at the entrance to the park, Farrand kept dozens of American beech trees in place, creating a natural grove atmosphere. Finally, in a larger area of the park, Farrand created a meadow-

Park ranger and visitors in Dumbarton Oaks Park, April 16, 1961. Notice the waterfalls and daffodils, both the works of Farrand. *National Park Service.*

like area with carriage roads, benches for sitting and contemplation and bluebells, a blue-blooming, low-to-the-ground flowering plant.[256]

"Farrand succeeded in creating the illusion that the Dumbarton Oaks [Park] property is larger than its actual size, while simultaneously treating visitors to small-scale localized scenes," notes historians Maureen De Lay Joseph, Kay Fanning and Mark Davison. Seven of Farrand's key design elements were "spatial organization, circulation, scale, topography, water features, vegetation, and color."[257]

Although the Blisses donated their land in 1940, Farrand continued her association with Dumbarton Oaks Park into the 1950s. For several years, as a collaborator with the National Park Service, she took an active role in the management and planting plan for the park. Farrand designed the wooden entrance sign that is still standing today to welcome visitors into her landscape during this time.

Mid-1900s visitors did find the park artistic and romantic. It became a popular site for dates and photography, while in 1962, Secretary of the Interior Stewart Udall invited personal friend Robert Frost to recite poetry in the park during a special event honoring Henry David Thoreau on the 100th anniversary of his passing.[258]

Visitors getting photographed in Dumbarton Oaks Park, circa 1960. *National Park Service.*

Unfortunately, after Farrand's retirement, National Park Service resources were needed elsewhere, and Dumbarton Oaks Park degenerated. Today, practically every tree in Farrand's beech grove has been carved into by unlawful visitors, while invasive plants from the surrounding landscape are now prevalent throughout the park. Fortunately, the Dumbarton Oaks Park Conservancy was formed in 2010 in order to restore the historical landscape to its former glory.

In a eulogy to Farrand after her death in 1959, Mildred Bliss wrote, "Never did Beatrix Farrand impose on the land an arbitrary concept. She 'listened' to the light and wind and grade of each area under study."[259] Farrand's subtle yet significant contributions to Dumbarton Oaks Park can still be seen today.

New Deal and 1930s Federal Government Workers

No Area of the Park Left Untouched

Probably very few people in Rock Creek Park take a hike today without walking past at least one structure built by workers of the Civilian Conservation Corps, Works Progress Administration or Public Works Administration. FDR's 1930s New Deal agencies combated widespread unemployment and homelessness caused by the worst economic depression in American history, and three of these agencies in particular had a profound effect on Rock Creek Park.

Known as the Tree Army, or CCC boys, the Civilian Conservation Corps employed young men ages eighteen to twenty-five in conservation and recreation projects across the country. Working generally as unskilled laborers, the CCC boys completed a series of projects in and around Rock Creek Park.

In matters of conservation, the Tree Army planted trees and shrubs along Rock Creek and Potomac Parkway, which was formally opened in 1936. They also created riprap, an erosion control measure involving piling rocks and boulders on stream banks to stabilize soil. Finally, the CCC removed litter from the watershed and historically restored Fort Stevens.[260]

Regarding recreation-based projects, the CCC constructed two and a half miles of bridle trails, complete with jumps; landscaped around Peirce Mill and repaired the picturesque dam; and built a rustic-looking comfort station across from Miller Cabin on Beach Drive that still stands today. They also filled in the Brightwood Reservoir bordering Sixteenth Street and landscaped the area with ball fields and tennis courts. Finally, the CCC completed numerous recreation projects at Fort Bunker Hill Park and constructed the now D.C. Parks and Recreation–administered Takoma and Taft recreation centers.[261]

Looking back at complaints from CCC workers in Rock Creek Park, it is a wonder that they completed any work at all, as supervision was apparently inadequate. "A great deal of the work embraces engineering skill and requires competent supervision," wrote a worker in a letter to the CCC director. But "many of the important jobs are now being directed by CCC enrollees [regular workers]." In another letter, a worker complained that of the five crew leaders, two were on sick leave, two were illiterate and one was the cousin of the District commissioner, "who was being paid an engineer's salary to pull weeds."[262]

A key difference between the CCC and other New Deal agencies is that the CCC housed its employees in on-site work camps. Rock Creek Park was home to CCC Camp NP-14-DC. Located at the current site of the police stables just off Oregon Avenue and grown out of Camp Goodwill, a former summer camp for low-income white families, NP-14-DC was built to include two long sleeping barracks, two bathhouses, a large mess hall and kitchen, a recreation center, an education center, a headquarters building, an infirmary, a supply room, an officer's quarters, two large garages and—probably best of all for the workers, thanks to the previous children's camp—a swimming pool. The camp operated from 1938 to 1942 and included 150 men.[263]

Not only did CCC workers get free room and board in exchange for an honest day's labor, but they also had the opportunity to take courses in order to be better equipped for landing an outside job. Instructors taught the CCC boys nightly at the Rock Creek Park camp in courses including "literacy, citizenship, blacksmithing, carpentry, cooking and baking, photography, truck driving, business and 'social courtesy,' first aid, and 'how to get and hold a job.'"[264]

While the CCC housed its workers, the Works Progress Administration (WPA) and similar-sounding Public Works Administration (PWA) did not. Furthermore, CCC work camps were segregated, and Rock Creek Park's camp was white only. However, due in part to the progressive views of Secretary of Agriculture Harry Hopkins, head of the WPA, and Secretary of the Interior Harold Ickes, head of the PWA, many African American workers did complete important projects in Rock Creek Park.[265]

The WPA employed day laborers from the surrounding community to complete numerous projects. Workers built the boulder-strewn U.S. Park Police Station now known as D-3 in the "Colonial Revival style." They also graded and landscaped Fort Reno, turning D.C.'s highest point into the athletic fields that visitors know today. Finally, WPA workers constructed Fort Reno Road as part of the "Fort Circle Drive" plan (the road's name has been changed today, but parallels the fort park), Piney Branch Parkway and Klingle Valley Road.[266]

The PWA, more closely resembling President Barack Obama's American Recovery and Reinvestment Act, was a bit different than the WPA in that it allowed government agencies to hire contractors to then complete specific, short-term projects. PWA projects in Rock Creek Park were substantial and included the construction of numerous footbridges, renovation of Peirce Mill and improvements at Battleground National Cemetery.

Civilian Conservation Corps (CCC) enrollees standing at attention in Camp NP-14-DC in Rock Creek Park on October 14, 1941. Walking in business suites are (from left) CCC director J.J. McEntee; Edward, Duke of Windsor (and former king of England); and Leiutenant Hugo Ruggiero, commanding officer of the camp in Rock Creek Park. A highly controversial figure in British royalty, King Edward VIII abdicated the throne in 1936 after serving for only a few months, leaving the position to his brother George. King George VI is the main subject of *The King's Speech*, a recent Hollywood film. *National Park Service.*

WPA workers construct
Fort Reno Park in July
1936. *National Park Service.*

Replacing at least five wooden footbridges that were destroyed during a
1933 flood, many of the PWA footbridges are still standing and used today,
most noticeably Rapids Bridge, Rolling Meadows Bridge, Bluffs Bridge,
Riley Springs Bridge and Boundary Bridge. You might notice that the park's
footbridges are not quite as rustic in appearance as Boulder Bridge. This is due
to an apparent mishap. Albert H. Good, landscape architect consultant for the
National Park Service in the 1930s, recommended using picturesque stone as
the construction material. Due to the higher cost of this material, however, it
was ultimately decided that concrete would be the primary material. Good
criticized the finished bridges as "frankly concrete." Nevertheless, he noted that
the bridges get the job done and have been serving their purpose ever since.[267]

Regarding Pierce Mill, operations of the historic gristmill had ceased
in 1897, but restoration work under the direction of architect Thomas T.
Waterman brought the mill back to its former glory. The renovation work
included rebuilding the waterwheel and remodeling the mill's headrace
to make it look more square and artistic, as opposed to its original rugged
appearance. Inside the mill, automatic grain elevators were rebuilt.[268]

Although the mill's gadgets and gizmos were already considered historic
in the 1930s, Pierce Mill was lucky due to the fact that it was situated not too

Riley Springs Bridge. Every footbridge over Rock Creek in Rock Creek Park today was built by PWA laborers in the 1930s. *National Park Service.*

far from Pennsylvania Dutch country. The contractor was able to find gears as well as a "hopper boy" (flour-cooling machine) by purchasing them from Amish settlers who still used water-powered mills. At Peirce Mill today, all brown-painted objects are the product of PWA renovation.[269]

The other PWA project involved workers digging a drainage ditch to better control erosion at Battleground National Cemetery. It was during this project that laborers had a great scare. "The Battle of Fort Stevens, [a] crucial Civil War engagement in which General Jubal Early's raiders were repulsed in their attack upon the Union's capital, almost claimed another victim or two Friday," claimed the *Washington Post* dramatically seventy years after the battle. Apparently, one of the workers discovered an unexploded mortar left over from the Civil War when his pick struck near it. D.C. special police forces then swarmed in, and a few more unexploded cannonballs were unearthed. No one got hurt, fortunately.[270]

Last to be discussed, a couple other New Deal projects—unknown whether completed by the WPA or PWA—were the renovation of Joshua

Peirce's historic Linnaean Hill mansion and the construction of a park caretaker's residence on a hill just above Military Road. Built for housing Rock Creek Park's head maintenance employee, in the late 1950s, the caretaker's residence would be reconfigured into the present-day nature center. Regarding the Linnaean Hill mansion and grounds, both had fallen largely into disrepair after the park acquired it in the early 1890s. New Deal workers significantly fixed up the inside of the house and simplified and cleaned up the outside property. National Park Service historian William Bushong notes that the man who oversaw the Linnaean Hill improvements, C. Marshall Finnan, might have had ulterior motives in the project, as he planned on and did, in fact, move into the historic home after its renovations were completed.[271]

Just as quickly as African American and white New Deal workers came into the park in the 1930s, they left the park to join the war effort in the early 1940s. The CCC camp was briefly used by the army, but no remnants of either camp remain. However, the projects that New Deal employees completed silently stand all over Rock Creek Park to this day.

ENJOYING THE PARK
AT MIDCENTURY

While it was the park boundary that did most of the expanding through the course of the first several decades of the twentieth century, between 1950 and 1970, it was park recreations' turn to expand. Due to several factors—including but not limited to the booming economy of postwar America, the rise of suburbia and increased emphasis on urban recreation and urban parks—the two decades saw the construction of many of Rock Creek Park's most popular visitor facilities. Each has its own unique story that continues into the present.

CARTER BARRON AMPHITHEATRE

America's Greatest Played Here

Before there was the Meriwether Post Pavilion, Wolf Trap National Park for the Performing Arts or the Kennedy Center, there was Rock Creek Park's Carter Barron Amphitheatre. A 4,200-seat outdoor amphitheater just off Sixteenth Street on Colorado Avenue, the performance venue has served as an outdoor community gathering place for decades. The amphitheater is a product of the national capital's sesquicentennial.

The year 1950 marked the 150th anniversary of Washington, D.C. To celebrate this accomplishment, promote the city and strengthen community, the National Capital Sesquicentennial Commission was formed. Civic leader and commission vice-president Carter T. Barron was the spark plug behind the amphitheater project. A businessman with many connections, Barron was described as "the link between government and show business." He served as an executive manager of Loews Theaters and was also personal friends with FDR and Harry Truman. For the amphitheater, Barron envisioned an outdoor musical venue where "all persons of every race, color, and creed" could congregate.[272]

As a result of Barron's lobbying, a groundbreaking ceremony was held in December 1949 for Sesquicentennial Amphitheatre. U.S. secretary of the interior Oscar Chapman turned the first spade of dirt using a patriotic red, white and blue shovel, while New York City Metropolitan Opera singer Claudia Pinza sang the national anthem. During the swift construction phase that followed, the amphitheater was outfitted with a state-of-the-art communication system that allowed the stage manager, sitting at his or her desk offstage, to speak to actors and stagehands in the middle of their performances. Lighting and sound equipment was also cutting edge for the time.[273]

The amphitheater opened the following summer with its first show, *Faith of Our Fathers*, a "symphonic drama depicting the life of George Washington," the capital's founder. The play was created by Paul Green, a Pulitzer Prize–winning playwright and author of *The Lost Colony*, a play that is still performed annually at Fort Raleigh National Historic Site in Roanoke Island, North Carolina. U.S. president Harry Truman and other key politicians attended the grand opening.[274]

During the first off-season, when Barron died before his time at the age of forty-five due to a sudden bout of brain cancer, interior secretary Chapman swiftly moved to change the name of the amphitheater to honor the civic leader. Barron's death was not the only low point for the newly named Carter Barron Amphitheatre, as *Faith of Our Fathers* saw surprisingly only mixed reviews during the first couple seasons. As a result, in 1954, the amphitheater was in search of a savior. Fortunately, it found two.[275]

Irvin and Israel Feld, the Feld brothers, won the contract and, over the course of the next two decades, brought all the biggest names in music to Rock Creek Park's Carter Barron Amphitheatre. Among the largest draws were performances by Ella Fitzgerald, the Kingston Trio, Nat King Cole, Ethel Merman, Andy Williams, Louis Armstrong, Benny Goodman, Johnny Mathis, the Dave Brubeck Quartet and Peter, Paul and Mary. Most popular of all was perhaps Ella Fitzgerald, who performed year

Carter Barron Amphitheatre, nestled in the woods of Rock Creek Park. *National Park Service.*

The U.S. Army Band plays for a packed house at Carter Barron Amphitheatre, 1952. *National Park Service.*

after year at the amphitheater in the late 1950s and early 1960s. "There's something about a hushed audience listening to Ella Fitzgerald sing 'I'm Old Fashioned' in a tree-shrouded glen that is close to magic," noted a concert reviewer in 1963.[276]

Aside from straight musical concerts, the Feld brothers continued the tradition of dramatic plays. Besides a program by famed comedian "Red" Skelton, perhaps the most notable of presentations involved a musical known as *Ice Capades*. To arouse interest for the show, amphitheater staff made twenty tons of snow for children to sled on—in the middle of August! Irving quipped that "after two hurricanes, a transit strike, and a few other events too complex to describe, we figure snow in August makes perfect sense. We're making snow right now. Plan on a slide, but children will have to bring their own sleds." While the kids were sledding, parents were invited to meet the beautiful Judith Dunkle, newly crowned Miss Washington at the time, staged at Carter Barron before the show.[277]

After Israel passed away in 1972, his wife took over the reins with Irvin. Expanding their musical offerings, the venue began to include rock-and-

Louis Armstrong sings at Carter Barron Amphitheatre, 1959. *National Park Service.*

Richard Bernard "Red" Skelton, American entertainer and comedian, at Carter Barron Amphitheatre in 1962. Skelton is best remembered for the *Red Skelton Show*, which aired from 1937 to 1971. *National Park Service.*

roll and blues musicians. During this era of Carter Barron Amphitheatre, Ray Charles, B.B. King, Stevie Wonder, Smokey Robinson and Bruce Springsteen performed on stage.[278]

After a great run, the Felds began to struggle in the mid-1970s due to "competition from other centers for performing arts and changes in production values." The family cashed in, and in 1976, Rock Creek Park staff took direct control of the operation. During this time, as larger music venues opened in the greater Washington area, Carter Barron Amphitheatre came to be used more and more as a neighborhood venue, becoming an important community space for a predominantly African American crowd.[279]

One of the more popular musical groups to perform during the National Park Service era of Carter Barron Amphitheatre has been the Blackbyrds. The all-male band produced their hit single "Rock Creek Park" in 1975 and performed it at the amphitheater for decades afterward. Its simple, sexual, repetitive lyrics are well known by a generation of Washingtonians:

Doing it in the park.
Doing it after dark.
Oh yeah, Rock Creek Park.
Oh yeah, Rock Creek Park.

The last time the Blackbyrds performed the song at Carter Barron was in 2006, and "Rock Creek Park" to this day can be played on the jukebox at Ben's Chili Bowl. Quietly, however, the leader of the band, jazz trumpeter and former Howard University music instructor Donald Byrd, passed away in 2013.[280]

Other than the Blackbyrds, National Park Service staff host themed evenings at the amphitheater, including reggae night, blues and jazz festivals, poetry slams, movie nights and more. Unfortunately, though, with budget cuts in recent years, the number of performances at the historic amphitheater in the woods of Rock Creek Park has decreased. In 2013, a record low of one performance was held. The number of amphitheater performances for future summers remains unknown.

ROCK CREEK PARK DAY

Fun and Games during the Park's Birthday Bash

Rock Creek Park was established on September 27, 1890, as the first federally managed urban nature park in the country. To celebrate the park's birthday in late September, visitors of all ages enjoy educational and recreational programs and children's activities during the annual Rock Creek Park Day. The festival tradition goes back to 1955, and although it has occurred in different months over the years, young and old alike have always enjoyed the informative fun.

The first Rock Creek Park Day festivals included archery shooting, pie-eating contests, a "Fun-O-Rama show featuring Washington's top entertainers," dog shows put on by the U.S. Park Police and their specially trained dogs and performances by military bands as well as the Camp Fire Girls of America at Carter Barron Amphitheatre. Worthy of noting, one early festival included a short talk by Howard Zahniser, executive director of the Wilderness Society. "You can keep a beautiful wild frontier like this in a great modern city only by making it a park and using it rightly and appreciating it and protecting it. That's the significance of Rock Creek Park Day," Zahniser said to the crowd.[281] In another festival, First Lady Mamie Eisenhower was made chairwoman of the Rock Creek Park Day committee.

Rock Creek Park Day 1956 was particularly noteworthy in that five hundred orphans experienced the wonders of nature and the excitement of the park, thanks to a local charity. The 1956 festival also witnessed the grand opening of the Rock Creek Nature Center at Klingle Mansion, the historic Peirce family estate just south of Peirce Mill. National Park Service director Conrad Wirth wrote an article in the newspaper advertising the special exhibits and "work-it-yourself devices" (see next article).[282]

In another festival around 1970, D.C. mayor-commissioner Walter Washington officially proclaimed the day as Rock Creek Park Day during a special ceremony. NPS director George Hartzog and other officials attended the

Boy Scouts promoting Rock Creek Park during an early Rock Creek Park Day festival. Walter Washington, D.C.'s first mayor, can be seen in the background behind and in between the letters *A* and *R*. *National Park Service.*

U.S. Park Police officer and dog during Rock Creek Park Day dog show. *Library of Congress.*

signing. The official proclamation was made in order to increase appreciation for D.C.'s largest and oldest park. Walter Washington would later become the first mayor of D.C., an important step for the national capital in its ongoing battle to have a truly representative government.[283]

Throughout the disco era of the 1970s, Rock Creek Park Day was hosted at Peirce Mill in addition to the nature center. At the mill, the park's birthday bash evolved into a cultural celebration based around international cuisine. Embassies promoted the culture of their countries, and ethnic food was enjoyed by many. As popular as this international festival was, park managers eventually terminated it, believing it didn't fit in with the traditional Rock Creek Park Day themes.[284]

During practically every Rock Creek Park Day festival, whether past or present, nature programs and history talks have been offered by park rangers. Programs with live birds of prey have proved quite popular recently, as have general bird walks. By late September, neotropical migrants such as the Canadian warbler and Baltimore oriole make their fall migration southward. Searching for these colorful species is a

Park ranger leads a nature hike in Rock Creek Park, circa 1965. *National Park Service.*

delight to the growing number of birders. Aside from bird programs, face painting, conservation puppet shows and climbing walls have also been popular attractions.

Recently, the 2011 Rock Creek Park Day was morphed into Fall Heritage Day at Pierce Mill, where, for the first time in two decades, the mill produced stoneground cornmeal. Hundreds of visitors turned out to watch the old waterwheel and millstones in action. Demonstrations on blacksmithing, bread making and 1800s medicine were also popular. The mill was brought back to life thanks in large part to Friends of Pierce Mill, a nonprofit organization that raised significant funds for the restoration.

Fun festivals, check. Educational festivals, check. But what about bizarre ones? Well, during one year, Girl Scout troops cooked hamburgers on a fire, coated them with cornflakes and then ate them—gross!

Nature Center and Planetarium

"The Next Planetary Stop Is...'Ooooooh, Mars!'"

Many national park units have visitor centers, but just a handful have nature centers. Only one has a planetarium. Yet while the current Rock Creek Park Nature Center and Planetarium was opened in 1960, many readers will be surprised to know that there was a previous nature center in the park. Here's the story of Rock Creek Park's two nature centers.

Located inside the 1820s mansion of Joshua Peirce on his original Linnaean Hill estate, Rock Creek Park's first nature center was short-lived but nevertheless on the cutting edge for its time. Officially opened in 1956 during the Rock Creek Park Day festival, for five years, the facility introduced children to the wonders of nature by way of various hands-on displays. A "Ye Olde Nature Curio Shop" enabled youngsters to feel the different kinds of tree seeds and nuts, while a "Rock Quiz" tested their knowledge of geology. In another area of the nature center, "Freddy the Talking Crow" was on display. Smokey the Bear posters made several appearances, and just

Above and opposite: Young visitors enjoying the exhibits inside Rock Creek Park's first nature center, located at Linnaean Hill, 1956. *National Park Service.*

before children left the nature center, rangers made sure they took Smokey's conservation pledge: "I give my pledge as an American to save and faithfully to defend from waste the natural resources of my country—its soil and minerals, its forests, waters, and wildlife."[285]

The nature center at Linnaean Hill was a popular place for children to visit during school on field trips, after school and on weekends. Unfortunately, because of this popularity, it was forced to relocate. Because it was situated at the end of a dead-end road in an extremely wealthy, white neighborhood, when neighbors complained of the traffic and noise caused by the nature center, racism might have been at work. As much of the nature center's clientele was African American, a series of newspaper editorials from a D.C.-area schoolteacher accused the neighbors of overt racism. Because of this, numerous environmental nonprofit organizations, most notably the National Parks Conservation Association, sided with the children and requested that the facility remain on its Linnaean Hill location. The National Park Service decided differently, though, and built a new facility out of an employee residence two miles north.[286]

Located in the noncontroversial woods away from park neighbors, the current Rock Creek Park Nature Center and Planetarium was built quickly and officially dedicated by children on June 4, 1960. While the new nature center exhibits remained similar to the ones at the first location, the planetarium was a totally new feature. Deemed controversial at the time, Bill Yeaman, longtime Rock Creek Park employee, recalls that "many National Park Service officials did not see the connection between nature and astronomy. But the sun itself, which can be studied in a planetarium, makes the forest in Rock Creek Park grow and is responsible for life on earth." Yeaman notes that the planetarium was constructed primarily due to the lobbying efforts of the National Capital Astronomers Association (NCA), a science group that has met once a month in the park for decades to provide free stargazing programs to the public. In particular, the NCA's Bob McCracken was the driving force. "He loved to talk and was passionate about astronomy. The planetarium probably would not have been constructed were it not for Bob."[287]

The first planetarium in the nation's capital and the only one in the entire National Park System, Rock Creek Park's night-sky room has been a staple in Rock Creek Park from its grand opening. Yeaman says that the 1970s were especially a fun time in the planetarium due to the almost daily new astronomical discoveries coming in from NASA. Indeed, this was the era of the *Voyager*, *Pioneer* and *Viking* spacecraft missions, and children loved learning about the discoveries in the planetarium. A newspaper journalist at the time, sitting in on one of Yeaman's programs, noted this enthusiasm:

> *The next planetary stop is…"Ooooooh, Mars!" Screams a little boy as satellite pictures of the red planet appear. Yeaman tells how the* Pioneer *craft landed on Mars to take pictures. Several kids ask if Martians really exist, just as a pair of cartoon-character Martians fly across the ceiling. After the delighted commotion dies down, Yeaman dispels the notion of little green men in real life…For every star there's a story…The ranger tells the kids several stories about the constellations and how they're derived from Greek and Roman as well as Indian and Eskimo mythology. A favorite is the tale of what's now called the Seven Sisters, a cluster of stars found on the shoulder of Taurus. The stars are faint, so Yeaman has the audience spot and count them out loud: The chorus builds, "One, two, three, four, five, six, SEVEN"—with a final "eight" from one little boy who forgets to put on the brakes.*[288]

The planetarium projector that Yeaman and park staff used in the 1970s was named George by the rangers, and it replaced the original A-1

Ranger-led astronomy program in the Rock Creek Park Planetarium, circa 1965. *National Park Service.*

Rock Creek Park Nature Center exterior, circa 1965. *National Park Service.*

planetarium system. George itself was replaced with "Ms. Seymour," a more high-tech projector and accompanying planetarium software, in 2008. One of the things that rangers, especially I, like about the new software is how it can showcase light pollution. In urban settings such as D.C., only in a planetarium can you see a dark night sky with thousands of stars. Outside in reality at night, due to city lights and particularly the fact that many streetlights shine up into the night instead of down on streets and sidewalks, a light cloud, known as light pollution, erases the view of most stars. But with a simple click of the computer mouse, rangers can switch between light pollution and a dark night sky in the planetarium, thus "shedding light" on the issue.

While planetarium projectors have changed through the ages, so too have the nature center's exhibits. The first two exhibit series, operating from the '60s to the '80s, largely promoted hands-on, kinetic learning. "The interpretive approach in the new building, which aimed at identification and taxonomy and served primarily as an introduction to the outdoors, initially followed that of the Peirce-Klingle Mansion programs. Exhibits focused on interactive ways of identifying plants, animals, and rocks," notes a recent National Park Service report.[289]

In the early 1980s, with the evolution of theories in interpretation and visitor education, new exhibits were created with the goal of bringing about "greater awareness and understanding of nature and the ecological relationship within Rock Creek Park…Hands-on, interactive exhibits, for instance, gave visitors the opportunity to create a balanced food chain pyramid by correctly stacking blocks of different plants and animals." Unfortunately, the interactive second exhibition series suffered from chronic machine, lighting and wiring breakdowns. Due to these factors, it was replaced after less than a decade by today's nonmechanical exhibits that spotlight the flora and fauna of the park. While some believe this switch away from hands-on learning was a shame, many visitors in contemporary times, perhaps surprisingly, state their approval of the current exhibits.[290]

One thing that has remained more constant in the nature center over the years is its use of live animals for educational purposes. From the facility's very beginning, it has been home to live critters. Today, these critters include snakes, turtles and fish, but in the past, they have included animals such as honeybees, woodchucks, screech owls, skunks, opossums, mallard ducks and flying squirrels! While Pokey the eastern box turtle is the most famous critter today, from 1972 until 1991, Max the barred owl stole the spotlight. When Max died, the *Washington Post* even wrote an obituary for him:

Max, the large barred owl loved by a generation of Washington area children, died this week while exercising outside his home at the Rock Creek Nature Center, officials said yesterday. Even though he perched sullenly and silently on a tree trunk at the rear of the exhibit hall, Max was the undisputed star of the center for nearly 19 years…He wasn't really friendly and visitors couldn't pet him…But kids loved him anyway, devoting to him more attention than to the center's stuffed animals, working beehive, preserved butterflies, two live snakes, and an opossum.[291]

With the exception of fish, none of the nature center's live critters were removed from the park. Instead, most were given to the park by D.C. urbanites who didn't want their pets anymore but also didn't want them to be put down. At least one of the nature center's critters had previously been the subject of animal cruelty—a screech owl, who lived in the nature center until the early 2000s, had gotten an eye shot out by a BB gun.[292]

Don't pet this at home, kids! Ranger showcases a possum to children, circa 1965. The possum was a nature center resident in the '60s and '70s. *National Park Service.*

Ranger showcasing a resident snake to children inside the current nature center, circa 1965. *John DeFerrari Collection.*

Aside from the exhibits, planetarium and live critters, a final popular attraction to the facility over the years has been special presentations. While rangers have always presented the vast majority of curriculum-based environmental education programs, interpretive programs and guided hikes, in the 1970s, the nature center hosted Bob Brown Puppets. A puppeteer company consisting of married duo Bob and Judy Brown, Bob Brown Puppets made over fifty appearances on the famous *Mr. Roger's Neighborhood* children's television program, bringing delight and smiles to thousands of young children in the D.C. area over their fifty-year career. At the Rock Creek Park Nature Center, park management paid for Bob and Judy Brown to present conservation- and environmental-themed puppet programs. Their programs on topics such as recycling and the importance of bees always drew a full house in the nature center's auditorium.[293]

The first nature center and first planetarium in the national capital area, the Rock Creek Park Nature Center and Planetarium has now been around for decades yet remains popular. Adults use the facility as a staging ground for hiking on weekends, while children, families and elementary school classes continue to enjoy the exhibits and ranger-led planetarium programs.

Horse Center
Therapeutic Riding in Rock Creek Park

While horseback riding and equestrian events have always been popular in Rock Creek Park, two public horse centers for recreational riding opened up in the park in the late 1950s. Ironically, the one public stable in the park that remains today went bankrupt in 1970, while the horse center that at first did well is now a U.S. Park Police facility for its horse-mounted units.

The first public facility, the Edgewater Riding Academy, was built at the southern end of Rock Creek Park. The academy was popular among horseback riders due to its location at the trailhead for a popular riding path that paralleled the Rock Creek and Potomac Parkway. Unfortunately for the riders, Edgewater closed when the Washington Metropolitan Area Transit Authority (WMATA) used the building as a staging ground for construction of the red line metro underneath Rock Creek and downtown D.C. The riding facility never reopened after the building project and was instead converted into a U.S. Park Police stable. It remains a police facility to this day.[294]

The other horse center was initially planned to be developed at the current Oregon Avenue community garden site. However, neighborhood opposition to this was widespread. "We believe our sixteen year old daughter will not be safe alone in our home, with the stable help required to care for forty horses, and the people who 'hang around' a stable, nearby," wrote one neighbor. Siding with the neighborhood, a park division chief said in a memorandum, perhaps ignorantly, that "the contemplated location is very near to a rather exclusive residential area. Rental stables notoriously attract a 'trashy' class of help and hangers-on, such as will be a continual source of friction with the neighboring residents."[295]

As a result of these fears and complaints, the horse center came to be built at its current location in between the nature center and park maintenance facility. This horse center struggled at first and went bankrupt. Fortunately, WMATA came to the rescue. Since it had displaced the Edgewater Riding Academy, WMATA paid for a new and improved public facility at the Glover Road location, and the Rock Creek Park Horse Center has been a popular attraction ever since. Furthermore, it has not attracted "trashy" citizens but rather hundreds of mentally and physically disabled persons determined and excited to train on horses as well as volunteer at the facility.[296]

Indeed, aside from housing horses and providing public horseback tours, riding lessons and summer camps for children, a commendable and long-standing tradition at the horse center has been its therapeutic riding program. Created in 1974, the program was designed to offer handicapped and mentally disabled children and adults a positive, outdoor experience. The horse center manager noted in 1981 that "our basic goal is not to teach them how to ride a horse but to help them become a total being, physically and mentally, to work on motor skills, conceptual skills and eye-hand coordination. We build confidence, and when the kids return to the classroom it is all put together."[297]

Perhaps the most well-known therapeutic rider over the years has been James S. Brady, the White House press secretary who got shot in the head during the 1981 Reagan assassination attempt that took place in D.C. Brady is permanently disabled with brain damage to this day, but his wife reported the benefits of his riding a horse at the Rock Creek Park Horse Center: "Jim loves it. He would go every day if he could…One of the greatest satisfactions is that it has given Jim a sense of control over himself and his horse."[298]

Therapeutic riding sometimes has gone both ways, as on at least one occasion, a horse's mood improved dramatically after moving to the horse center. Jackson was the horse's name, and according to staff, he hated almost all grown men, most likely due to the fact the he was abused by a male in his early years. He lived at the horse center for fifteen years and helped hundreds of children learn to ride:

> *He was the horse who always took the frightened, the small and the nervous children. He had a pitch-perfect trot for kids, and somehow the intuition to know just when to go a little harder, a little softer, to lean one way or another to balance the newbie rider, without the help of expert grown-ups…Eventually, the staff learned that Jackson allowed a very select group of adults on his back, too—the injured and disabled. He tossed able-bodied riders, but had a soft spot and special intuition for carrying wounded troops or adults with cerebral palsy…The horse had a special relationship with Christoph Ruesch, 29, who can move only his neck and head. Jackson became Christoph's muscular chest and strong legs so that for one hour a week, Christoph could move among the trees, 10 feet tall, striding with a swagger.[299]*

After several years, when Jackson started slowing down and showing signs of pain, staff retired him, only to discover a depressed Jackson with head down and body turned to the back of his stall. "He clearly needed them [children]. He knew what his job was, and he wanted to do it," said Amber Power-Shickler, the horse center manager, of Jackson. "So we let him." And so Jackson kept up a three-hour riding schedule up until three weeks before his death. When he did pass away in September 2012 after a good life of thirty-three years, horse center staff found it very hard to announce and accept his death. "He was the heart of the horse center," a young female rider noted in Jackson's *Washington Post* obituary.[300]

Today, the horse center continues its therapeutic riding program and partners with the U.S. Park Police to extend its services to wounded warriors (war veterans). The horse center also makes it a point to recruit volunteers with mental disabilities, enabling them to work in the great outdoors among friendly beasts of burden.

THOMPSON BOAT CENTER

Water Sports for the National Capital

The same year that the current horse center and nature center opened saw the opening of the National Capital Water Sports Center at the mouth of Rock Creek. Its construction was completed only after much debate, as many opposed the facility at the site due to its being a combined sewage–stormwater discharge point. Furthermore, some claimed that the center would mar the beauty of the mouth of the creek. But National Park Service National Capital Region director Harry T. Thompson pushed strongly for the facility's construction and, just like Carter Barron with the amphitheater, saw it through to fruition. When Thompson died just five months after the National Capital Water Sports Center's grand opening, the name was officially changed to the Harry T. Thompson Boat Center.[301]

For over fifty years now, the boat center has provided canoe and other small watercraft rentals to the public. It also stores boats for a fee and hosts major regattas, or rowing competitions. Operating under a concession contract with Rock Creek Park, Thompson Boat Center has proved perhaps most popular among area high school and college students. These young rowers, most notably from Georgetown University and George Washington University, train and compete in regattas on the Potomac River annually. Two rowing clubs also are based out of Thompson Boat Center.[302]

In addition to rowing races, in 1965, Thompson Boat Center hosted a major river cleanup the day before the White House Conference on Natural Beauty "in order to demonstrate in practice what will be discussed

Monday [at the conference] in theory." Known as Potomac Pick-Up Day and sponsored by the Citizen's Council for a Clean Potomac, the event included "five units of walking groups and people in canoes and power boats" removing litter and unnatural debris from the river. At the end of the day, U.S. senator Daniel Brewster of Maryland as well as Secretary of the Interior Stewart Udall informally addressed and thanked the participants.[303]

Today, just a half mile up the bank of the Potomac from Thompson Boat Center, the Key Bridge Boathouse is a newer Rock Creek Park concessioner. Its wooden dock, multicolored kayaks and stand-up paddleboard (SUP) rentals make it a popular recreational facility.

JOHN INSCOE AND HIS MULES

A Familiar and Friendly Face to Visitors

While not a recreational activity, a key attraction for Rock Creek Park visitors and commuters once involved a senior citizen employee and his mules. For forty years, a physically fit Arlington man had a daily ritual:

> *Eighty four year old John Inscoe, who drives the mule-drawn lawn mowers in Rock Creek Park, keeps on the go about 17 hours a day. He figures that's about enough. Inscoe is up at 2:45 a.m. every week day and doesn't quit working and walking until about 7:00 p.m. He goes to bed an hour later…His schedule is staggering. He's up at 2:45 a.m. and walks three miles to his stable at MacArthur Boulevard and Foxhall Road NW. After completing his stable chores, he's out cutting grass by 6 a.m. He knocks off at 3 p.m., returns to the stable, performs more chores, and then walks home.*[304]

According to the article, John owned ten mules. On any given day, eight of them would be out in the park in teams of two, cutting grass on "slopes that can't easily be reached efficiently by the hand-pushed or tractor-pulled mowers." The other two mules pulled canal boats for tourists along the Chesapeake and Ohio Canal.[305]

Inscoe, whose "blue denim jacket and khaki trousers are a familiar sight to motorists," took just one day "off" per week: "Sunday is a snap. He sleeps later and merely walks three miles to the stable to check on things and do some leftover chores." With a devout love for his mules, during

John Inscoe and his mules get ready to mow around the southern portion of Rock Creek Park. *National Park Service.*

winter when the grasses did not need mowing, Inscoe still often walked down to the stables to check on them and see that they were getting fed and exercised properly.[306]

Perhaps because of his hardy exercise in the great outdoors, Inscoe was sharp as a tack and physically fit well into his late eighties: "Inscoe's memory is pretty good, and he can't recall ever losing a day's work because of sickness. He figures his long-term health is the result of clean living. 'I get up early and go to bed early. I don't smoke,' he said. Asked whether he drinks, the ruddy-faced octogenarian replied, 'Yes, water.'"[307]

Part IV

Recently in Rock Creek Park

9

ENVIRONMENTAL PROBLEMS

Throughout the first several chapters of this book, hints have been dropped alluding to the fact that not all is well with the landscape and water of Rock Creek Park. Due primarily to its urban surroundings, Rock Creek Park is diverse not only in its abundant recreational opportunities but also, unfortunately, in its environmental problems. Although these challenges did not begin in the past fifty years, which is the general focus of this chapter, traffic and, perhaps most notably, water pollution did get more publicity then. Indeed, in the mid-1960s, heightening environmental awareness on the part of citizens led President Lyndon Baines Johnson to refer to the Potomac River as a "national disgrace" due to its pollution problems. A small stream that directly feeds into the "national disgrace" is Rock Creek itself. Unfortunately, as you will see, many of Rock Creek Park's environmental problems are yet to be significantly mitigated. The park's history is not all fun and nostalgic; some of its past—and present—is quite serious and sobering.

HIGHWAY PROPOSALS, CAR TRAFFIC AND THE PARK RESPONSE

Pave Paradise?

Rock Creek Park is unique among national park units in that its primary use today is as a commuter corridor. Hundreds of visitors enjoy cycling, hiking and jogging in the park on nice-weather weekends, but thousands of automobilists commute down Beach Drive and feeder roads every weekday. But hey, at least there is not a four- to six-lane expressway running through the length of the park—a common proposal throughout the 1940s and '50s to improve traffic flow in the nation's capital.

A first call for such a grand highway occurred in 1938. Just a couple years after the Rock Creek and Potomac Parkway was completed in the southern Rock Creek Valley, District commissioner Melvin C. Hazen proposed a four-lane, high-speed artery paralleling Rock Creek into Maryland in the northern valley (ironically, a Rock Creek tributary is named after Hazen). Proposed to mitigate commuter traffic, Hazen's plan was criticized by the *Evening Star* as just "about the worst thing that could happen to Rock Creek Park." As a result, District engineers proposed a different speedway that would parallel the creek only along the southern section of the park and then parallel Broad Branch and Oregon Avenue in the north. While some supported this plan, World War II helped table the debate for a few years.[308]

However, with the postwar economic boom and massive increase in population on the outskirts of the capital—this was the rise of suburbia—highways through the park were proposed again, this time to connect U.S. Route 240 (presently Interstate 270) in Maryland with downtown Washington. While District commissioners, some newspapers and others supported the plan, conservation and environmental organizations, the U.S. secretary of the interior and the National Park Service opposed it. "The Department of the Interior will vigorously oppose any use of the Rock Creek Valley for arterial highway purposes or any other use contrary to the intent of Congress in the establishment of this important park area," interior secretary Douglas McKay wrote in 1953.[309] Sigurd Olson, noted conservationist and then president of the National Parks Association (later renamed the National Parks Conservation Association), said it perhaps more succinctly:

The real issue is whether or not our national capital is willing to sacrifice one of the grandest parks of its kind in the world, an asset that with our growing population becomes more and more valuable over time…We have a real sanctuary in Rock Creek Park. Let us cherish it and protect it so that future generations will not point to us and say, "They had no understanding or vision for this place."[310]

Although a highway never did get built through the park, National Park Service officials didn't just sit back and do nothing during this era of road building. As commuters, D.C. officials and even some NPS landscape architects criticized Rock Creek Park's rustic and antiquated road system, major steps

TRAFFIC ACCIDENTS IN CHEVY CHASE CIRCLE

Highway proposals and car traffic have not just affected the main stem of Rock Creek Park over the years; they have also touched—quite literally—several of the park's satellite units. While an expressway was proposed to travel the length of Glover Archbold Park, perhaps the most notable story involves the one-acre Chevy Chase Circle. Straddling the D.C.- Maryland boundary along Connecticut Avenue, the circle was formally landscaped in 1933 as a picturesque entrance into the city as well as public relaxation spot. A memorial fountain with thirty-foot geyser, Potomac bluestone walkway and benches were constructed, while willow oaks, yews and azaleas were planted around the site.[311]

Unfortunately, however, with the park being surrounded by the increasingly busy roundabout, Chevy Chase Circle has borne the brunt of several car accidents over the years. Since 1960, automobiles have smashed into the oaks, fountain and benches on multiple occasions, causing significant damage. From 1985 to 1990, the fountain sat idle due to a car accident, while in 2001, destruction to the fountain caused by a driver returning from a New Year's Eve outing resulted in the entire circle park being closed with chain-link fence for over a year—the National Park Service refused to spend money and time fixing the park only to have another accident occur. Only after D.C. Department of Transportation installed striping and delineators on the roadway lanes did the NPS agree to spend $40,000 in repair work.[312]

Even so, the author carefully crossed the busy lanes of traffic to the circle park in late March 2013 and saw broken benches, likely from another car accident. Furthermore, after he crossed back over, a neighborhood resident asked, "How did you manage to get over there? I applaud you for doing so. This is the most dangerous circle in the city. We call it Suicide Circle. The danger goes both ways. It's dangerous for pedestrians to cross the street to get to the park, and it's dangerous for cars to navigate around the circle and stop for pedestrians."[313]

were taken to modernize the park in the '50s and '60s. It was thought that if Rock Creek Park widened and straightened its roadways in key locations, expressway promoters would back off. As a result, the period witnessed the closing of many fords and the razing of several rustic bridges (Pebble Dash Bridge, for example) in return for more modern, fast-paced structures.[314]

During this road-modernization era, the Rock Creek Golf Course was forced to shrink in size by 25 percent. What was once a spacious eigtheen-hole golf course stretching out to Sixteenth Street and Military Road became significantly condensed in the late 1950s when Joyce Road was constructed and Military Road went from being a "narrow, winding, two-lane road into a high speed thoroughfare" of four lanes. Ever since, golf course fairways have bordered one another with practically no buffer zone.[315]

Causing even more change, the biggest construction project and the one with the most far-reaching effects involved the construction of the "Beach

U.S. secretary of the interior Stewart Udall, at podium, presides over the official dedication of the Beach Drive Zoo tunnel. The project was approved and started before Udall began as interior secretary in 1961, putting the conservation-minded secretary in an odd position. The second the tunnel opened, Rock Creek Park's automobile traffic increased dramatically. *National Park Service.*

Drive-Zoo tunnel," located on Beach Drive just below the National Zoo. Though the tunnel had been promoted for years by NPS officials as a way to connect the Rock Creek and Potomac Parkway with Rock Creek Park, it was not until landscape architect Conrad Wirth became National Park Service director that the tunnel was carried through to fruition. Compromising with the National Zoo, which for two decades opposed the tunnel on the grounds that it didn't want its animals upset by car horns and traffic, construction began in earnest in the late 1950s and was completed in 1966.[316]

Prior to the tunnel's construction, Beach Drive had followed the U bend in the creek. Located generally where the multiuse trail broadly curves around the tunnel today, the road forded the creek twice. Due to the fact that the fords were sometimes closed during high water and at night and also due to the roadway not being that straight, Beach Drive did not serve as a primary commuter corridor. The tunnel completion changed this. The tunnel bypassed the fords and directly connected Beach Drive to the Rock Creek and Potomac Parkway. And so, essentially the moment after the ribbon-cutting ceremony was completed by Secretary of the Interior Stewart Udall, traffic rolled through the tunnel and has continued to this day. Park officials learned to despise the tunnel the moment it opened.[317]

Although an expressway was not constructed through Rock Creek Park in the 1950s and '60s, Beach Drive became a two-lane highway of sorts.

THE 1952 SEWAGE LEAK

Old Faithful Geyser in Rock Creek Park

Stream valley parks such as Rock Creek Park are ideal locations for large underground pipes for two reasons. First, the valley slopes downhill, enabling sewer lines to follow the flow of gravity in pipes to the Blue Plains Treatment Plant. Second, parks tend to have less aboveground structures to deal with during construction. The problem comes, however, when pipes are not enlarged to keep up with increasing urban and suburban population growth and when they age, break, leak and collapse. The worst of these accidents occurred in 1952.

As a precursor, the main Rock Creek Park sewer line was constructed in 1917. Running generally north to south through the park, its construction caused sections of Beach Drive to be closed for a year. The pipe was built five feet in diameter in the northern section of the park, but just north of Military Road, the pipe decreased in size to two and a half feet. As suburbia in Maryland expanded during the post–World War II economic boom, so too did the raw sewage traveling through the pipe.[318]

This came to the forefront in 1952 and 1953 in Rock Creek Park, when the narrower section of pipe finally went over capacity. The dishwasher fluid, shower water and toilet waste shot up the nearest manhole. The manhole cover then burst open, and five thousand tons of raw sewage poured out into Rock Creek and adjacent picnic areas—today's picnic groves six, seven and eight—every day for almost a year.[319]

Harold Kemp, director of Sanitary Engineering for Washington, D.C., at the time, spoke out boldly in the beginning of the leak: "We're…trying to operate on the small amount of money we have. This Rock Creek situation could be a good thing if it makes the people and Congress aware of the need for new sewers." Fortunately, funds did come through quickly, but it took time to build a new pipe.[320]

As city workers scrambled to build an additional sewer through the park, the gushing continued. Workers compared the exploding manhole to Yellowstone National Park's most famous geothermal geyser: "It's called 'Old Faithful' by the construction gang working on the new sewer. It keeps up a steady flow that reaches fountain proportions during the 'peak hours' of midmorning, early afternoon, and evening," noted the *Washington Post*.[321]

The good news is that a sewage leak at the 1952 level proved to be an isolated incident. The bad news, however, is that sewage leaks are still commonplace in the Rock Creek watershed.

Rock Creek Floods and Water Pollution

The High Cost of High Water

The power of water is awesome, and when exacerbated by stormwater runoff, combined sewer overflows (CSOs) and anthropogenic climate change, it's even more awesome. On numerous occasions during the last century, Rock Creek floods caused by tropical storms have wreaked havoc on park infrastructure as well as the overall creek environment. While a few of the most significant floods will be spotlighted in this section, it's important

Flood debris and damage along the Rock Creek and Potomac Parkway. *Library of Congress.*

The aftermath of a Rock Creek flood shows stream bank erosion and a picnic table in an unlikely place. *Library of Congress.*

to note that dozens of additional floods have proved detrimental as well.

An early well-documented flood occurred as far back as 1933. Prior to the park's cement footbridges of today, which were constructed by the Public Works Administration in 1934, there were a series of wooden footbridges across the creek. The 1933 flood destroyed each of the eight wooden bridges. The water level of Rock Creek was so high during the flood that it flowed through a tunnel (removed between 1939 and 1941) below Massachusetts Avenue on the Rock Creek and Potomac Parkway.[322]

Probably Rock Creek Park's most damaging flood occurred forty years later during Tropical Storm Agnes. During this event in 1972, at peak flood stage, the first floor of Peirce Mill was three feet under water (the high-water mark can still be seen inside the mill today), as was the inside of Thompson Boat Center at the mouth of Rock Creek. All the boat center's docks washed away, and the inside damage was substantial.[323]

Regarding roads and trails in the park, National Park Service officials noted that one-third of the newly constructed multiuse trail along the parkway and parts of the road itself were damaged. Finally, the Rock Creek Water Environmental Trail—an interpretive, self-guiding trail beginning at Boundary Bridge—was destroyed by Agnes. Park management decided to not replace the trail afterward. Damage and repairs from Agnes cost Rock Creek Park $1 million. This amount of damage today would cost over $3 million if you factor in inflation.[324]

Later in the same decade, Tropical Storm David in September 1979 caused sixty-mile-per-hour wind gusts and submerged much of Beach Drive and over a dozen park picnic groves. Rock Creek floodwater from David destroyed the hiker-biker bridge just south of Peirce Mill, while parts of the paved trail farther south simply disappeared. Park superintendent Jim Redmond noted that 175 picnic tables, seventy-five trash receptacles and seventy-five benches washed away and over two hundred trees, both mature and young, toppled and met their end. Finally, parts of the southbound lanes of Rock Creek and Potomac Parkway were washed away yet again.[325]

Erosion caused by flooding and stormwater has caused almost all of the trail, road and bridge damage in Rock Creek Park, and these factors continue to affect park infrastructure into the present. In 1991, Klingle Valley Road was closed when its roadway was deemed unsafe for travel due to the loose soil below it, and it's been closed ever since. More recently, in 2013, the road bridge over the Fenwick Tributary of Rock Creek was closed for the same reason.

Although floods are natural and occurred on Rock Creek prior to large-scale urbanization, over the years, the water volume has increased due to

High water flowing over the dam near Peirce Mill. Due to periodic flooding of the mill's basement and the fact that fresh cornmeal drops into bins in the basement after being "ground" by the millstones, the park is no longer permitted to sell Peirce Mill cornmeal. It would be a violation of U.S. Department of Health and Human Services standards to do so. *National Park Service.*

expansion of the urban surroundings. Roads, sidewalks, driveways, parking lots and rooftops are impervious, meaning water cannot filter through them. As a result, during heavy rainfall, the urban surfaces act as waterways in their own right, flushing litter, spilled car oil and other pollutants into storm drains. These storm drains then dump directly into Rock Creek and its tributaries, leading to a negative chain reaction: the powerful stormwater sends massive amounts of litter into the park and chews away at stream banks, causing erosion; the erosion topples trees, eats away at park infrastructure and carries sediment downstream; the sediment decreases oxygen levels in the creek; and the low oxygen levels makes it difficult for fish to breathe.[326]

All of Rock Creek's water pollution and erosion problems are exacerbated by the fact that much of the lower Rock Creek Valley is served by a combined sewer–stormwater system. Because this system conveys both sanitary sewage and stormwater in one piping system, the District of Columbia Water and Sewer Authority (D.C. WASA, known today more as D.C. Water) notes the differences that take place in combined sewer–stormwater system between dry and wet weather:

> *During normal dry weather conditions, sanitary wastes collected in the combined sewer system are diverted to the Blue Plains Advanced Wastewater Treatment Plant. The sanitary wastes are diverted at facilities called regulators…* [But] *during periods of significant rainfall, the capacity of a combined sewer may be exceeded. When this occurs, regulators are designed to let the excess flow, which is a mixture of stormwater and sanitary wastes, to be discharged directly into the Anacostia River, Rock Creek, the Potomac River, or tributary waters. This excess flow is called Combined Sewer Overflow (CSO). Release of this excess flow is necessary to prevent flooding in homes, basements, businesses, and streets.* [327]

Because of this antiquated system of combined sewer–stormwater, which was designed prior to 1900, millions of gallons of combined sewage–stormwater flows into Rock Creek annually—52 million gallons in 2004, according to D.C. Water. [328] Besides erosion, the negative consequences of this are many: bad odor, no longer being able to swim in the national capital's creek, fish kills and aquatic habitat impairment, among other things. [329]

Fortunately, under a court-ordered consent decree in 2005, the U.S. Environmental Protection Agency (EPA) has required D.C. Water to construct three large-scale tunnels, or underground reservoirs, to significantly decrease the amount of combined sewer overflow in Rock Creek, the Anacostia River and the Potomac River. The idea is that the tunnels will temporarily hold sewage and stormwater until it can flow to Blue Plains Water Treatment Plant and be filtered sustainably after storm events.

Anacostia's tunnel is being constructed at the time of this book's publication, and when the tunnel is completed in 2016, D.C. Water estimates that this holding reservoir will keep 96 percent of the dirty fluids out of the Anacostia River. Unfortunately, however, regarding Rock Creek's holding tunnel, D.C. Water has decided to deify the EPA ruling and solve the combined sewer overflow problem in its own way, through small-scale green infrastructure projects. While the author supports rain gardens, green roofs, porous pavements and rainwater harvesting, he finds D.C. Water's change of plans regrettable.

The Rock Creek tunnel should be constructed posthaste to finally stop the decades-old problem of raw sewage, not to mention tens of millions

EXCERPTS FROM THE U.S. DEPARTMENT OF THE INTERIOR 1967 REPORT ENTITLED *THE CREEK AND THE CITY: URBAN PRESSURES ON A NATURAL STREAM...ROCK CREEK PARK AND METROPOLITAN WASHINGTON*

"Rock Creek—like the city of Washington—belongs to all the people of America. We must ask ourselves how can we expect to clean up any river in the nation, if we cannot clean up Rock Creek. Here is a small watershed which serves a politically astute community. It is surrounded by one of this country's finest metropolitan parks. Rock Creek can and must be clean."
—Stewart Udall, U.S. Secretary of the Interior

This is our program to clean up, restore, and preserve Rock Creek...

Street cleaning practices in the Rock Creek basin should be more rigidly overseen to do away with the large quantities of litter and trash that find their way into the storm sewer systems and the creek...

Both combined storm and sanitary sewer systems of the District of Columbia and the separate sewers of the Maryland suburbs will continue to be heavy sources of pollution for Rock Creek in time of rainstorms until they are supplanted or modified by new and better methods of waste and runoff collection. These problems are not only difficult but widespread in the United States, and we consider that Rock Creek merits "pilot" status in a major research and demonstration program to provide underground temporary storage of excessive flows or other means of assuring their treatment and proper disposal...

The most essential single element in this program is an urgent plea to the responsible citizens of the area to form a strong organization whose interest is focused on the creek, its problems, and their solution[s]. It must come soon and it must last. Its purposes should include informing the general public about the creek, continued vigilance against bad planning and sanitary practices and laxity in enforcement of regulations, and if necessary, harassment by means of publicity and political or legal action of organizations and official agencies responsible for abuses.

of gallons of dirty stormwater, from dumping into the national capital's creek. With the large amount of pavement and asphalt in the Rock Creek watershed, creating dozens of small-scale green infrastructure projects will only decrease combined sewer outfall levels slightly. Furthermore, D.C. Water's green infrastructure project can be seen as a stall tactic, as the private company wants to complete a multiyear exploratory period, while following the EPA's orders would have the tunnel done sooner. The author believes that now is not the time to change plans, defy orders, stall and experiment with other solutions; now is the time to follow orders from the leading environmental protection bureau in the land.[330]

Since the 1930s, National Park Service and Department of the Interior reports have suggested time and time again numerous ways that Rock Creek's intermingled flooding, stormwater and sewage problems can be mitigated. The bad news is that these reports have largely gone ignored. The good news is that they hold the key to solving Rock Creek's water woes.

Illegal Dumping Down Storm Drains

150,000 Fish Killed

The water of Rock Creek is polluted not only by sewage leaks, stormwater runoff and combined sewer overflows but also, several times each year, by chemicals. While it is illegal to dump any type of chemical into a storm drain that feeds into Rock Creek, select homeowners and businesses in the Rock Creek watershed have either ignored this rule or not known about it. The result has been the death of hundreds of thousands of fish in an already overpolluted watershed.

In 1990, a tank beneath a condominium on Connecticut Avenue adjacent to the Melvin Hazen Tributary of Rock Creek leaked and spilled an estimated eight thousand gallons of heating oil into the watershed. Bob Ford, the park's first chief of natural resources and who worked in the park from the late '60s until the early 2000s, told reporters at the time that about fifteen booms, or oil-stopping devices, were placed across the tributary to intercept the floating oil before it reached the creek. Still, one must wonder how much of the oil made it into the creek.[331]

A decade later, in the spring of 2000, the park's largest fish kill incident occurred when an employee at an exterminating company in Silver Spring spilled pesticides in a parking lot and then hosed them down the nearest storm drain. The pesticide, specifically known as PrevailT and containing the highly toxic chemicals cypermethrin and bifenthrin, emptied into Rock

Creek, and an estimated 150,000 fish died along an eight-mile section of the national capital's creek. The chemicals attacked fish gills, and the EPA notes that seven of sixteen fish species, four of eight minnow species and twenty of the total forty-six macro-invertebrates found in Rock Creek—including stonefly, caddisfly and mayfly—went temporarily extinct along Rock Creek.[332] Gary Sikora, longtime environmental protection volunteer for the park, claims that the spring migrations of various fish species up Rock Creek has never recovered. "In the 1990s I would see thousands of herring and shad swimming up the creek to hatch their young. These days, I see a couple of dozen—that's it," Sikora notes.[333]

While a multilateral investigation was conducted and charges were eventually pressed against the business owner for violating the Clean Water Act and Federal Insecticide, Fungicide and Rodenticide Act, it is unknown how much the business was forced to pay. Furthermore, the damage was already done.[334]

Another recent illegal chemical dump occurred in 2006 between Blagden Avenue and Park Road in the vicinity of Peirce Mill. Two hundred fish were reported dead in one day, including minnows, crayfish and large channel catfish, not to mention numerous aquatic insects. "Fortunately, it happened over a fairly short stretch of the stream," noted Bill Yeaman in an interview with the *Washington Post*.[335]

When harmful chemicals enter the creek, one of the first indications involves bizarre movements of fish. They are often found making circles around the surface of the water, breathing their last breaths and trying to find a way out of their predicament. Unfortunately, they are doomed. And unfortunately, illegal chemical dumps into Rock Creek occur often due to the park's urban surroundings.

INVASIVE, NONNATIVE PLANTS

An Exotic Plant History of Rock Creek Park

In the beginning, in the very beginning, all plants were native to the Rock Creek Valley. But then along came man. Indigenous Virginia bluebells, stately cedars and other native plants and trees were crowded out and overtaken by invaders like Japanese honeysuckle and English ivy. Today, an astounding one-third of park plant species are considered nonnative and invasive, meaning that they don't naturally belong in the park and, in many cases, outcompete and kill plant species that do, thus decreasing biological diversity. How did these invasive plants enter and then spread through signficant sections of the park?

One reason is by unintended consequences. Early photos of Klingle Mansion show English ivy climbing up the historic stone walls of the home. Indeed, Joshua Peirce, the original owner of Linnaean Hill, planted, harvested and sold English ivy all over the city in the mid-1800s.[336] After Perice's property was abandoned, the ivy spread unchecked.

The blame does not belong solely on Shoemaker, however, as many other invasive plants now prevalent in Rock Creek Park were introduced in the 1800s through different means. Garlic mustard, for instance, an edible invasive species also known for its medicinal values, was introduced from Europe into New York City in 1868 and used originally by rural settlers. Additionally, mile-a-minute and Japanese stiltgrass were introduced accidently onto America's public lands from East Asia. Stilt grass in particular was used as packaging material for porcelain dishware. These exotic plants and others probably gained a footing in the park directly after it was established. Farmers within the Rock Creek Valley were forced to leave, and "after cultivation was abandoned, these [farmland] tracts suffered from invasion by weedy, mostly exotic species," notes former Rock Creek Park botanist Peggy Fleming.[337]

A second reason for invasive plant infestation is, perhaps surprisingly to some readers, through park staff's planting of them. Indeed, English ivy was part of the original landscape plans for Montrose Park, Meridian Hill Park and certain bridges, while Japanese honeysuckle was planted along the banks of Rock Creek to stabilize soil and decrease erosion. Ironically, the Olmsted brothers' 1918 Rock Creek Park report, which served as the park's first de facto general management plan, called for the widespread planting of the sweet-smelling, pretty-flowering, yet highly invasive Japanese honeysuckle. Realizing this problem, fine arts commissioner Charles Moore wrote a letter to park management in the early 1920s noting that the honeysuckle "will kill anything but the largest trees, and unless pains are taken to keep it down, for it cannot be exterminated, it will ruin Rock Creek Park."[338]

It wasn't until the 1960s that official National Park Service policy changed to reflect the Fine Arts Commission's view on invasive plants. And only in the mid-1970s did park managers and staff begin actively seeking to remove the nonnative species. In fact, Rock Creek Park's very first position dedicated to natural resource management wasn't created until the late 1970s. By this time, though, it was the park neighbors' turn to do damage.

The third reason for widespread invasive plants in Rock Creek Park is due to its urban surroundings—namely, park neighbors and illegal dumpers. By the 1980s, Washington, D.C.'s diamond had filled out with development. Rock Creek Park was surrounded on all sides by urbanity, primarily residential homes and apartments. Some of these residents purchased and planted—and continue to plant—evergreen English ivy and other invasive, nonnative plants in their gardens. Birds, hiking boots, wind and other transporters then carry these seeds into the park. They also illegally dump yard waste clippings in the park. In an interview with first Chief of Natural Resources Bob Ford in 1990, the *Washington Post* noted:

> *Exotic pest plants such as English ivy, Asian bittersweet, and porcelainberry* [are] *introduced by well-intending neighbors who dump yard waste containing the pesky seeds in the park. The ivy has spread across some of the forest floor, choking out fawn lilies and spring beauties, while other vines are growing up and over native trees and slowly smothering them...Ford worries that the battle against tenacious vines will be lost because of tighter*

Invasive plant infestation on the Pinehurst Tributary of Rock Creek before being treated with herbicide, 1996. *National Park Service.*

The same location after being sprayed with herbicide in 1998. The minimal ground cover is the sign of a healthy and natural mid-Atlantic region forest ecosystem. Unfortunately, herbicides have been deemed controversial and are not generally used over large areas of infestation. *National Park Service.*

budget cuts that include no funding for extra help next year to cut them back and discourage new growth.[339]

Small-scale landscaping companies, trying to avoid going to the dump, are also a problem. Former chief of maintenance Dave Newman stated in the 1980s that "it's getting to the point where Rock Creek Park is like a landfill." U.S. Park Police captain Dale Dickerhoff noted that "we're getting hammered by illegal dumping. We're getting sinks and toilet bowls. It's a disgrace."[340] They were also getting invasive seeds.

Fortunately, although invasive plants are now prevalent in Rock Creek Park, in the past several years, Weed Warrior volunteers and park partners such as the Rock Creek Conservancy and Dumbarton Oaks Park Conservancy have joined in the battle against invasive species. However, these pesky plants are resilient, and most plant nurseries continue to sell invasive species to their customers, thus undermining the problem. Furthermore, the most effective means of eradicating invasive species is by using herbicides, but herbicides themselves are frowned on by some environmentalists. And so, well into the twenty-first century at this point, Rock Creek Park and hundreds of other public landscapes across the country and world are in a huge predicament when it comes to the problem of invasive, nonnative plants.

VANDALISM

Some Park Visitors Are "Full of Devilment"

While flooding and the spread of invasive plants in Rock Creek Park have become more severe over the course of the last several decades, so too has park vandalism. Defacing of government property has, in fact, a history in Rock Creek Park, going back to at least the 1960s.

During this decade, a *Washington Post* article reported that rambunctious children broke several windows in historic Peirce Mill. "Fifty nine panes have been broken out of the 22 windows in the building. Watt [the miller] said boys who are 'full of devilment' throw stones at the Mill windows, and sometimes, if no one is inside, the boys break in to take a soft drink from a cooler kept for tourists."[341]

A few years later, in 1968, due to the widespread racial riots and protests that occurred directly after the assassination of Dr. Martin Luther King Jr., a formal armillary sphere in Meridian Hill Park was severely vandalized to the point that park staff removed it. Since this tumultuous period, formal statues in Meridian Hill Park have been defaced continually. Currently, the statue of *Serenity* is missing its right hand and nose, and a huge crack has enveloped most of the marble monument. In 2013, an unlawful citizen spray-painted *Serenity*'s nipples and face black. "It's very disappointing," park user Erika Castillo noted in a newspaper article. "This park, it's beautiful, and to have this happen—it's a family park—it's disappointing."[342] Meanwhile, *Joan of Arc*'s sword was removed, stolen and missing for several years and was just recently replaced, while spray paint is common throughout Meridian Hill Park on its historic walls.

In Rock Creek Park proper, the most common form of vandalism is carving into park trees, specifically American beech trees due to their smooth bark and light color. Very few of these biologically important tree species seem to remain untouched. Bridge railings have also been vandalized, as one S.E. Banker writes disturbingly in his 1982 poem entitled "Rock Creek Park," apparently not realizing the illegality behind his actions:

We walked the rock alley
Saving our favorite stones
Then through the storm sewer
Our passage to the park
Where we carved obscene words
With my brother's Boy Scout knife
On the railings of the bridges
That crossed Rock Creek Park.

ENVIRONMENTAL PROTECTION AND SUSTAINABILITY

Although its environmental problems and vandalism issues need to be taken seriously, fortunately, Rock Creek Park's environmental history is not all doom and gloom. The other side of the environmental history coin is the park's sustainability and environmental protection success stories. While some of these success stories have already been highlighted—the establishment of the park, parkway and tributaries; much of the work of the Civilian Conservation Corps; and environmental education at the Nature Center, for examples—many have occurred in the last few decades. One notable exception to this, however, is the green movement that started in World War II.

BLAIR ROAD AND FORT STEVENS COMMUNITY GARDENS

World War II Victory Gardens Now Go Green

Working-class neighborhoods are perhaps not the first place someone thinks of when they think of sustainability in the national parks, but this is the case when it comes to Rock Creek Park. The park administers several community gardens throughout the northwest quadrant of D.C., two of which include the Blair Road Community Garden and Fort Stevens Community Garden.

These gardens, like many others in the area and nation, were established during World War II as victory gardens.

During the war, in order to conserve gas and food for the hundreds of thousands of American soldiers fighting Hitler and Japan overseas, millions of Americans began planting vegetable and fruit gardens in their backyards, windowsills or neighborhood parks. Rock Creek Park interpretive park ranger Deanna Ochs notes that "gas and food were critically short. Transportation systems were overwhelmed with masses of troops and supplies. Yet Americans were full of patriotism and eager to do their part. The weapons of choice: a garden hoe and watering can."[343] Indeed, the idea of victory gardens spread like wildfire, and by 1943, there were an estimated 20 million gardens raising 8 million tons of produce annually.[344]

The gardens were incredibly beneficial to the war effort. Unfortunately, though, at the end of the war, many victory gardens reverted back to vacant lots and lawns. However, in the nation's capital, when citizens requested that the land be retained for gardening, the National Park Service complied as much as it could. Thus, several of Rock Creek Park's community gardens were founded, including the ones at Blair Road and across from Fort Stevens. The gardens run independently, with members paying dues to the NPS once per year and then democratically electing a garden supervisor to oversee things. [345]

Since the 1940s, despite plans at different times to turn the Blair Road Community Garden into a parking lot and later a Metro stop, the garden survives. At five acres, Blair Road Community Garden is one of the largest in D.C.[346]

Many of the gardeners at Blair Road take great pride in their plots. According to a National Park Service oral history report, one such gardener is James Bishop, an African American man who has had a garden plot there since 1973. In the early days of the garden, when he applied for a plot, Bishop was rejected by the all-white garden association on the grounds that there was not enough room. When he noticed the many vacant plots in the garden, Bishop paid a visit to a Department of the Interior official and was afterward immediately given a plot of land. Then, things changed:

Within the next two years, after the former garden president suffered a stroke and moved to Florida, an African American garden president took over—within three years the demographics of the garden completely changed with Caucasian gardeners moving out and African American gardeners moving in. Mr. Bishop and his fellow gardeners battle with the rabbits, squirrels, and birds for the successful collards, kale, string beans, squash, black eyed peas, beans, sweet potatoes, and others…To Mr. Bishop, the benefits of growing home vegetables are clear…it's cheaper, the vegetables taste better, and they aren't coated with pesticide spray. But the therapy that one achieves from such an activity is by far what keeps this gardener coming back year after year.[347]

Different from the garden at Blair Road, the Fort Stevens Community Garden across the street from the Civil War fortress was traditionally African American, reflecting the Brightwood neighborhood's rich heritage. Since the late 1980s, though, the demographic makeup of the garden members has changed with the changing makeup of the surrounding community. "A primarily African American garden became more international with Hispanic, African, Caribbean, and Asian members," the report notes. Common vegetables grown for healthy consumption at this international garden include tomatoes, okra, green beans, eggplant, pole beans and lettuce. Garlic, figs, cabbage, peppers, beets, zucchini, lettuce, peas and peanuts are also grown. Finally, sunflowers tower over parts of the community garden in the summertime.[348]

Although there are many advantages to community gardening, one benefit that's being realized more and more is its role in the modern "go green" movement. Ochs notes that by growing produce near home as opposed to driving to a grocery store, park roads have less car traffic:

Today, community gardens are perhaps an expression of a new kind of patriotism: the "greening of America." While large grocery stores haul produce from far afield, locally grown food reduces the need for transportation. This generates less air pollution and frees up space on crowded D.C. roads. There's no bulky packaging for the landfills, and gardeners use earth-friendly pest controls and fertilizers. Perhaps most significantly, the gardens offer their caretakers an awareness of nature's ability to soothe the city dweller's soul. That is exactly why Rock Creek Park was established and why the gardens remain popular for those who don't mind getting a little dirt under their nails.[349]

Superintendent Jim Redmond and the Rise of the Bicycle
Commuting without Polluting

"The late Jim Redmond had a deep appreciation for the park he superintended. He valued its importance as a natural oasis in the nation's capital," notes Barry Mackintosh in the first two sentences of *Rock Creek Park: An Administrative History*.[350] Indeed, if Colonel Lansing Beach was the guardian angel of the park in the 1890s, seventy years later, the angel, according to many, was Jim Redmond. Anyone who enjoys bicycling in the park or believes in energy conservation and sustainability should be interested in Redmond's legacy.

It is not a coincidence that the park began experimenting with alternative uses of park roads directly after Redmond arrived as manager of Rock Creek Park in the late 1960s. The first such experiment involved closing sections of Beach Drive to vehicles on Sundays so that walkers, joggers and cyclists could enjoy a safer and more serene experience in the park. This closure

Beach Drive road closure in Rock Creek Park. *Author's collection.*

200

Rock Creek Park superintendent Jim Redmond (right) and maintenance worker Michael Deas. *National Park Service.*

proved successful over time and in 1981, in a ribbon cutting ceremony somewhat mocking the opening of the traffic-causing Beach Drive-Zoo tunnel fifteen years earlier, Redmond, park staff and area bicycle lobbyists closed the section of roadway on both weekend days.[351]

While the Beach Drive road closure between Broad Branch Road and Joyce Road, as well as other park road closures, succeeded and continue on weekends and holidays to this day, another experiment most definitely did not. In 1971, one lane of the four-lane Rock Creek and Potomac Parkway was closed in order to allow bicyclists the opportunity to commute. Not enough bicyclists used the lane, however, and frustrated drivers sitting in traffic noticed the empty lane that they were not allowed to utilize. As a result, the lane closure lasted at most a week—one report suggests it lasted only a day. However, as a compromise with the increasingly powerful Washington Area Bicyclists Association and other environmental nonprofits, the paved multiuse trail that parallels the entire length of the parkway was constructed quickly. Although this trail terminated the long-standing tradition of horseback riding—riders commonly used the previous dirt trail—the use of the multiuse trail by joggers, cyclists and walkers has paid dividends over the years in the form of less car exhaust and carbon dioxide gas released into the atmosphere, not to mention the opportunity for healthy exercise.[352]

In the late 1970s, with President Carter pushing for energy and natural resource conservation programs, Jim Redmond and the park he superintended followed suit with bolder bicycle policies. With Redmond's support, the general management plan of the time was written to include an objective "to improve the quality of the visitor's experience by reducing excessive automobile commuter traffic on roads within Rock Creek Park, and encourage the shift of such traffic to mass transit, bicycle, and other more appropriate forms of transportation." Studies were made, and a few years later, the People's Alliance for Rock Creek Park (PARC), a loose group of environmental nonprofits, worked with Redmond on a proposal. According to it, Beach Drive between Broad Branch Road and Joyce Road were to be permanently closed to automobile traffic after the completion of the red line metro (D.C.'s subway system) in the mid-1980s. (It was thought that the metro line would decrease the traffic on roadways.) As a result, this closure would have terminated the tradition of the park being used as a commuter corridor. Thousands less vehicles per day would have used Beach Drive, thus turning the majority of the park into a bicycle-friendly area not only on weekends but on weekdays as well.[353]

Redmond supported the plan officially, despite the fact that many park neighbors, due to the threat of increasing traffic in their neighborhoods, did not. Perhaps if Redmond had not passed away in the middle of the debate, bicycle users would have gotten their way. After succumbing to a quick degeneration caused by cancer, Redmond died in middle age in 1983. Almost immediately afterward, National Park Service officials did an about-face and began opposing the plan. PARC, the National Parks Conservation Association, Washington Area Bicyclists Association (WABA) and other nonprofit groups were outraged by this change of heart. They protested, but to no avail.[354]

Fortunately, before his death, Redmond was instrumental in other park endeavors. While significant snowfall is not that common in the park, Redmond, again promoting recreation, made it a policy to have Ross Drive, Ridge Road, Sherrill Drive and Bingham Drive closed when snow accumulated. The roads were then not opened again until all the snow melted, enabling cross-country skiers to use the roadways as trails. This practice continues as a legacy of Redmond to this day.[355]

In terms of energy conservation, park enthusiasts might be surprised to know that from the 1950s into the 1980s, many park roads and especially intersections were lined with streetlights. In order to decrease electricity usage in the park, in the late '70s, Redmond and staff turned off all the lights. Though controversial and a practice opposed by some, the park manager noted that not many nighttime drivers utilized the park's roadways anyway and that the trails and grounds of the park beyond the roads were in fact closed at night. After Reagan and the rise of anti-environmentalism in the 1980s, the park continued to keep the streetlights off before finally removing all of them later in the decade.[356]

One final legacy of Redmond was his getting citizens involved in the park. The superintendent was one of the original founders of Friends of Rock Creek's Environment, or FORCE, now known as Rock Creek Conservancy. The park's nonprofit friends group, volunteers and staff from the group over the years have removed hundreds of tons of litter from the park. Redmond also brought in the Potomac Appalachian Trail Club, a volunteer-led organization, to maintain several trails in the park. Both organizations remain active in protecting and maintaining the park today.[357]

Throughout his fifteen-year tenure at Rock Creek Park, Redmond was highly regarded by his staff as well as environmental-minded citizens. "He was very much in touch with the park and wanted to protect it," notes Bill Yeaman, veteran natural resource manager who worked with Redmond for over a decade. Yeaman says that Redmond was constantly out and about in the park on both weekdays and weekends, always searching for ways to improve the visitor experience while at the same time protecting the park's natural integrity.[358]

After his death, in a small ceremony, park staff and Mrs. Redmond planted and dedicated a small grove of viburnum and flowering dogwoods in a field near the nature center.[359] These trees, as well as the weekend road closures and bicycle trails, among other things, stand as quiet memorials to Superintendent Jim Redmond.

Peggy Fleming and Park Meadows

Promoting Biodiversity Since 1977

Superintendent Jim Redmond was not the park's only nature protector in recent years. Peggy Fleming, the first and only official botanist the park has ever had, was instrumental as well. In order to conserve energy, reduce the use of gas-guzzling lawn mowers and increase biodiversity in the park, Fleming, under the direction of Bob Ford, created and then oversaw the year-to-year maintenance of approximately one dozen natural meadows throughout Rock Creek Park.

Begun in 1977, the meadows were mowed once a year and given year-round tender loving care in order to keep invasive plants in check. Native plants were also planted. The result was "not lawn, not woods, but something in between. The next results: new flora and fauna that flourish only under such circumstances."[360] Indeed, in the Military Field meadow located near the intersection of Glover Road and Military Road, milkweed now rules supreme. In the spring and early summer, hundreds of tall, green milkweed chutes race upward for the sun. Growing to heights of four feet, a light pink "ball" flower then blooms at the top of the chute. Fleming, who conducted research with her children in the meadows, also observed the comeback of numerous swallowtail butterflies (the yellow-and-black butterfly commonly seen in the park), short-tailed shrews, American goldfinches and dozens of insect species that are important for providing rich soil and flower pollination.[361]

While many of the meadows now suffer from invasive plant infestations, many still host unique native plants and wildlife found nowhere else in the

Milkweed and yellow swallowtail butterfly in the Military Field meadow. *Author's collection.*

park. A meadows brochure, developed by park natural resource staff in 2013, goes into more detail about the unique ecosystems.

Fleming's other major contribution to Rock Creek Park was her documenting and cataloguing of park plant species. Together with dedicated park volunteer Raclare Kanal, Fleming spent countless hours in the field exploring and documenting the vegetation in every nook and cranny of Rock Creek Park. The result was the *Annotated Checklist of Vascular Plants of Rock Creek Park, National Park Service, Washington, DC*, Rock Creek Park's first and only comprehensive list of plant species. The report documents both native and invasive plants and has proved invaluable to natural resource managers and researchers ever since.[362]

After sixteen years in Rock Creek Park studying and documenting its flora and implementing the meadow plan, Fleming moved on to her second career in the mid-1990s. Since then, she has served as a community promoter and environmental activist, having produced three photo-essay books documenting lesser-known stories of contemporary D.C. In 2013, Fleming co-directed, wrote and produced the documentary film *Potomac: A River Runs Through Us*. The thirty-minute film, available to watch for free on YouTube, discusses the benefits that the mighty river provides, the contemporary challenges it faces and the responsibility each person living in the Potomac watershed—the Rock Creek watershed is a part of the Potomac watershed—has to protect it.

Still a regular visitor to Rock Creek Park, Fleming notes, "When I walk in the park now, I still pull up Japanese honeysuckle along the sides of the paths. But I am in awe that this park exists…It has been 20 years since I retired. My children said they were glad to go in the park with me after I retired because I wasn't focused on the problems [as much], and we could just enjoy the gift of this forest to Washington."[363]

GARY SIKORA, PEG SHAW AND THE BLACK FOREST

Seasons' Greenings with Christmas Trees!

Anthropologist Margaret Meade once recommended to "never doubt that a small group of thoughtful, committed citizens can change the world. Indeed, they are the only ones that ever have." Regarding environmental protection in Rock Creek Park, two thoughtful, committed citizens include long time volunteers Gary Sikora and Peg Shaw. If a couple hundred citizens were as dedicated as Sikora and Shaw, the park would be much closer to "pristine."

Since 1988, Sikora and Shaw have spent an average of twenty hours a week, or a little over one thousand hours per year, bringing back biological diversity to a mile-long section of stream bank and adjacent slope. Their section of the park is known informally as the Black Forest and is located along Rock Creek and adjacent Rock Creek and Potomac Parkway between P Street and the Whitehurst Freeway overpass. Of their work area, Sikora and Shaw note that "we dream of a natural preserve with a single foot trail at the very top of the hill, with erosion stabilized and the park populated with native vegetation."[364]

Sikora, a soft-spoken individual and former bicycle and motorcycle messenger who has completed numerous natural history and stream bank restoration courses through Graduate School USDA and the Isaac Walton League, and Shaw, a general practice lawyer, live in an apartment in West End, a small neighborhood bordering Adams Morgan and Dupont Circle, just across the creek from Georgetown. They've completed numerous environmental protection projects in their neck of the woods, all as volunteers and therefore without compensation. One major task has been removing myriad social trails, caused over the years by park users. In their report to the park after twenty-five years of service, Sikora and Shaw noted:

> We closed 7,975 feet of linear feet of foot trail…We covered the soil with branches, scattered leaves and spread [native plant] seeds. The leaves prevent erosion, conserve soil moisture and add organic material to the soil when they decay. The branches and leaves hide the existence of former trails and give the area a natural appearance. We [also] planted 50 hazelnut trees on one closed trail and ash and redbud seedlings on other newly closed trails.[365]

Sikora, Shaw and occasional friends in the Black Forest have removed significant amounts of invasive plant species in their work area as well. They've practically eradicated all of the once prevalent Japanese knotweed. "It once grew six to eight feet tall and dominated the bank for almost the entire mile of the creek," the married couple note. Sikora and Shaw over the years have also removed tons of porcelainberry, Japanese honeysuckle, garlic mustard and English ivy, not to mention litter in rather bizarre variety.[366]

Going one step further than just removing invasive plants, the two park protectors have also encouraged growth of native plants. "The spread of Virginia creeper is perhaps our chief triumph. We encourage it by transplanting runners and distributing seeds into erosion-prone areas." Sikora and Shaw have also noted the comeback of poison ivy, a native plant that is good for wild animals. Due to its harmful oils that can cause itchiness for days on human skin, many park users and even some volunteers believe that poison ivy is bad and should be removed. Sikora and Shaw, however, advocate the fact that poison ivy is a protected species in Rock Creek Park.[367]

Other native plant species have been reintroduced to the slopes of the Black Forest by partners. In 2008, the National Arboretum donated half a dozen common milkweed seedpods to Sikora and Shaw, while in 2005, "Behkne Nursery trucked six cubic yards of oak leaves to our area for our use…The goal is to create conditions favorable for an oak-hickory forest." Finally, Sikora and Shaw obtained two hundred pawpaw and hazelnut seedlings between 2005 and 2007 and planted them with help from the Anacostia Watershed Society.[368]

Perhaps the couple's most unique project of all has been its means of mitigating stream bank erosion: the two placed over 4,500 Christmas trees at the edge of Rock Creek in order to rebuild the creek's most vulnerable sections. Sikora and Shaw's thought is that the "Christmas trees become part of the bank after they fill with sediment deposited by the creek's flowing waters…Our Christmas tree project is based on the hypothesis that roots of growing plants will gradually replace decaying Christmas trees and hold the trapped sediment in place." For this reason, they have started to plant trees with extensive root systems among the Christmas trees. The trees themselves get donated as "leftovers" from Christmas tree lots.[369]

With all the work they have done over the years, what is the reward? Due to improved natural habitat in their work area, Sikora and Shaw now occasionally observe native wildlife including red fox, deer, salamanders, a black rat snake and even a hive of honeybees. Symbolically, this wildlife thrives just ten blocks west of the White House in the Black Forest.[370]

REGENERATIVE STORMWATER CONVEYANCES
A Cutting-Edge Solution to Stormwater Runoff

By eroding stream banks, toppling trees and sending sediment and other pollutants into waterways, stormwater runoff is a major environmental problem for Rock Creek and all its tributaries. To purify this dirty water, slow it down, decrease erosion and recharge underground aquifers, the District Department of the Environment worked with Rock Creek Park and constructed two Regenerative Stormwater Conveyances, or RSCs, in the park in 2011. Viewable from the paved multiuse trail paralleling Oregon Avenue roughly one-third of a mile north of the Military Road intersection, the RSCs offer hope for a cleaner and greener Rock Creek.

Here's how they work. First, dirty water that picks up spilled car oil and sediment from streets and parking lots pours into the tributary of Rock Creek. Rather than racing straight down to the creek, though, the stormwater funnels into a series of step pools making up the RSC. The pools have a thick layer of sand below them, which acts as a natural purifier as some of the water filters underground. Most water, however, slowly filters downward from pool to pool. In between each pool are walls of stone and sand, which again act as purifiers. And so each pool contains slightly less contaminated water, until by the time the water reaches the creek, it is significantly cleaner than when it first entered the park.[371]

Aside from recharging groundwater, decreasing erosion and cleaning the dirty water, RSCs also provide new habitat in the form of ponds. Natural Resource Management specialist Bill Yeaman and the author have observed frogs and toads hopping into the pools as well as tall, native blooming flowering plants nearby.[372]

Rock Creek Park's RSCs were constructed carefully. Workers made their footprint on the land as light as possible by using preexisting roadways to dump construction material. Afterward—working with Casey Trees, a D.C. nonprofit—Rock Creek Conservancy volunteers and Yeaman planted about two hundred trees bordering the RSCs to stabilize the soil. In September 2013, Yeaman and the author led a large group of Discovery Channel volunteers in a "TLC for RSC Trees" community service event. Volunteers and staff meticulously weeded and mulched around each tree to reinvigorate it. They also enlarged deer fences around each tree to keep white-tailed deer from overbrowsing.

Regenerative Stormwater Conveyance in Rock Creek Park just off Oregon Avenue.
Author's collection.

Although the RSCs are pricey, costing around $1 million each, one could argue that when it comes to cleaner water, no price is too expensive. "The potential for additional RSCs in Rock Creek Park are good. Of course, it depends on funding in the long run, but RSCs are cost effective because they don't need much maintenance after their construction," Yeaman says.[373] In 2014, an additional RSC was completed on the upper portion of the Broad Branch Tributary, and with foresight and funding, additional RSCs will be constructed in the park and throughout other streams in the area facing the same problems.

11
NEW TRENDS AND RECENT RECREATION

A lthough front and center, it's not just environmental problems and the mitigation thereof that park managers and staff have been dealing with the past few decades. Throughout Rock Creek Park's history, new additions have been added, new forms of recreation have begun and new trends have started. This continues into the present, perhaps bringing the park's history full circle.

VOLUNTEERS AND INTERNS

Increasingly Important Staff of the National Park Service

Partisan politics over the federal government budget, as well as emphasis on increasing funding for the military and Department of Defense in recent years, has led to a decrease in the number of staff in Rock Creek Park. An early 1980s park photo depicts eighty-three full-time National Park Service employees working in Rock Creek Park. Today, this number has dwindled to fewer than fifty. The reality is that many positions in the park have gone unfilled. Although park maintenance workers do a lot with a little, much of the work they used to do is now contracted out in order to save money. Furthermore, in recent years, the Division of Interpretation staff has been cut substantially. An ever-increasing management and employee solution to this decreasing number of park staff has been the hiring and supervising of dedicated volunteers and interns. Although their seasonal or intermittent work does not make up for a year-round employee, interns and volunteers, serving in varying capacities, have proved integral over the last several decades and will continue to do so into the future. This brief article will spotlight the rise of volunteerism in Rock Creek Park.

While National Park Service director George Hartzog formalized the Volunteer in Parks (VIP) program in 1972, select citizens were volunteering in Rock Creek Park for years prior. From the moment Old Stone House opened to the public in 1960, for instance, volunteers were used to provide living history interpretation and demonstrations to visitors. In period costume, Girl Scouts baked and cooked old-timey style, spun yarn and knitted clothing, all using historic methods. In the '80s and '90s, adult volunteers took over these tasks. While the practice of living history interpretation proved popular, it terminated in the early 2000s because there was not enough full-time staff to provide the necessary oversight.[374]

In addition to Old Stone House volunteers, a park volunteer group that began in the '70s was the Potomac Appalachian Trail Club (PATC). A nonprofit, volunteer-run organization based on enhancing the hiking experience for outdoor recreationalists, PATC constructed new trails and formally established the green-blazed Western Ridge Trail and blue-blazed Valley Trail. PATC volunteers also constructed bridges over wet areas and repaired trails after storms. For example, in 1990, sixty members of the U.S. Marine Corps' Twelfth Battalion assisted the organization and park staff in returning the Melvin Hazen trail footbridge to its proper location after it had been moved downstream by floodwater. The PATC continues to maintain most trails in the park to this day.[375]

Recent volunteers and interns have done much for the park. Interpretive volunteers, generally volunteering once or twice a month, work to enhance the visitor experience. They staff the front desk at the Nature Center and provide visitor information and orientation. Meanwhile, interpretive volunteers working at historic Peirce Mill, many of whom are members or serve on the board of directors of Friends of Peirce Mill, provide informal tours of the inner workings of the mill during the summer months when it is open.

In a volunteer capacity as assistant miller, Richard Abbot served for several years as "jack of all trades for the mill" before formally establishing the friends group. Other mill volunteers (just two of many) have been Leah Yale Potter, who served as a living history interpreter during her teen years, and Marcia

Cole. A 1989 park volunteer newsletter notes that, joining the volunteer force in 1986, Cole "planned, planted, weeded, and nurtured Peirce Mill's herb garden. You can find Marcia working in the garden at any time and if asked, she gladly takes time to explain the use of the herbs grown here."[376]

In addition to interpretive volunteers, park partnerships with the Student Conservation Association, Geological Society of America and Washington Center have brought in passionate, hardworking college-aged interns to do everything from conducting interpretive geology hikes and children's archaeology programs to developing the first interpretive product related to climate change in park history. Interns differ from volunteers in that they generally volunteer full time in the park for a three- to four-month period. They sometimes receive housing and/or a small stipend for room and board, and they usually work in the park to gain career experience.

Not only have the park's trails and visitor experience benefited from volunteerism in recent years, but the park's naturalness and biological diversity have improved as well, as seen with Gary Sikora and Peg Shaw. Over the years, a countless number of unpaid individuals have rid the watershed of tens of thousands of pounds of trash and invasive, nonnative plants. Rock Creek Conservancy staff, its stream team leader volunteers and park staff have led countless community groups in volunteer projects over the years. Popular annual volunteer events include the Potomac Watershed Clean-Up in April (sponsored by the Alice Ferguson Foundation), the Martin Luther King Jr. National Day of Service in January and National Public Lands Day in September.

Specific commendable environmental protection projects include Rock Creek Conservancy's current goal of removing 100 percent of arborized English ivy. The ivy vines block sunlight from reaching the tree and also weigh it down, slowly killing it. And so by removing English ivy from the infested trees in the park, the tree's health is significantly improved. Current U.S. secretary of the interior Sally Jewel has volunteered with the conservancy to remove English ivy on at least two separate occasions.

Another good goal has been set farther south in the park by Dumbarton Oaks Park Conservancy, which was formally chartered in 2010. With only one part-time staff member, the conservancy nevertheless leads numerous invasive plant removal events with volunteers each year. Dumbarton Oaks Park Conservancy's goal is to restore the historic park to the way it looked in the 1950s. In the spring of 2014, the conservancy completed a restoration project that involved removing all invasive plants and planting native species in their place on the two-acre entrance to the park.

Boy Scout volunteers during and just after completing a litter cleanup on August 1, 1960. The current U.S. Park Police substation, known as D-3, is in the background of the above photo. Rock Creek Park's Litter Bug—or rather, anti-Litter Bug—is here as well. *National Park Service.*

Outside the main Rock Creek corridor, two friends groups in the late 1980s and early 1990s worked to benefit specific satellite units administered by Rock Creek Park. Volunteers of Friends of Battery Kemble Park, an organization since disbanded, worked to clean up the park and plant over one hundred trees. At the same time, Friends of Meridian Hill Park volunteers worked to make their namesake park safer. Described by a police officer in the early '80s as "a supermarket of drug dealing," Meridian Hill Park was a crime haven. Steve Coleman, executive director of D.C. nonprofit Washington Parks and People, which served as an umbrella organization over Friends of Meridian Hill Park, notes what volunteers and concerned citizens then did about the crime. "They organized a park patrol, which wore orange hats and carried no weapons but said, 'Hello' to everyone they met in the park. It's a simple thing, and it sounds corny but it really works," he says.[377]

Aside from friends groups' volunteers, several unique individual volunteers and interns have lent a helping hand to Rock Creek Park over the years. Recent notables include a former member of the U.S. men's Olympic soccer team, a young woman from Japan's Department of the Environment and a passionate young man who got arrested when he helped his Greenpeace team lower a banner with the words "Stop Global Warming" over the presidential faces of Mount Rushmore in 2010.

Although they should never act as a substitute for full-time, paid employees and although it takes full-time, paid employees to successfully recruit, manage, coordinate and supervise volunteers and interns, this unpaid labor force has been and will continue to be a major positive asset to Rock Creek Park.

POPULAR CULTURE AND THE MEDIA

Is Rock Creek Park the Most Dangerous Park in the United States?

Volunteers have majorly benefitted the park, but in many cases, popular culture and the media have not. Many U.S. citizens who were not born and raised in D.C. have heard of Rock Creek Park. They've heard of it thanks to the overdramatization of park violence by news outlets and popular culture.

Most of this attention is due to the Chandra Levy murder—a rare, ruthless incident involving a Capitol Hill intern who was killed in the park while she was jogging on the Western Ridge Trail by a sex offender. They might have also heard of the park thanks to television dramas. Popular shows, including *CSI*, *Bones* and *House of Cards*, have spotlighted fictional homicides, violence and/or suspense in the park. Finally, fictional murder-mystery novels also promote the myth of a violent Rock Creek Park. For example, the back cover of Simon Conway's *Rock Creek Park* reads, in part, "Former soldier Michael Freeman is now a homicide detective in Washington, D.C. As a massive snowstorm engulfs the city, a late night jogger in Rock Creek Park discovers the brutally beaten body of a once beautiful young woman." Popular culture and the media can and should be blamed for many of America's ills, and one of these ills has been to wrongly suggest over the past few decades that Rock Creek Park is incredibly violent. Nothing is farther from the truth.

Regrettably, murders, dumped bodies, the death of a homeless person and suicides do occur in the park—they occur all over America. In one way, shape or form, there is perhaps one visitor death in the park every couple years. However, compare this with overall violence and homicides in Washington, D.C., and Rock Creek Park is the safest place in the capital. Murder maps of the district show the park's large swath of land practically void of violence. At the same time, many neighborhoods that people believe to be safe are, in fact, more violent—for example, Columbia Heights.[378]

Compared with other large, urban parks around the country, Rock Creek Park also stands up well. New York City's Central Park, at half the size of Rock Creek Park, had nine violent crimes (including murder, rape and felony assault) in 2013 compared to one in Rock Creek Park. In 2001, Central Park had fourteen violent crimes. San Francisco's Golden Gate Park also has more hard crime than Rock Creek Park.[379]

Rock Creek Park is not the most dangerous park in the United States. On the contrary, it's one of the safest large, urban parks in the country. It's also the safest area of D.C. Female park visitors can make themselves even safer by hiking or jogging with a friend or family member rather than alone. Rock Creek Park should not be avoided on account of its myth of widespread violence.

Professional Tennis Tournaments

Andre Agassi Being Andre Agassi in Rock Creek Park

During a weeklong event from late July to early August every summer, tennis enthusiasts from around the region and professional tennis players from around the globe congregate at the William H.G. Fitzgerald Tennis Stadium located off Sixteenth Street in the vicinity of the Carter Barron Amphitheatre in Rock Creek Park. The tournament, known now as the Citi Open and previously known as the Legg Mason Classic, has hosted the biggest names in tennis over the years. Rock Creek Park is the only unit of the National Park System with a professional tennis stadium, and here's its history.

Although recreational tennis was enjoyed by many in the park for decades, the proposal of a professional tournament began in the late 1960s. At the time, the Washington Area Tennis Patrons Foundation, today known as the Washington Tennis and Education Foundation and hereafter referred to as WTEF, approached the National Park Service to see if it could use the existing NPS-built tennis stadium to hold tennis tournaments for charity and fundraising purposes. A D.C. nonprofit focused on improving the life prospects of at-risk, low-income, underserved youth through athletics and academic assistance, WTEF needed to increase funds to stay afloat. The NPS obliged, and in 1969, the Washington Star International Tennis Championships were held.[380]

With the first tournament's success, it became an annual event. As stadium seating expanded, major tennis stars began competing on Rock Creek Park's humble courts. African American tennis star Arthur Ashe, described as "one of the most visible and socially-conscious athletes of his day," who died later of AIDS, won the singles competition in 1973 and the doubles competition (playing with Bob Hewitt) in 1978. Other big-name winners prior to the construction of the present tennis stadium included Guillermo Villas, who is the only Argentinian tennis player to ever be elected into the Tennis Hall of Fame, in 1977 and 1979 and crowd favorite Jimmy Connors, who, over the course of his long career, was known for yelling at opponents, officials and the crowd.[381]

In the late 1980s, as tennis as a sport grew in popularity, so too did WTEF. In order to increase mentoring, educational and athletic services for the low-income African American youth whom it served and in addition to promoting tennis, WTEF approached the National Park Service as it had twenty years earlier. The idea now was for the construction of a tennis stadium "worthy of the nation's capital." The proposal and ultimate stadium construction was deemed controversial, however. Many neighbors did not want the added noise and traffic, while some park officials believed that a national park was not a place for professional sports. Furthermore, the limited number of parking spaces was an issue.[382]

After heated debate, the 7,500-seat tennis stadium was built and paid for by the tennis foundation. The stadium opened in 1989 as the William H.G.

William H.G. Fitzgerald Tennis Stadium in Rock Creek Park. *Guest Services, Inc.*

Fitzgerald Tennis Stadium, Fitzgerald being an area tennis enthusiast who donated significant funds for the facility's establishment. Although park and WTEF officials have continued to butt heads over the years—most notably in 1993, when the NPS ruled to permit only one large-scale event at the stadium per year—the annual tennis tournaments have proved wildly popular.[383]

In the two-and-a-half-decade existence of the park's large tennis stadium, spectators have perhaps most enjoyed watching superstar Andre Agassi. A regular at the tournament into the early 2000s, Agassi won the singles event in 1990, '91, '95, '98 and '99. A much newer addition to the tournament has been the women's competition, taking place alongside the men's since 2012.

For fifty weeks per year, the William H.G. Fitzgerald Tennis Stadium inside Rock Creek Park is enjoyed by recreational tennis players getting their afternoon workout on, as well as WTEF staff and the youth it serves. During the fifty-first and fifty-second weeks, though, the facility and parking lot turns into a professional venue, complete with VIP area, tennis vendors and, of course, an abundance of exceptional tennis matches for the public to enjoy. This is how things currently stand.

Oddisee's Rock Creek Park

Bringing the Beat Back

While professional tennis in a national park unit is unique, another recent piece of recreation makes Rock Creek Park unique as well. In 2010, national capital area musician Amir Mohamed, better known by his stage name Oddisee, became the first (and only to date) African American in the United States to produce an album about a national park unit. The park he chose? None other than the national capital's largest and most natural.

Singles off Oddisee's instrumental-soul album *Rock Creek Park* include "Skipping Rocks," "The Carter Barron," "Beach Drive" and more. The album represents a unique take on the musician's view of the park: "If the park were to have a soundtrack, what would it be? What does walking along the trails of the park sound like? What does driving on the narrow tree-lined roads sound like? This album is my interpretation of Rock Creek Park through break beats, samples and live instrumentation." Oddisee continues:

Rock Creek Park is and has always been one of my favorite places in Washington, DC. It has a way of aging with you and adapting to where you are in life. When I was younger, it was a place for skipping rocks, bike rides and imaginary adventures in the woods. As a teen it was a place where I played basketball, had cookouts with friends & walked through with dates. As an adult it's my short cut through the city, my quickest way from Silver Spring to Georgetown. One thing it still is and always will be is my retreat.[384]

In addition to *Rock Creek Park*, Oddisee has been a workhorse in his fifteen-year career, producing an astounding twenty-one albums since going professional in 1999. Though his music has been featured on ESPN and National Public Radio, the musician considers himself non-mainstream and is proud of it. Quietly recording and performing, Oddisee has toured nationally and internationally and spends his time today between Washington, D.C., and New York City. Oddisee was born to a Sudanese father and African American mother in Prince Georges County.

CONCLUSION

This book has attempted to shed light on the incredibly diverse and rich heritage of Rock Creek Park, the largest and first park in the nation's capital, one of the largest urban nature parks managed by the National Park Service and one of the largest urban nature parks, period.

The park's history continues into the present, specifically in regards to official names of the park and park units. In 2014, D.C. congresswoman Eleanor Holmes Norton introduced a bill to reclassify Rock Creek Park as "Rock Creek National Park in the District of Columbia" in order to "clarify the difference between Rock Creek Park under federal jurisdiction in the District and the contiguous portion owned by the state of Maryland." Additionally, Norton hopes that

> *in renaming the park, "Rock Creek National Park in the District of Columbia," the bill will highlight the park's significance to the nation, the residents of the District and region, and visitors to the nation's capital…"This redesignation would highlight the importance of the park and its place among our nation's other magnificent national parks," said Norton. "I hope that it would help in our efforts to attract even more visitors from our city and every part of the region and nation to the park to enjoy the unusual outdoor space located in the midst of a great city."*[385]

Renaming the park "Rock Creek National Park" would indeed give the park more recognition. It would also resolve its identity crisis; the fact that Rock Creek Park is a unit of the National Park System but does not have the word "national" anywhere in its title confuses a lot of visitors. The problem of park identities is actually an issue for many national park units. Fortunately, there is a growing school of thought within the National Park Service and some of its partners to redesignate all national park units as official National Parks to solve this issue.[386] All this said, Rock Creek Park has been the official name of the park for 125 years now, and one could argue that the name itself has become historical in its own right and should not be changed.

At any rate, Congresswoman Norton also introduced a bill reclassifying the Civil War Defenses of Washington, which includes the Rock Creek Park–administered Civil War sites, to "Civil War Defenses of Washington National Historical Park."[387] For much the same reason that Fort Stevens–Lincoln National Military Park was proposed by its namesake association over one hundred years ago, the new title would promote the importance and significance of sites such as Fort Stevens and Battleground National Cemetery. It would also promote the fact that the parks are managed by the National Park Service.

Regardless of park naming issues, as Rock Creek Park continues its path of existence and evolution further into the twenty-first century, it will continue to need help. It needs help in sharing its heritage as well as help in protecting its sensitive environment and cultural resources. With or without your pocket book, there are several ways you yourself can assist the park:

- Continue learning about the park by virtually visiting the park website and park partner websites. The official Rock Creek Park website for the National Park Service is www.nps.gov/rocr/, while Meridian Hill Park's own website is www.nps.gov/mehi/. Park partner websites include www.rockcreekconservancy.org for Rock Creek Conservancy, www.peircemill-friends.org/ for Friends of Peirce Mill and www.dopark.org for Dumbarton Oaks Park Conservancy. Other park partners include the Alice Ferguson Foundation (http://fergusonfoundation.org/), Potomac Appalachian Trail Club (http://www.patc.net/PublicView/) and Student Conservation Association (http://thesca.org/).

- Continue learning about the park by attending a ranger-led program in person. Rock Creek Park interpretive park rangers offer a wide variety of programs for all ages on topics varying from astronomy and nature to history and environmental education. The official park website has a link to its schedule of events. You can also grab a schedule of events and/or sign up for the park's weekly schedule e-mail blast at the Rock Creek Park Nature Center.

- Volunteer for one of the park partners and then share your experience and talk about what you learned with friends and family. The Rock Creek Conservancy and Dumbarton Oaks Park Conservancy host several volunteer events each month in order to restore the naturalness of park ecosystems and garner community involvement and activism.

- Become a national parks philanthropist and donate to one of Rock Creek Park's many partners so that they can continue and even expand what they do. Nonprofit partners of Rock Creek Park include Rock Creek Conservancy, Dumbarton Oaks Park Conservancy, Friends of Peirce Mill, Alice Ferguson Foundation, the National Tennis and Education Foundation and Student Conservation Association, among others.

- Enjoy and explore Rock Creek Park. Take a hike. Trail run. Bicycle. Play tennis. Watch tennis. Visit the nature center. Visit Peirce Mill. Visit Old Stone House. Visit Fort Stevens. Visit Fort DeRussy. Attend a concert at Carter Barron Amphitheatre. Golf. Go horseback riding. Visit history sites spotlighted in this book. Sit and write a poem by the creek. Picnic with the family. Do yoga in the park. Walk with your dog. The opportunities for recreation in Rock Creek Park are endless. Be sure to share and discuss your experiences in the park with friends and family.

ROCK CREEK PARK:
SOMETHING TO CELEBRATE

[In 2015, Rock Creek Park celebrates its 125th birthday.] *Only a handful of national parklands have existed longer as such. The occasion will be something to celebrate.*

The century [and a quarter] *of this urban natural park—almost a contradiction in terms—has been one of challenges. As its birth was achieved only after much effort, so was its extension by the Rock Creek and Potomac Parkway and other additions. The natural qualities for which it was set aside have been perennially threatened by pressures for incompatible development and uses—some of which have prevailed. The park will not satisfy those who seek solitude in wilderness.*

But it is not supposed to. Rock Creek Park was envisioned to preserve some attractive natural scenery for public enjoyment in the midst of a growing city, whose outer reaches were largely rural in 1890 but whose total urbanization was even then a certainty. It would be set aside from the city, yet it would be of the city. Washington residents and visitors would come on foot, on horseback, by carriage, and soon by automobile to enjoy an hour's or an afternoon's contrast from the neighboring streets and buildings. Increasingly, they would just pass through on their way to other destinations—yet even such brief windshield contacts with natural surroundings would enrich.

The law of supply and demand operates for natural preserves as much as for other commodities. Thus, as the urban and suburban encirclement of the park has become complete, its value has increased. Its presence in the midst of the nation's capital, so much taken for granted, is in fact a marvel. Driving through such a valley in remote country would be a pleasant experience but hardly an extraordinary one. Coming south from Maryland along Beach Drive, knowing that one is bisecting the capital yet seeing only the creek, rocks, and forested valley slopes until one is virtually at the city center—that is indeed an extraordinary experience for those who pause to ponder it.

A small jewel on a contrasting cloth can appeal as much as a large jewel in a setting of other gemstones. Rock Creek Park is not Yosemite, its fellow 1990 centenarian. But to those who appreciate the wonder of its existence, it gleams no less brightly.

—Barry Mackintosh, National Park Service historian

NOTES

CHAPTER 1

1. National Park Service, "Native Americans in the Rock Creek Valley," http://www.nps.gov/pimi/forteachers/upload/nativeindepth.pdf. Today, only one of the animals on the list can still be found in Rock Creek Park: the American beaver. The others became extinct in the region due to changing climates and, more recently, overhunting and more extensive land use.
2. William Henry Holmes to Clarence Sherrill, Washington, D.C., April 6, 1925, in Jennifer Moran, *Rediscovering Archeological Resources at Rock Creek Park* (Washington, D.C.: Department of the Interior, National Park Service, 1997), Rock Creek Park, Interpretation Subject Files.
3. National Park Service, "Native Americans in the Rock Creek Valley."
4. John Bedell, Stuart Fiedel and Charles LeeDecker, *Bold, Rocky, and Picturesque: The Archeology and History of Rock Creek Park* (Philadelphia: Eastern National, 2013), 7–8; National Park Service, *Ancient Native Americans in Rock Creek Park*, brochure.
5. Bedell, Fiedel and LeeDecker, *Bold, Rocky, and Picturesque.*
6. History is technically the study of written past.
7. Marie MacNeil, *Ninian Beall and the Rock of Dumbarton: A Preliminary Study* (1938). A copy of Beall's will is included in the study.
8. Ibid.
9. Ibid.
10. Ibid.
11. National Park Service, "Georgetown Historic District," http://www.nps.gov/nr/travel/wash/dc15.htm.

12. National Park Service, "Old Stone House History," in *Old Stone House Volunteer Handbook* (1978), Old Stone House, Interpretation Subject Files.

13. National Park Service, *Owners of Old Stone House*, Old Stone House, Interpretation Subject Files.

14. Cornelius Heine, *Old Stone House History* (Washington, D.C.: Department of the Interior, National Park Service, 1955), 14.

15. *Washington Post*, "How Sam Rayburn's Speech Saved the Old Stone House."

16. Heine, *Old Stone House History*.

17. Allen C. Clark, "Suter's Tavern," *Records of the Columbia Historical Society*, Vols. 42–43, 117. Quoted in Heine, *Old Stone House History*.

18. Heine, *Old Stone House History*.

19. National Park Service, *The War of 1812*, http://www.nps.gov/subjects/warof1812/index.htm.

20. National Park Service, *James Lingan's Funeral in Parrott's Woods*, Old Stone House, Interpretation Subject Files.

21. National Park Service, "First Blood: the Baltimore Riots," http://www.nps.gov/stories/first-blood.htm.

22. Ibid.

23. National Park Service, *James Lingan's Funeral in Parrott's Woods*.

24. Ibid.

25. Ibid.

26. Arlington National Cemetery, http://public.mapper.army.mil/ANC/ANCWeb/PublicWMV/ancWeb.html. Lingan's grave location is in Section 1, Grave 89-A; National Park Service, *James McCubbin Lingan Funeral*, Old Stone House, Interpretation Subject Files.

27. National Park Service, *Cultural Landscape Inventory: Linnaean Hill*, Part 2A, 5, Rock Creek Park, Cultural Resource Subject Files.

28. Steve Dryden, *Peirce Mill: Two Hundred Years in the Nation's Capital* (Washington, D.C.: Friends of Peirce Mill, Inc., 2009), 33; National Park Service, *Cultural Landscape Inventory: Linnaean Hill*, Part 2A, 4.

29. Dryden, *Peirce Mill*; National Park Service, *Cultural Landscape Inventory: Linnaean Hill*, Part 4, 15.

30. Peirce Shoemaker, *Historic Rock Creek* (Washington, D.C.: Columbia Historical Society, April 14, 1908), http://archive.org/stream/jstor-40066992/40066992_djvu.txt; Dryden, *Peirce Mill*, 28.

31. Dryden, *Pierce Mill*, 28.

32. John D. Rhodes, "How Rock Creek Park Was Established," *Atlantic Monthly* 12, no. 6 (October 1954).

33. Bedell, Fiedel and LeeDecker, *Bold, Rocky, and Picturesque*, 47; National Park Service, *Cultural Landscape Inventory: Linnaean Hill*, Part 2A, 6.

34. Dryden, *Peirce Mill*; Jessica Carlton, *The Peirce Family and Their Former Slaves* (Washington, D.C.: Department of the Interior, National Park Service, 2013), 14.

35. Ibid.

36. Pernell Holmes, Sabina Wiedenhoeft and Cynthia R. Field, "The History of the Columbia Mill," Smithsonian Institution, http://www.si.edu/ahhp/h_mills. Peirce Mill was also built in the Oliver Evans automated-mill style. Evans's patent for his automated mill system was U.S. patent number three, signed into effect by Thomas Jefferson. A largely unknown yet significant figure of the Industrial Revolution, Evans was a cutting-edge New Jersey miller. His new, advanced mill design, with features such as automatic grain elevators and an automatic hopper boy, decreased the need of labor at the mill from several workers down to just one, the miller. Unfortunately for Evans, he was often taken advantage of. Most mill owners who designed their mills after Evans's automated system never compensated him. Early failures of the patenting system like this eventually led to the very stringent standards and laws that are in place today.

37. Ibid.

38. Smithsonian Institution, "Records Relating to Pre-National Zoological Park Purchases," http://www.si.edu/ahhp/h_prezoo.

39. Holmes, Wiedenhoeft and Field, "History of the Columbia Mill."

40. William Bushong, *Rock Creek Park Historic Resource Study* (Washington, D.C.: Department of the Interior, National Park Service, 1990), 36.

41. National Park Service, *Blagden Mill*, exhibit at Peirce Barn.

42. Ibid., *Historic Mills of Rock Creek*, Rock Creek Park, Interpretation Subject Files.

43. Ibid.

44. Stephen H. Lewis, *Historical Report: Godey Limekilns, Washington, D.C.*, (Washington, D.C.: Department of the Interior, National Park Service, 1965), Old Stone House, Interpretation Subject Files.

45. Part of Harpers Ferry National Historical Park, the hike up and around Maryland Heights is 6.5 miles round trip from the historic town and travels past lime quarries, such as the ones Godey used.

46. Lewis, *Historical Report: Godey Limekilns.*

47. Ibid.

48. Ibid.

49. Joaquin Miller, *Joaquin Miller's Poems*, vol. 1 (San Francisco, CA: Whitaker and Ray Company, 1909), 2.

50. Walt Curtis, "Joaquin Miller," Oregon Cultural Heritage Commission, 1995, http://www.ochcom.org/miller/.

51. Martin Severin Peterson, *Joaquin Miller: Literary Frontiersman* (Palo Alto, CA: Stanford University Press, 1937), 88; M.M. Marberry, *Joaquin Miller: Splendid Poseur* (New York: Thomas Y. Crowell Company 1953), 24, 32.

52. Marberry, *Joaquin Miller*, 58–59.

53. Curtis, "Joaquin Miller."

54. Marberry, *Joaquin Miller*, 158–60.

55. Ibid., 179.

56. Kathy Morrison-Taylor, "The Poet's Cabin: Joaquin Miller in Washington, D.C.," *Beltway Poetry Quarterly*, http://washingtonart.com/beltway/jmiller.html.

57. Marberry, *Joaquin Miller*, 224–25.

58. Quoted in National Park Service, "Rim Road Celebrates 100 Years: Construction of the Skyline Boulevard Began in 1913," *Crater Lake National Park Newspaper*, summer 2013.

CHAPTER 2

59. "C-SPAN Historians Presidential Leadership Survey," http://legacy.c-span.org/PresidentialSurvey/Overall-Ranking.aspxA. The survey ranks Buchanan as dead last. An article on the U.S. News and World Report website also ranks Buchanan as the worst president: http://www.usnews.com/news/history/features/the-10-worst-presidents.

60. Frank Freidel and Hugh Sidey, "James Buchanan," White House Historical Society, 2006, http://www.whitehouse.gov/about/presidents/jamesbuchanan. Aside from the statue of Buchanan himself, the Buchanan Memorial includes two allegorical figures, one representing diplomacy and the other law. These are fitting statues, considering Buchanan's background and decades as a lawyer and diplomat.

61. Jean H. Baker, *James Buchanan* (New York: Henry Holt and Company, 2004), 60–62.

62. Ibid., 114.

63. Ibid., 25–26.

64. Ibid., 124–25.

65. Ibid., 137.

66. Ibid., 3.

67. National Park Service, "Civil War Defenses of Washington," http://www.nps.gov/cwdw/planyourvisit/upload/Civial%20War%20defenses%20of%20Washington_final.pdf.

68. National Park Service, "Fort DeRussy," http://www.nps.gov/cwdw/historyculture/fort-derussy.htm.

69. William Todd, *The Seventy-Ninth Highlanders: New York Volunteers in the War of the Rebellion 1861–1865* (Albany, NY: Brandon, Barton and Co., 1886), 12–13, https://archive.org/details/seventyninthhigh00toddrich.

70. Zack Spratt, *Rock Creek's Bridges*, (Washington, D.C.: Columbia Historical Society, 1953), 106.

71. William A. Spicer, *History of the Ninth and Tenth Regiments, Rhode Island Volunteers, and the Tenth Rhode Island Battery, in the Union Army in 1862*

(Providence, RI: Snow & Farnham, 1892), 259–61, http://archive.org/historyninthand01spigoog.

72. Quoted in Benjamin Franklin Cooling III and Walton H. Owen II, *Mr. Lincoln's Forts: A Guide to the Civil War Defenses of Washington* (Lanham, MD: Scarecrow Press, 2010), 170–71.

73. Ibid., 171.

74. *Washington Post*, "Wild Target Shooting," September 16, 1883.

75. Jubal Anderson Early and Ruth Hairston Early, *Leiutenant General Jubal Anderson Early, C.S.A.* (Philadelphia: J.B. Lippincott Company, 1912), 390, http://books.google.com/books?id=0xtCAAAAIAAJ&pg=PA390&lpg=PA390&dq=%22on+the+right+was+rock+creek%22+jubal+early&source=bl&ots=d2aZaysE_7&sig=smTNZLUrj_IFfhNrmUlQ2CCqcw8&hl=en&sa=X&ei=yGQxU9udOsezqQH304HgAw&ved=0CCwQ6AEwAQ#v=onepage&q=%22on%20the%20right%20was%20rock%20creek%22%20jubal%20early&f=false.

76. National Park Service, *Battle of Fort Stevens*, Brochure; U.S. Army, *Report of Captain John Norris, Second Provisional Pennsylvania Heavy Artillery, of the Defenses of Washington* (Fort DeRussy, D.C., July 16, 1864), Rock Creek Park, Interpretation Subject Files.

77. U.S. Senate, *Letter from the Assistant Clerk of the Court of Claims Transmitting a Copy of the Findings of the Court in the Case of Elizabeth Thomas Against the United States*, 58th Cong., 3rd sess., December 15, 1904.

78. National Park Service, "Elizabeth Proctor Thomas," http://www.nps.gov/history/cultural_landscapes/People-Thomas.html. Although the website states that Thomas was finally compensated for her property when she was ninety-five years old, most other accounts say she was never compensated.

79. National Park Service, "Fort Stevens," http://www.nps.gov/cwdw/historyculture/fort-stevens.htm.

80. Author discussion with Mary Brazell, Rock Creek Park interpretive park ranger.

81 National Park Service, *Civil War Defenses of Washington*, brochure.

82. Quoted in National Park Service, "Civil War Defenses of Washington," www.nps.gov/cwdw.

83. National Park Service, *Civil War Defenses of Washington: Historic Resource Study*, http://www.cr.nps.gov/history/online_books/civilwar/hrs1-7.htm.

84. Joseph Judge, *Season of Fire: The Confederate Strike on Washington* (Berryville, VA: Rockbridge Publishing Company, 1994), 235–36. Quoted in Benjamin Franklin Cooling III, *The Day Lincoln Was Almost Shot: The Fort Stevens Story* (Lanham, MD: Scarecrow Press, 2013), 129.

85. National Park Service, *Civil War Defenses of Washington: Historic Resource Study*.

86. Cooling, *Day Lincoln Was Almost Shot*, 152–53.

87. National Park Service, *Battle of Fort Stevens*. The exact story of Lincoln standing on top of the parapet at Fort Stevens has been debated for decades. Some accounts claim that Elizabeth Thomas was the one who yelled at Lincoln to get down, while an even more popular account credits U.S. Supreme Court justice Oliver Wendell Holmes for the commentary.

88. Ibid.

89. Quoted in National Park Service, *Battle of Fort Stevens*.

90. National Park Service, *Battleground National Cemetery Superintendent's Lodge Physical History and Condition Assessment*, March 1, 2004, Rock Creek Park, Interpretation Subject Files.

91. George T. Stevens, *Three Years in the Sixth Corps: A Concise Narrative of Events in the Army of the Potomac, From 1861 to the Close of the Rebellion, April, 1865* (Albany: S.R. Gray, Publisher, 1866), 368, http://www.gutenberg.org/files/21976/21976-h/21976-h.htm. In the book, Stevens also gives an account of army life at Meridian Hill, then a Civil War camp.

92. Ron Harvey, *Buried in History: The Five Misidentified Graves at Battleground National Cemetery* (Washington, D.C.: Department of the Interior, National Park Service, 2008), Rock Creek Park, Interpretation Subject Files.

93. Ibid.

94. *Washington Post*, "Campbell, Last of City's Defenders, Dies," March 11, 1936.

95. Harvey, *Buried in History.*

96. U.S. Army Corps of Engineers, "Commanders of the Corps of Engineers," http://www.usace.army.mil/about/history/commanders.aspx.

97. National Park Service, *Preserving Fort Jefferson*, http://www.nps.gov/drto/upload/Restoration%20site%20bulletin4.pdf.

98. Cooling and Owen, *Mr. Lincoln's Forts*, 61.

99. Cooling, *Day Lincoln Was Almost Shot*, 16.

100. National Park Service, "John Gross Barnard," http://www.nps.gov/cwdw/historyculture/john-gross-barnard.htm.

101. John Gross Barnard, *Professional Papers of the Corps of Engineers U.S. Army, No. 20, A Report on the Defenses of Washington to the Chief of Engineers, U.S. Army*, U.S. Army, 1871.

102. Henry L. Abbot, *Biographical Memoir of John Gross Barnard*, National Academy of Sciences, April 17, 1902, http://www.nasonline.org/publications/biographical-memoirs/memoir-pdfs/barnard-john.pdf. Barnard himself presented a biographical lecture on the life and legacy of Joseph Totten to the National Academy of Sciences. This publication can also be accessed online.

103. National Park Service, "Living Contraband: Former Slaves in the Nation's Capital during the Civil War," http://www.nps.gov/resources/story.htm?id=227.

104. Ibid.

105. Ibid.

106. John Hampton, e-mail message to author, January 6, 2014.

107. John Munro Longyear, "Georgetown during the Civil War," *Georgetown Today*, March 7, 1975, 10. Quoted in National Park Service, *Civil War Defenses of Washington: Historic Resource Study*.

108. George Alfred Townsend, *Washington, Outside and Inside: A Picture and a Narrative of the Origin, Growth, Excellences, Abuses, Beauties, and Personages of Our Governing City* (Hartford, CT: James Betts & Co., 1873), 219–20. Quoted in National Park Service, *Civil War Defenses of Washington: Historic Resources Study*.

109. Ibid.

110. National Park Service, *Meridian Hill Park History*, Rock Creek Park, Interpretation Subject Files.

111. *The Baptist Encyclopedia: A Dictionary of Doctrines*, vol. 2, edited by William Cathcart (Philadelphia: Louis H. Everts, 1881), 1,223, http://books.google.com/books?id=h0g4AQAAMAAJ&pg=PA1223&lpg=PA1223&dq=Wayland+Seminary+Meridian+Hill&source=bl&ots=7u-ug7L9b-&sig=nZpqRyhRMDalBOjYfkHX729g8Gk&hl=en&sa=X&ei=amb-UpiRCOnOyQHxvoDIBg&ved=0CDMQ6AEwBTgK#v=-onepage&q=Wayland%20Seminary%20Meridian%20Hill&f=false.

CHAPTER 3

112. Barry Mackintosh, *Rock Creek Park: An Administrative History* (Washington, D.C.: Department of the Interior, National Park Service, 1985), 1.

113. Pamela Scott, *Capital Engineers: The U.S. Army Corps of Engineers in the Development of Washington, D.C. 1790–2004* (Alexandria, VA: U.S. Army Corps of Engineers 2005), 160.

114. U.S. Army Corps of Engineers, *Report of Brevet Brigadier General N. Michler, Major of Engineers, United States Army, in Charge of Public Buildings, Grounds, Works, &C.*, Washington, D.C., 1867.

115. Much of Michler's engineering and mapmaking tools are on display at Chamizal National Memorial in El Paso, Texas. Ironically, and simply by chance, the author worked at Chamizal from 2008 to 2010. He discovered the Michler link between Chamizal and Rock Creek Park only after becoming a ranger at Rock Creek Park.

116. U.S. Army Corps of Engineers, *Report of Brevet Brigadier General N. Michler*, 15–16.

117. Scott, *Capital Engineers*, 74.

118. U.S. Army Corps of Engineers, *Report of Brevet Brigadier General N. Michler*, 15–16.

119. Ibid. Perhaps not all of Michler's proposals were out of place, though. The author agrees with one: removing select trees in specific park locations in order to give visitors outstanding views of the Rock Creek Valley. "Beautiful vistas, artistically arranged, can be cut through them, exhibiting distant points of landscape," he noted. Removing a few trees from atop Pulpit Rock and on a trail overlooking Boulder Bridge so that visitors can gain a romantic view might be a worthwhile endeavor.

120. Ibid.

121. Timothy Davis, *Rock Creek Park Road System*, Historic American Engineering Record, HAER No. DC-55 (Washington, D.C.: Department of the Interior, National Park Service, 1996), http://lcweb2.loc.gov/pnp/habshaer/dc/dc0900/dc0966/data/dc0966data.pdf, 31.

122. Ibid.

123. *Washington Post*, "Underground Engineering: Captain Hoxie's Report of the Sewers and Water Supply," November 25, 1883.

124. Newbold Noyes, "Tribute to Charles Carroll Glover," Columbia Historical Society, January 4, 1938, http://www.jstor.org/discover/10.2307.

125. John D. Rhodes, "How Rock Creek Park Was Established," *Atlantic Monthly* 12, no. 6 (October 1954).

126. Carlton Fletcher, "Charles Carroll Glover," http://gloverparkhistory.com/estates-and-farms/alliance-farm/charles-carrol-glover/.

127. *Washington Post*, "Capital Mourns Charles Glover, City Benefactor," February 26, 1936. Glover Archbold Park is an administrative unit of Rock Creek Park.

128. Rhodes, "How Rock Creek Park Was Established."

129. Ibid.

130. Mackintosh, *Rock Creek Park*, 12–13; Davis, *Rock Creek Park Road System*, 33. One example of Shepherd's ruthlessness is accounted for by DC Cultural Tourism. The nonprofit group notes that in the Shaw neighborhood, Shepherd ordered the razing of a marketplace in the middle of the night without warning any residents. As a result, several African Americans inside the market were killed: http://www.culturaltourismdc.org/portal/c/document_library/get_file?uuid=5bf6de4f-5382-4fc6-a69c-b68939e98e3e&groupId=701982.

131. Bushong, *Rock Creek Park Historic Resource Study*, 71.

132. *Washington Post*, "Capital Mourns Charles Glover, City Benefactor," February 26, 1936.

133. U.S. Congress, *An Act Authorizing the Establishment of a Public Park in the District of Columbia*, 51st Cong., sess. I, September 27, 1890.

134. Quoted in Cornelius W. Heine, *The Contributions of Charles Carroll Glover and Other Citizens to the Development of the National Capital* (Washington, D.C.: Department of the Interior, National Park Service, 1952), 10.

CHAPTER 4

135. U.S. Supreme Court, "*Shoemaker v. United States* - 147 U.S. 282 (1893)," http://supreme.justia.com/cases/federal/us/147/282; Bushong, *Rock Creek Park Historic Resource Study*, 77.

136. Dryden, *Peirce Mill*, 60.

137. Shoemaker, *Historic Rock Creek*.

138. Ibid.

139. U.S. Army Corps of Engineers, "Commanders of the Corps of Engineers," http://www.usace.army.mil/about/history/commanders.aspx.

140. *Washington Evening Star,* October 3, 1903. Quoted in Bushong, *Rock Creek Park Historic Resource Study*; Davis, *Rock Creek Park Road System*, 39.

141. National Park Service, *Cultural Landscape Report: Rock Creek Park Historic Trails*, 2012, 30.

142. Davis, *Rock Creek Park Road System*, 58.

143. Ibid., 40–41.

144. U.S. Congress, *Park Improvement Papers of the District of Columbia*, Senate Committee on the District of Columbia, Washington, D.C., 1903, 113, https://ia600600.us.archive.org/26/items/parkimprovementp00moor/parkimprovementp00moor.pdf; Davis, *Rock Creek Park Road System*, 44.

145. Davis, *Rock Creek Park Road System*, 58.

146. National Park Service, *Boulder Bridge*, HAER No. DC-12, 1988, http://lcweb2.loc.gov/pnp/habshaer/dc/dc0600/dc0625/data/dc0625data.pdf.

147. Gail Spilsbury, *Rock Creek Park* (Baltimore, MD: Johns Hopkins University Press, 2003), 57; Spratt, *Rock Creek's Bridges*, 109–11.

148. Davis, *Rock Creek Park Road System*, 44.

149. Ibid., 45.

150. Quoted in Mackintosh, *Rock Creek Park*, 74.

151. U.S. Congress, *Park Improvement Papers of the District of Columbia*, 111.

152. National Park Service, *Milkhouse Ford*, HAER No. DC-25, Washington, D.C., 1992, http://lcweb2.loc.gov/pnp/habshaer/dc/dc0700/dc0762/data/dc0762data.pdf. In the Brightwood neighborhood, in between Fort Stevens and Rock Creek Park, there is a narrow roadway named Rock Creek Ford Road. This road originally went straight down to its namesake ford, now known as Milkhouse Ford.

153. *Washington Post*, "Boy, 9, Drowned Wading in Rock Creek Park Ford," August 7, 1932; Spratt, *Rock Creek's Bridges*, 116–17.

154. National Park Service, *Historic Landscape Report: Historic Trails of Rock Creek Park*, Historic Trails Map, 2012, Rock Creek Park, Cultural Resource Subject Files.

155. William P. Richards to the engineer commissioner, December 1, 1903. Quoted in National Park Service, *Historic Landscape Report: Historic Trails of Rock Creek Park*, 34, Rock Creek Park, Nature Center Subject File.

156. Ibid.

157. Spratt, *Rock Creek's Bridges*, 106; National Park Service, *Historic Landscape Report: Historic Trails of Rock Creek Park*, 40.

158. National Park Service, *Historic Landscape Report: Historic Trails of Rock Creek Park*, 39–40.

159. Frederick Law Olmsted Jr. and John Charles Olmsted, *Rock Creek Park: Report by Olmsted Brothers* (Washington, D.C.: National Park Service, 1918), 22, http://www.nps.gov/history/history/online_books/rocr/olmsted_brothers.pdf.

160. U.S. Congress, *Statements before the Subcommittee on Appropriations, United States Senate*, 63rd Cong., 2nd sess., H.R. 10523, 68–69, http://books.google.com/books?id=GrctAAAAMAAJ&pg=RA1-PA68&lpg=RA1-PA68&dq=Henry+Cabot+Lodge+Rock+Creek+Park&source=bl&ots=3L8ClOR7YQ&sig=agrKSIcCShVHsn6S9Uw1bnr5mzI&hl=en&sa=X&ei=dY4MU8LQC-m2yAHixoCwDQ&ved=0CCcQ6AEwAQ#v=onepage&q=Henry%20Cabot%20Lodge%20Rock%20Creek%20Park&f=false.

161. U.S. Forest Service, *Species:* Juniperus virginiana, http://www.fs.fed.us/database/feis/plants/tree/junvir/all.html.

162. Greenleaf to Sherrill, March 3, 1922; Moore to Ridley, May 22, 1920. Quoted in Mackintosh, *Rock Creek Park*, 37.

163. Columbia University, "Chestnut Blight Fungus," http://www.columbia.edu/itc/cerc/danoff-burg/invasion_bio/inv_spp_summ/Cryphonectria_parasitica.htm.

164. Dewey to Biddle, March 9, 1907, Office of the Engineer Commissioner. Quoted in Mackintosh, *Rock Creek Park*, 32.

165. Mackintosh, *Rock Creek Park: An Administrative History*, 36.

166. *Washington Post*, "Gators in Rock Creek," July 30, 1916.

167. U.S. Congress, *Botanical Gardens*, House of Representatives, 64th Cong., 1st sess., May 5, 1916, Report No. 641; ibid., *Removal of Botanical Gardens*, 64th Cong., 1st sess., May 8, 1916, Rock Creek Park, Interpretation Subject Files.

168. Olmsted and Olmsted, *Rock Creek Park: A Report by Olmsted Brothers*, 17–18.

169. Mackintosh, *Rock Creek Park: An Administrative History*, 35.

170. *Washington Post*, "Plans for Reservoir," December 22, 1898.

171. David Swerdloff, *Crestwood: 300 Acres, 300 Years* (Washington, D.C.: Humanities Council of Washington, D.C., 2013), 64.

172. U.S. Congress, *State Exhibition Buildings in Rock Creek Park, District of Columbia*, Senate, 55th Cong., 2nd sess., Report No. 614.

173. Ibid.

CHAPTER 5

174. Theodore Roosevelt, *Outdoor Pastimes of an American Hunter* (New York: Scribner Publishing, 1906), 384, http://books.google.com/books?id=Fjji xuGgB70C&pg=PA611&lpg=PA611&dq=Theodore+Roosevelt+An+A utobiography+rock+creek+park&source=bl&ots=xnjRWR44hf&sig=Df uSKlNBokvj_Ht_ZloEFvWHlNU&hl=en&sa=X&ei=xAgNU6ChMPH JsQTihIGACA&ved=0CFEQ6AEwBw#v=onepage&q=Theodore%20 Roosevelt%20An%20Autobiography%20rock%20creek%20park&f=false.

175. *Washington Post*, "Fifty Follow Hounds: Society Folk in Drag Chase at Rock Creek Park," March 31, 1912. Although today it is considered a native species, the red fox was actually introduced into North America by the British for the sake of foxhunting. A popular sport in England historically, it became a sport of nobility across the ocean for an extended period of time.

176. Ibid.

177. Quoted in Thomas Chused, "Brightwood Reservoir: The Story of Carter Barron and the Tennis Stadium," Crestwood History blog, 2013, http//:www.crestwood-dc.org.

178. *Washington Post*, "1,500 See 155 Vie in Horse Show in Park," May 16, 1938.

179. National Park Service, *Peirce Mill Teahouse Menu*, Rock Creek Park, Interpretation Subject Files.

180. John DeFerrari, *Historic Restaurants of Washington, D.C.* (Charleston, SC: The History Press, 2013), 72.

181. Newman to Sherrill, June 23, 1921. Quoted in Mackintosh, *Rock Creek Park*, 28.

182. Mackintosh, *Rock Creek Park*, 29.

183. Sherrill to Mrs. Powell Clayton, November 4, 1921. Quoted in Mackintosh, *Rock Creek Park*, 29.

184. Bushong, *Rock Creek Park Historic Resource Study*, 115.

185. *Washington Post*, "500 Scouts Rough It for a Night and 2 Meals at Park Camporee," June 7, 1936.

186. Although there is very little information out there on these swimming holes, the author viewed historic photos during a trip to the Historical Society of Washington, D.C., that proclaim them as such.

187. Unsigned copy of letter to Colonel Chester Harding, June 16, 1913. Quoted in Mackintosh, *Rock Creek Park*, 25.

188. Kathleen M. Lesko, Valerie Babb and Carroll R. Gibbs, *Black Georgetown Remembered: A History of Its Black Community from the Founding of "The Town of George" in 1751 to the Present Day* (Washington, D.C.: Georgetown University Press, 1991), 6.

189. Davis, *Rock Creek Park Road System*, 81.

190. Scott, *Capital Engineers*, 212.

191. *Evening Star*, "Night Parking Prohibition Rule in Rock Creek Exempts Families," July 18, 1922. Quoted in Mackintosh, *Rock Creek Park*, 25.

192. *Washington Post*, "Life Sized Replica Carved in Rock Creek Park Draws Eyes of Passersby," December 23, 1932.

193. Ibid., "Skating in City Begun at Rock Creek Pond," January 27, 1922.

194. Mackintosh, *Rock Creek Park*, 26–27; Bushong, *Rock Creek Park Historic Resource Study*, 118–19; *Washington Post*, "Rock Creek's Links Are Opened," April 3, 1926.

195. *Washington Post*, "Turkey Golf Planned at Rock Creek Course," November 7, 1933; "Rippy Takes Rock Creek Golf Title," April 7, 1934.

196. "About Us—Rock Creek Golf Course," http://www.rockcreekgolfcourse.com/sites/courses/layout11.asp?id=694&page=43365.

Chapter 6

197. John Burroughs, "Spring in Washington: With an Eye to the Birds," *Atlantic Monthly* (May 1869).

198. Ibid.

199. Ibid.

200. Edward J. Renehan Jr., "Portrait of a Friendship," New York State archives, winter 2004, 22, http://www.archives.nysed.gov/apt/magazine/archivesmag_winter04.pdf.

201. Theodore Roosevelt, *An Autobiography* (New York: Macmillan Company, 1916), 47, http://www.theodore-roosevelt.com/images/research/autobiography.pdf.

202. Quoted in Renehan, "Portrait of a Friendship."

203. Roosevelt, *Outdoor Pastimes of an American Hunter*, 384. Roosevelt actually dedicated this book to John Burroughs, whom he referred to affectionately as "uncle."

204. Tom Sterling, "Lost Ring. If Found Return to 1600 Pennsylvania Avenue," Ghosts of DC blog, 2013, http://www.ghostsofdc.org. As fun as this story is, there's a competing story from the *Washington Post* in 1921. In "How Boulder Bridge Became Famous," the newspaper writer notes that Roosevelt was actually living at 20 Jackson Place at the time due to White House renovations.

205. *Washington Post*, "President Has Quiet Day," November 27, 1908.

206. Quoted in National Park Service, Jusserand Memorial wayside exhibit.

207. William Roscoe Thayer, *Theodore Roosevelt: An Intimate Biography*, http://www.gutenberg.org/cache/epub/2386/pg2386.html.

208. Vylla Poe Wilson, "Jusserand Memorial Recalls Many Stories of His Distinguished Service Here," *Washington Post*, October 25, 1936.

209. Docent-led tour of Woodrow Wilson House, November 29, 2010.

210. Woodrow Wilson quoted in memorandum, Ridley to Gillen, May 10, 1920. Quoted in Mackintosh, *Rock Creek Park*, 33.

211. Woodrow Wilson to Colonel Clarence Sherrill, June 21, 1921. Quoted in Mackintosh, *Rock Creek Park*, 34.

CHAPTER 7

212. Mackintosh, *Rock Creek Park: An Administrative History*, 65.

213. William Henry Holmes to Colonel Clarence Sherrill, April 6, 1925, in Moran, *Rediscovering Archeological Resources at Rock Creek Park*.

214. Davis, *Rock Creek Park Road System*, 85.

215. Mackintosh, *Rock Creek Park*, 65–66.

216. Charles W. Eliot II, *Park System for the National Capital, Washington Region*, February 1927. Quoted in Mackintosh, *Rock Creek Park*, 66-67.

217. Macintosh, *Rock Creek Park*, 66–69.

218. John DeFerrari, "Mary Foote Henderson: The Iron-Willed Empress of Meridian Hill," Streets of Washington blog, 2011, http://www. streetsofwashington.com/2011/07/iron-willed-empress-of-meridian-hill.html.

219. Ibid.

220. National Park Service, "Mary Henderson," http://www.nps.gov/mehi/historyculture/henderson.htm.

221. *Washington Times*, "Joaquin Miller in Modern Washington," March 10, 1899, http://chroniclingamerica.loc.gov/lccn/sn85054468/1899-03-10/ed-1/seq-2/.

222. *Meridian Hill Park Cultural Landscape Report*, vol. 1 (Washington, D.C.: Department of the Interior, National Park Service; Architrave P.C., Architects, 2001), 38.

223. Ibid.

224. National Park Service, "Meridian Hill Park History and Culture: People," http://www.nps.gov/mehi/historyculture/people.htm. Horace Peaslee also developed Montrose Park in Georgetown, now an administrative unit of Rock Creek Park.

225. *Meridian Hill Park Cultural Landscape Report*, 91.

226. National Park Service, "Meridian Hill Park," www.nps.gov/mehi.

227. Commission of Fine Arts, Twelfth Report, July 1, 1929–December 31, 1934, 84. Quoted in National Park Service, *Meridian Hill Park*, Historic

American Building Survey, HABS No. DC-532, 13, http://lcweb2.loc. gov/pnp/habshaer/dc/dc0100/dc0188/data/dc0188data.pdf.

228. U.S. Grant III to Honorable William J. Harris, U.S. Senate, June 26, 1930. Quoted in *Meridian Hill Park Cultural Landscape Report*.

229. U.S. Congress, *Park Improvement Papers of the District of Columbia*, 47–74, under "Fort Stevens, Where Lincoln Was Under Fire."

230. U.S. Congress, *Journal of the Senate of the United States*, 58th Cong., 2nd sess. (Washington, D.C.: Government Printing Office, 1904), 119 (S3886). Quoted in National Park Service, *Civil War Defenses of Washington: Historic Resource Study*.

231. Ibid.

232. Horace Albright, *My Trips with Harold Ickes* (Washington, D.C.: Department of the Interior, National Park Service, n.d.) http://www.nps. gov/history/history/online_books/npsg/ickes/index.htm.

233. Ibid.

234. Lisa Pfueller Davidson and James A. Jacobs, *Civilian Conservation Corps Activities in the National Capital Region of the National Park Service*, Historic American Buildings Survey, HABS DC-858 (Washington, D.C.: National Park Service, n.d.), 44, http://lcweb2.loc.gov/pnp/habshaer/dc/ dc1000/dc1020/data/dc1020data.pdf.

235. Ibid., 39, 41, 96–97.

236. National Park Service, *Rapid Ethnographic Assessment of Park Users and Neighbors, Civil War Defenses of Washington, Anacostia Park, District of Columbia, for Park Management Plans* (Juarez and Associates, Inc., 1997), 153, Rock Creek Park Interpretive Resource Files.

237. Ibid. Author inspection and exploration of site on February 28, 2014.

238. For more information on Fort Circle Drive, see Chapter Three, "The Fort Park System," of National Park Service, *Civil War Defenses of Washington: Historic Resource Study*, Part II. http://www.cr.nps.gov/history/ online_books/civilwar/hrs2-3.htm.

239. *Washington Post*, October 10, 1937.

240. "Big Idea Intro and Fort Circle Parks," CapitalSpace, https://docs.google. com/a/nps.gov/file/d/0Bz3ZLaGJKAaBYTI4N2MwMDAtNmU5OS00 MmZlLWI0ZjYtNzkyNzJmYWU3M2Jl/edit?pli=1&hl=en#, 4.

241. Richard J. Beall to Engineer Commissioners of D.C., February 27, 1905. Quoted in Davis, *Rock Creek and Potomac Parkway*, 46, http://lcweb2. loc.gov/pnp/habshaer/dc/dc0800/dc0806/data/dc0806data.pdf.

242. Davis, *Rock Creek and Potomac Parkway*, 46–47.

243. Ibid, 48–52.

244. Charles Moore, ed., *The Improvement of the Park System of the District of Columbia*, U.S. Congress, Senate Report No. 166, March 1902, 57th Cong., 1st sess., 139, http://www.cr.nps.gov/history/online_books/mcmillan/ index.htm.

245. Davis, *Rock Creek and Potomac Parkway*, 77, 95–97.

246. Gail Spilsbury, *A Washington Sketchbook: Drawings by Robert L. Dickinson, 1917–1918* (Baltimore, MD: Chesapeake Book Company, 2011), 111.

247. National Park Service, *Highways in Harmony: Rock Creek and Potomac Parkway*, brochure.

248. Davis, *Rock Creek and Potomac Parkway*, 10.

249. Ibid., 13.

250. National Park Service, *Highways in Harmony*.

251. *Washington Evening Star*, "New Parkway Here to Rank with Finest," April 17, 1936.

252. National Park Service, *Highways in Harmony*.

253. Quoted in Judith B. Tankard, *Beatrix Farrand: Private Gardens, Public Landscapes* (New York: Monacelli Press, 2009).

254. Ibid.

255. Maureen De Lay Joseph, Kay Fanning and Mark Davison, *Cultural Landscape Report: Dumbarton Oaks Park, Rock Creek Park* (Washington, D.C.: Department of the Interior, National Park Service, 2000).

256. Ibid.

257. Ibid.

258. Ibid.

259. Ibid.

260. "Rock Creek and Potomac Parkway—Washington, DC," Living New Deal, https://livingnewdeal.berkeley.edu/projects/rock-creek-and-potomac-parkway-washington-dc/.

261. Davidson and Jacobs, *Civilian Conservation Corps Activities*; Bushong, *Rock Creek Park Historic Resource Study*, 143, 169. Prior to the establishment of Camp NP-14-DC in Rock Creek Park, many of the same CCC boys worked in and around the park but lived in other nearby camps.

262. Ibid., 190.

263. Ibid., 43.

264. Ibid.

265. Davidson and Jacobs, *Civilian Conservation Corps Activities*, 44.

266. Bushong, *Rock Creek Park Historic Resource Study*, 135–36; National Park Service, Rock Creek Park Historic Photos Collection, Cultural Resource Subject Files.

267. National Park Service, *Riley Springs Footbridge*, HAER, No. DC-32, http://www.loc.gov/pictures/item/dc0769/. Accessed through http://lcweb2.loc.gov/.

268. Bushong, *Rock Creek Park Historic Resource Study*, 137–38; Dryden, *Peirce Mill*, 71.

269. Dryden, *Peirce Mill*, 71.

270. *Washington Post*, "Workmen Almost Victim of Battle Fought 70 Years Ago," February 25, 1944.

271. Bushong, *Rock Creek Park Historic Resource Study*, 140; National Park Service, Rock Creek Park Historic Photos Collection, Cultural Resource Files.

CHAPTER 8

272. *Washington Post*, "Carter Barron Dies of Cancer, D.C. Leader, President's Friend," November 17, 1950.

273. National Park Service, "Carter Barron History," www.nps.gov/rocr/planyourvisit/cbhistory.htm; *Washington Post*, "Diva Will Sing in Park Today," December 17, 1949.

274. National Park Service, "Carter Barron History."

275. Ibid.

276. Leroy F. Aarons, "Ella Makes Magic with Old Favorites at Carter Barron," *Washington Post*, July 24, 1963.

277. Richard L. Coe, "Bring Sleds to the Park," *Washington Post*, August 17, 1955; Library of Congress, "Red Skelton," http://www.loc.gov/pictures/item/lmc1996001546/PP/.

278. National Park Service, "Carter Barron History."

279. Ibid.

280. Chris Richards, "These Blackbyrds Have Lots to Crow About: Three Decades On, D.C. Band Still Provides a Fitting Accompaniment to Summer," *Washington Post*, August 20, 2006.

281. *Washington Post*, "First Lady Named Head of Park Day," September 23, 1955.

282. Conrad L. Wirth, "Visit Rock Creek Park Sunday," *Washington Post*, October 5, 1956. The nature center was designed as part of the National Park Service's very first Mission 66 project. Mission 66 was a ten-year project designed to update visitor facilities in the park in time for the NPS's fiftieth anniversary in 1966.

According to a sign in front of Klingle Mansion, the official title of the nature center was the Rock Creek Nature Center. At the center's present location, signs have referred to it as both the Rock Creek Nature Center and Rock Creek Park Nature Center.

283. National Park Service, Rock Creek Park Historic Photos, Cultural Resource Subject Files.

284. Bill Yeaman, interview by author, Washington, D.C., January 10, 2014.

285. National Park Service, Rock Creek Park Historic Photos Collection, Cultural Resource Subject Files.

286. Mackintosh, *Rock Creek Park*, 102–03.

287. Yeaman, interview by author.

288. Steven Allen, "Up All Night in the Middle of the Day," *Washington Post*, mid-1970s.

289. *National Capital Region Administrative History, 1952–2005* (Washington, D.C.: National Park Service; Robinson & Associates, Inc., 2008), 97.

290. Ibid., 97–98.

291. Nancy Lewis, "Star of Rock Creek Nature Center Dies," *Washington Post*, fall 1991.

292. Yeaman, interview by author.

293. Ibid.

294. Mackintosh, *Rock Creek Park*, 93–96.

295. Report of meeting and letters in Stables file, Rock Creek Park, NCR-NPS records; Memorandum, Selby to Kelly, Oct. 14, 1957. Quoted in Mackintosh.

296. Ibid., 95–96.

297. Barbara Gamarkelian, "A Horse Is a Horse Is a Therapeutic Horse," *New York Times*, June 6, 1985, http://www.nytimes.com/1985/06/06/us/a-horse-is-a-horse-is-a-therapeutic-horse.html.

298. Ibid.

299. Petula Devorak, "The Passing of Jackson: An Appaloosa Gentle to Those Who Needed Him Most," *Washington Post*, September 3, 2012, http://www.washingtonpost.com/local/washington-mourns-a-much-loved-horse/2012/09/06/e856741c-f80e-11e1-8b93-c4f4ab1c8d13_story.html.

300. Ibid.

301. Mackintosh, *Rock Creek Park*, 116–17.

302. Ibid., 117; "The History of Thompson Boat Center," http://www.thompsonboatcenter.com/history.htm.

303. *Washington Post*, "Clean Up Set Today Along the Potomac," May 23, 1965.

304. *Washington Post*, "Driver of Mule-Power Park Mowers Is on Go 17 Hours a Day at Age 84," September 14, 1958.

305. Ibid.

306. Ibid.

307. Ibid.

CHAPTER 9

308. Davis, *Rock Creek Park Road System*, 111.

309. McKay to Nye, June 17, 1953. Quoted in Mackintosh, *Rock Creek Park*, 86.

310. *Washington Post*, "Plan for Highway in Rock Creek Park Called 'Intolerable' and an 'Outrage,'" May 26, 1955.

311. National Park Service, *Cultural Landscape Inventory: Chevy Chase Circle*, 23, Rock Creek Park, Cultural Resource Subject Files.

312. Ibid., 23–24, 36.

313. All this during the author's first visit to the circle on March 24, 2013!

314. Davis, *Rock Creek Park Road System*.

315. Davis, *Rock Creek Park Road System*, 148; "About Us—Rock Creek Golf Course."

316. National Park Service, *Rock Creek and Potomac Parkway*, 111–14.

317. Ibid.

318. *Washington Post*, "Sewer Eruption in Park Held Symptom of Decrepit System," June 22, 1952; "5 Million Gallons of Sewage Pours into Rock Creek Daily," March 22, 1953; Davis, *Rock Creek Park Road System*, 58.

319. *Washington Post*, "Sewer Eruption in Park Held Symptom of Decrepit System," June 22, 1952; "5 Million Gallons of Sewage Pours Into Rock Creek Daily," March 22, 1953.

320. Ibid., "Sewer Eruption in Park Held Symptom of Decrepit System."

321. Ibid., "5 Million Gallons of Sewage Pours Into Rock Creek Daily."

322. Spratt, *Rock Creek's Bridges*, 106; Library of Congress, Rock Creek Park Flood Photos.

323. John Katz, "Area Slowly Cleaning Up Flood Debris," *Washington Post*, July 11, 1972.

324. Ibid.

325. Thomas Morgan, "Rock Creek Park Damage by Storm Set at $374,000," *Washington Post*, September 12, 1979.

326. To learn more about park water pollution and stormwater runoff in Rock Creek Park, visit http://www.rockcreekconservancy.org/index.php/rock-creek/water-quality. The National Park Service's *Rock Creek Watershed Conservation Study*, a much larger and longer read, also sheds light on the matters.

327. D.C. Water, "Combined Sewer System," http://www.dcwater.com/wastewater_collection/css/.

328. D.C. Water, "CSO Overflow Predictions for Average Year," August 2004, http://www.dcwater.com/wastewater_collection/css/CSO%20 Overflow%20Predictions%20%20for%20Average%20Year.pdf.

329. U.S. Environmental Protection Agency, Combined Sewer Overflows, http://www.epa.gov/nrmrl/wswrd/wq/stormwater/cso.pdf.

330. Although it is not ideal for a stormwater–sanitary tunnel to be built under a national park unit (Piney Branch Tributary), the author strongly believes that the end justifies the means. For more information on D.C. Water's plans, see http://www.dcwater.com/education/pdfs/green_infrastructure_brochure.pdf, and http://www.dcwater.com/green#comments.

331. Stephen Buckley, "Tank in NW Leaking Oil into Rock Creek Branch; Condo Loses about 8,000 Gallons of Fuel," *Washington Post*, January 3, 1990.

332. U.S. Environmental Protection Agency, "Case Studies—Bioassessment and Enforcement: Using Bioassessment as Evidence of Damage and

Recovery following a Pesticide Spill," http://water.epa.gov/scitech/swguidance/standards/criteria/aqlife/biocriteria/enforcement.cfm.

333. Gary Sikora, interview with author, March 14, 2014.

334. U.S. Environmental Protection Agencu, "Case Studies."

335. David A. Fahrenthold, "Dead Fish Found in Rock Creek." *Washington Post*, September 1, 2006.

336. Dryden, *Peirce Mill*, 28.

337. Peggy Fleming and Raclare Kanal, *Annotated Checklist of Vascular Plants of Rock Creek Park* (Washington, D.C.: Department of the Interior, National Park Service, n.d.), 5.

338. Olmsted and Olmsted, *Rock Creek Park: A Report by Olmsted Brothers*, 31; National Park Service, *Montrose Park Cultural Landscape Report*, 168; *Meridian Hill Park Cultural Landscape Report*; Greenleaf to Sherrill, March 3, 1922. Quoted in Mackintosh, *Rock Creek Park*, 44. Ironically, Frederick Law Olmsted Jr. was a previous member of the D.C. Commission of Fine Arts. He was requesting the planting of Japanese honeysuckle in the park at the same time his colleagues on the commission were requesting that the park stop the harmful practice; Moore to Ridley, May 22, 1920. Quoted in Mackintosh, *Rock Creek Park*, 37.

339. Linda Wheeler, "A Diamond Ever Rough: Rock Creek Park Turns 100 Unspoiled, Underused," *Washington Post*, September 26, 1990.

340. Anne Chase, "Illegal Dumping in Rock Creek Park a Growing Problem," *Washington Post*, March 10, 1988.

341. George Eagle, "Peirce Mill Abused by Boys with Rocks," *Washington Post*, n.d.

342. Chris Gordon, "Vandals Deface 'Serenity' Statue in Columbia Heights Park," *NBC Washington*, April 24, 2013, http://www.nbcwashington.com/news/local/Vandals-Deface-Serenity-Statue-in-Meridian-Hill-Park-204574951.html.

Chapter 10

343. Deanna Ochs, "A Tomato Grows in Rock Creek Park," *Respite: The Official Newspaper of Rock Creek Park*, Summer 2008 edition, http://www.nps.gov/rocr/parknews/upload/Summer2008.pdf.

344. National Park Service, *The Community Gardens of Rock Creek Park: Oral History Project*. Rock Creek Park, Interpretation Subject Files.

345. Ibid.

346. Ibid.

347. Ibid.

348. Ibid.

349. Ochs, "A Tomato Grows in Rock Creek Park."

350. Mackintosh, *Rock Creek Park*, VII. Redmond served as park manager from the late 1960s until the mid-1970s and then served as Rock Creek Park's first official superintendent until his untimely death in 1983. During the mid-'70s, reorganization of the National Capital Region of the National Park Service occurred, resulting in Rock Creek Park's becoming, for the first time, a separate unit of the National Park System. Prior to this reorganization, Rock Creek Park, the National Mall, the Chesapeake and Ohio Canal, the George Washington Memorial Parkway and National Capital Parks–East were overseen by a single superintendent.

351. Davis, *Rock Creek Park Road System*, 151.

352. Ibid.

353. Ibid., 152.

354. Ibid.

355. Yeaman, interview by author.

356. Ibid.

357. Ibid.

358. Ibid.

359. Ibid.

360. "Rock Creek's Meadows," *Hour*, August 17, 1989, http://news.google.com/newspapers?nid=1916&dat=19890817&id=bjIiAAAAIBAJ&sjid=uXQFAAAAIBAJ&pg=1215,2700743.

361. National Park Service, *Meadows*, brochure, 2012; Bill Yeaman, interview by author.

362. Peggy Fleming, e-mail with author.

363. Ibid.

364. Gary Sikora and Peg Shaw, *Habitat Restoration Project, Rock Creek Park: 20th Anniversary Report to the National Park Service*, 2008, 1.

365. Ibid., 1, 4.

366. Ibid., 5–6. The litter is, in fact, used condoms and ripped condom wrappers. Large urban parks attract diverse crowds, sometimes *very* diverse. The "P Street Beach" area of the Rock Creek and Potomac Parkway has long been known as a cruising, or gay sex, spot.

367. Ibid., 6–7.

368. Ibid.

369. Ibid., 1–2.

370. Ibid., 8.

371. D.C. Department of the Environment, *Regenerative Stormwater Conveyences in Rock Creek Park*, Rock Creek Park, Natural Resource Subject Files.

372. Yeaman, interview with author.

373. Ibid.

CHAPTER 11

374. National Park Service, "Old Stone House Historic Photos," Rock Creek Park, Interpretation Subject Files; *Washington Post* "Old Stone House to Cut Hours," n.d.

375. National Park Service, Rock Creek Park Volunteer Newsletter, January–February 1990, Rock Creek Park, Interpretation Subject Files.

376. Ibid., July–August and April–June 1989, Rock Creek Park, Interpretation Subject Files.

377. Ibid., April–June 1989, Rock Creek Park, Interpretation Subject Files; "Neighborhood Reclaims Meridian Hill Park in Washington, DC," Project for Public Spaces, 1998, http://www.pps.org/reference/successwashington-3/.

378. Some maps that depict the fact that very little crime occurs in Rock Creek Park can be found at http://www.spotcrime.com/dc/washington or http://www.popville.com/2012/07/crime-map-of-washington-dc/.

379. New York City Police Department, *Central Park Precinct CompStat*, http://www.nyc.gov/html/nypd/downloads/pdf/crime_statistics/cs022pct.pdf; "Golden Gate Park Crime," http://www.mapreport.com/na/west/ba/news/subtopics/c/cities/golden_gate_park.html.

380. National Park Service, *Rock Creek Park Tennis Stadium: Environmental Impact Statement*, 11, Rock Creek Park, Interpretation Subject Files.

381. Carter Bonn, "Tournament History," www.citiopentennis.com; "Citi Open," http://www.atpworldtour.com/Tennis/Tournaments/Washington.aspx.

382. National Park Service, *National Capital Region Administrative History, 1952–2005*, Appendix E, 77, Rock Creek Park, Interpretation Subject Files.

383. Ibid.

384. "Rock Creek Park by Oddisee," http://mellomusicgroup.bandcamp.com/album/rock-creek-park.

CONCLUSION

385. U.S. Congress, *Norton's Bill to Rename Rock Creek Park for 125ᵗʰ Anniversary Highlights Its Significance to D.C., the Region and the Nation*, January 16, 2014, http://norton.house.gov/media-center/press-releases/norton-s-bill-to-rename-rock-creek-park-for-125th-anniversary-highlights.

386. For an insightful, informative article on this, see David Harmon's essay entitled *Beyond the 59ᵗʰ Park: Reforming the Nomenclature of the US National Park System*. The article can be accessed at http://www.georgewright.org/292harmon.pdf.

387. See *Norton Introduces Bill to Preserve D.C. Region Civil War Defenses*, http://norton.house.gov/media-center/press-releases/norton-introduces-bill-to-preserve-dc-region-civil-war-defenses.

Selected Bibliography

The following list of publications includes the main sources used for this work. For a full list of sources, please refer to the notes.

Baker, Jean H. *James Buchanan*. New York: Henry Holt and Company, 2004.

Bedell, John, Stuart Fiedel and Charles LeeDecker. *Bold, Rocky, and Picturesque: The Archeology and History of Rock Creek Park*. Philadelphia: Eastern National, 2013.

Bushong, William. *Rock Creek Park Historic Resource Study*. Washington, D.C.: Department of the Interior, National Park Service, 1990.

Cooling, Benjamin Franklin, and Walton H. Owen. *Mr. Lincoln's Forts: A Guide to the Civil War Defenses of Washington*. Lanham, MD.: Scarecrow Press, 2010.

Davis, Timothy. *Rock Creek and Potomac Parkway*. Historic American Building Survey, HABS No. DC-697. Washington, D.C.: Department of the Interior, National Park Service, 1992. http://lcweb2.loc.gov/pnp/habshaer/dc/dc0800/dc0806/data/dc0806data.pdf.

———. *Rock Creek Park Road System*. Historic American Engineering Record, HAER No. DC-55. Washington, D.C.: Department of the Interior, National Park Service, 1996. http://lcweb2.loc.gov/pnp/habshaer/dc/dc0900/dc0966/data/dc0966data.pdf.

DeFerrari, John. Streets of Washington blog. http://www.streetsofwashington.com/.

Dryden, Steve. *Peirce Mill: Two Hundred Years in the Nation's Capital*. Washington, D.C.: Friends of Peirce Mill, Inc., 2009.

Heine, Cornelius W. *The Contributions of Charles Carroll Glover and Other Citizens to the Development of the National Capital.* Washington, D.C.: Department of the Interior, National Park Service, n.d.

Mackintosh, Barry. *Rock Creek Park: An Administrative History.* Washington, D.C.: Department of the Interior, National Park Service, History Department, 1985.

Marberry, M.M. *Joaquin Miller: Splendid Poseur.* New York: Thomas Y. Crowell Company, 1953.

Meridian Hill Park Cultural Landscape Report. Vol. 1. Washington, D.C.: National Park Service; Architrave P.C., Architects, 2001.

Montrose Park: Cultural Landscape Report. Washington, D.C.: National Park Service; Architrave P.C., Architects, 2004.

Moore, Charles, ed. *Park Improvement Papers: A Series of Twenty Papers Relating to the Improvement of the Park System of the District of Columbia.* Washington, D.C.: Senate Committee on the District of Columbia, 1903. https://archive.org/stream/parkimprovementp00moor#page/n5/mode/2up.

National Capital Region Administrative History, 1952–2005. Washington, D.C.: National Park Service; Robinson & Associates, Inc., 2008.

National Park Service. *Civil War Defenses of Washington Historic Resource Study.* http://www.cr.nps.gov/history/online_books/civilwar/hrst.htm.

Peirce, Shoemaker. *Historic Rock Creek.* Washington, D.C.: Columbia Historical Society, 1907.

Peterson, Martin Severin. *Joaquin Miller: Literary Frontiersman.* Palo Alto, CA: Stanford University Press, 1937.

Ross, Deanna, and Frances McMillen. *Cultural Landscape Report: Historic Trails of Rock Creek Park.* Washington, D.C.: Department of the Interior, National Park Service, 2012.

Scott, Pamela. *Capital Engineers: The U.S. Army Corps of Engineers in the Development of Washington, D.C. 1790–2004.* Alexandria, VA: U.S. Army Corps of Engineers, 2005.

Spilsbury, Gail. *Rock Creek Park.* Baltimore, MD: Johns Hopkins University Press, 2003.

U.S. Army Corps of Engineers. *Report of Brevet Brigadier General N. Michler, Major of Engineers, United States Army, in Charge of Public Buildings, Grounds, Works, &C.* Washington, D.C., 1867.

Washington Post archives. http://pqasb.pqarchiver.com/washingtonpost/search.html.

INDEX

About the Author

A U.S. National Park Service interpretive park ranger since 2006, Scott Einberger has served as Rock Creek Park's volunteer coordinator and interpretive media specialist since 2010. He's also worked at Chamizal National Memorial in El Paso, Texas; Denali National Park in interior Alaska; Craters of the Moon National Monument in south-central Idaho; Gila Cliff Dwellings National Monument in southwestern New Mexico; and Lassen Volcanic National Park in northeastern California. A National Park System enthusiast and environmental historian, Einberger lives with his wife in between Rock Creek Park's Fort Slocum and Fort Stevens in Washington, D.C. The author welcomes your thoughts on park history, the book and anything else. E-mail him at Scott_Einberger@yahoo.com.

Visit us at
www.historypress.net
....
This title is also available as an e-book